D0322361

£14 99

ENGLISH POLITICAL CULTURE
IN THE FIFTEENTH CENTURY

English Political Culture in the Fifteenth Century is a new and original study of how politics worked in late medieval England. It throws new light on a much-discussed period in English history. Michael Hicks explores the standards, values and principles that motivated contemporary politicians, and the aspirations and interests of both aristocracy and peasants alike.

Hicks argues that the Wars of the Roses did not result from fundamental weaknesses in the political system but from the collision of exceptional circumstances that quickly passed away. Overall, he shows that the era was one of stability and harmony, and that there were effective mechanisms for keeping the peace. Structure and continuities, Hicks argues, were more prominent than change.

Students and teachers of late medieval England will find this a key text in the area, as it covers a broad spectrum in a particularly focused way.

Michael Hicks is Professor of Medieval History and Head of History at King Alfred's College, Winchester. He has published extensively on late medieval England and the Wars of the Roses. His previous publications include *Bastard Feudalism* (1995), *Warwick the Kingmaker* (1998) and *Richard III* (2000).

University of London Library

SHL

Reference Only

WITHDRAWN

THIS BOOK MUST NOT BE REMOVED
FROM THE LIBRARY

ENGLISH POLITICAL CULTURE IN THE FIFTEENTH CENTURY

Michael Hicks

Routledge
Taylor & Francis Group
LONDON AND NEW YORK

BIBL
LONDON
UNIV
WITHDRAWN

First published 2002
by Routledge
11 New Fetter Lane, London EC4P 4EE

Simultaneously published in the USA and Canada
by Routledge
29 West 35th Street, New York, NY 10001

Routledge is an imprint of the Taylor & Francis Group

© 2002 Michael Hicks

Typeset in Galliard by Taylor & Francis Books Ltd
Printed and bound in Great Britain by TJ International Ltd, Padstow,
Cornwall

All rights reserved. No part of this book may be reprinted or
reproduced or utilised in any form or by any electronic,
mechanical, or other means, now known or hereafter
invented, including photocopying and recording, or in any
information storage or retrieval system, without permission in
writing from the publishers.

British Library Cataloguing in Publication Data
A catalogue record for this book is available from the British Library

Library of Congress Cataloging in Publication Data
A catalog record for this book has been requested

ISBN 0–415–21763–6 (hbk)
ISBN 0–415–21764–4 (pbk)

TO CYNTHIA

CONTENTS

PREFACE

This book was to have been a short study of how politics worked in the fifteenth century and the standards to which it conformed. It presumed twenty years of research into fifteenth-century politics, bastard feudalism, idealism and motivation, and local case studies. A change of publisher and title, a doubling in length and an explosion in recent studies has made for a much longer and more elaborate book. The original thrust has not changed, but the range, level and depth of discussion undoubtedly has. It is the first synthesis of a new type of history of fifteenth-century England.

My own research, published or unpublished, has been important, but so has that of many others. The subject matter is vast, largely unre-searched and beyond the capacity of any individual to investigate in full. Studying even the English constitution is a tremendous task. Stanley Chrimes' classic *English Constitutional Ideas in the Fifteenth Century* studies particular reigns and particular texts, and a dozen *Fifteenth-Century Attitudes* have mapped parts of a jungle still largely uncharted. Who had thought of writing articles and books on the concept of service, on chivalry in domestic politics, or the culture of childhood twenty years ago? Although we differ in so many particulars, I acknowledge Christine Carpenter's identification and conceptualisa-tion of many key issues, her bold engagement with the thorniest of problems and her perception, which I share, that 'we are still in a state of ignorance in many important areas'. I have been fortunate to draw on many wholly new editions and re-issues of old editions of the prin-cipal sources. I have built on half a century of major monographs and volumes of essays on the structure of government, central and local, on the aristocracy and the peasantry, both as classes and in particular local-ities, on bastard feudalism and on local politics. The contributions of Ralph Griffiths, Gerald Harriss, Jack Lander, K.B. McFarlane, Tony Pollard and Colin Richmond have been more influential than specific references indicate. I have made extensive use of the work produced in the last thirty years. I have abridged the works of my predecessors and contemporaries, adapting and borrowing as appropriate, whilst subjecting them to my own themes and overriding framework and turning them to uses often unintended by the authors and perhaps unexpected. The interplay of motives and the interaction of different groups, individuals, ideas and factors has taken priority.

Every book selects. I chose some topics for study and rejected others. Researching the book has modified my understanding of where and how everything relates. Accessible material, primary and secondary, is growing apace. Topics originally excluded have become relevant. Further choices have had to be made. There is much that this book is not. That I am concerned primarily with political culture rather than other sorts of culture and with the rural aristocracy rather than urban townsmen makes it one sort of book rather than others that it might have been. It has focused more on England than its dependencies and on civil than foreign war. National generalisations and perceptions have crowded out the myriad regional variations of the original synopsis. There are more beginnings than endings and more topics are touched on than can be more fully explored. There is little here about symbolism, ceremony and ritual, folklore and literary culture, superstitions and the supernatural. And so on. Some such emphases are deliberate, inescapable, yet regrettable. I could not write about everything, nor indeed could I be comprehensive about everything I do write about. This book is interim and provisional to an unusual degree, since most current and future historical scholarship impacts upon it. I hope for future updates and revisions.

The first seven chapters are the foundation for the final three. Chapter 1 sets out the parameters and raises fundamental issues. Chapter 2 looks at the climate of ideas, which are explored in different contexts – monarchy, aristocracy and the other social classes, Chapters 3 to 5 respectively. Chapter 6 is about government. The pivotal Chapter 7 explores some alternative perceptions. Chapters 8, 9 and 10 explore concepts and systems in practice, through bastard feudalism, provincial communities and national politics in peacetime, and culminate naturally in Chapter 11, the collapse into and emergence from civil war.

I am solely responsible for what the book contains. I find it unusually difficult to acknowledge all those who have contributed to the thinking and subject matter of this book over the past thirty years. Almost everyone who taught me, whom I have heard, read or discussed, deserves my thanks. Specific identifiable debts are acknowledged, I believe, in the bibliography and notes. Some names feature especially frequently. Not present there, but thanked here, are my research students, especially Toby Purser, Richard Brown, Karen

Stoeber and Winifred Harwood, who have broadened my horizons and made me think more critically. I am grateful to Steve Rigby, who first proposed the project, and to successive editors, Heather McCallum and Victoria Peters. My family, as always, have been tolerant and supportive.

All quotations have been translated from their original language into modern English. Unless otherwise indicated, all places of publication are London.

Michael Hicks
Winchester
December 2001

ABBREVIATIONS

Armburgh	*The Armburgh Papers: The Brokholes Inheritance in Warwickshire, Hertfordshire and Essex c.1417–c.1453*, ed. C. Carpenter (Woodbridge, 1998)
BIHR	*Bulletin of the Institute of Historical Research*
Brown, *Governance*	A.L. Brown, *The Governance of Late Medieval England 1272–1461* (1989)
Carpenter, *Wars*	C. Carpenter, *The Wars of the Roses: Politics and the Constitution in England, c.1437–1509* (Cambridge, 1997)
CCR	*Calendar of the Close Rolls*
CPR	*Calendar of the Patent Rolls*
Chrimes	S.B. Chrimes, *English Constitutional Ideas in the Fifteenth Century* (Cambridge, 1934)
Concepts of Service	*Concepts and Patterns of Service in the Later Middle Ages*, ed. A.E. Curry and E. Matthew (Woodbridge, 2000)
Crowland	*The Crowland Chronicle Continuations 1459–86*, ed. N. Pronay and J.C. Cox (Gloucester, 1986)
Dockray	*Three Chronicles of the Reign of Edward IV*, ed. K. Dockray (Gloucester, 1988)
Dunham, *Hastings*	W.H. Dunham, *Lord Hastings' Indentured Retainers 1461–83,*

	Transactions of the Connecticut Academy of Arts and Sciences 39 (New Haven, 1956)
EHD	*English Historical Documents*, vol. 4, *1327–1485*, ed. A.R. Myers (1969)
EHR	*English Historical Review*
English Chronicle	*An English Chronicle of the Reigns of Richard II, Henry IV, Henry V, and Henry VI*, ed. J.S. Davies (Camden Society 64, 1856)
English Parliament	*The English Parliament in the Middle Ages*, ed. R.G. Davies and J.H. Denton (Manchester, 1981)
Fane Fragment	*The Fane Fragment of the 1461 Lords' Journal*, ed. W.H. Dunham (New Haven, 1935)
Fifteenth-cent. Attitudes	*Fifteenth-Century Attitudes: Perceptions of Society in Late Medieval England*, ed. R.E. Horrox (Cambridge, 1994)
Fifteenth-cent. England	*Fifteenth-century England 1399–1509: Studies in Politics and Society*, ed. S.B. Chrimes, C.D. Ross and R.A. Griffiths (Manchester, 1972)
Given-Wilson, *Chronicles*	*Chronicles of the Revolution 1397–1400*, ed. C. Given-Wilson (Manchester, 1993)
Given-Wilson, *Nobility*	C. Given-Wilson, *The English Nobility in the Later Middle Ages* (2nd edn, 1996)
Green, *Truth*	R.F. Green, *The Crisis of Truth: Literature and Law in Ricardian England* (Philadelphia, 1999)
Griffiths, 'For the might of the land'	'"Ffor the myght off the lande, aftir the myght off the grete lordes thereoff, stondith most in the kynges officers": the English crown, provinces and dominions in the fifteenth century', *Concepts and Patterns of Service in the Later Middle Ages*, ed. A.E. Curry and

E. Matthew (Woodbridge, 2000)

Griffiths, *Henry VI*
R.A. Griffiths, *The Reign of King Henry VI, 1422–61* (1981)

Griffiths, *King and Country*
R.A.Griffiths, *King and Country: England and Wales in the Fifteenth Century* (1991)

Griffiths, 'King's Council'
'The King's Council and the First Protectorate of the Duke of York, 1450–54', *King and Country: England and Wales in the Fifteenth Century* (1981)

Harl 433
British Library Harleian Manuscript 433, ed. R.E. Horrox and P.W. Hammond (4 vols, Upminster, 1979–83)

Harriss, 'Political Society'
G.L. Harriss, 'Political Society and the Growth of Government in Late Medieval England', *Past and Present* 138 (1993): 28–57

Harvey, *Cade*
I.M.W. Harvey, *Jack Cade's Rebellion of 1450* (Oxford, 1991)

Harvey, 'Popular Politics'
I.M.W. Harvey, 'Was there Popular Politics in Fifteenth-Century England?', *The McFarlane Legacy: Studies in Late Medieval Politics and Society*, ed. R.H. Britnell and A. J. Pollard (Stroud, 1995)

Henry V
Henry V: The Practice of Kingship, ed. G.L. Harriss (Oxford, 1985)

Hicks, *Clarence*
M.A. Hicks, *False, Fleeting, Perjur'd Clarence: George Duke of Clarence 1449–78* (rev. edn, Bangor, 1992)

Hicks, *Rivals*
M.A. Hicks, *Richard III and his Rivals: Magnates and their Motives during the Wars of the Roses* (1991)

Hicks, *Warwick*
M.A. Hicks, *Warwick the Kingmaker* (Oxford, 1998)

HPT
History of Parliament: The Commons 1386–1421, ed. J.S. Roskell, L. Clark and C. Rawcliffe

	(4 vols, 1992)
HR	Historical Research
Ingulph	Ingulph's Chronicle of the Abbey of Croyland, ed. H.T. Riley (1859)
James	M.E. James, Society, Politics and Culture in Early Modern England (Cambridge, 1986)
Lander	J.R. Lander, Crown and Nobility 1450–1509 (1976)
McFarlane, England	K.B. McFarlane, England in the Fifteenth Century (1981)
McFarlane, Nobility	K.B. McFarlane, The Nobility of Later Medieval England (Oxford, 1973)
McFarlane Legacy	The McFarlane Legacy: Studies in Late Medieval Politics and Society, ed. R.H. Britnell and A.J. Pollard (Stroud, 1995)
Myers	The Household of Edward IV: The Black Book and the Ordinance of 1478, ed. A.R. Myers (Manchester, 1959)
Original Letters	Original Letters illustrative of English History, ed. H. Ellis (11 vols, in four series, 1824–46)
Paston L & P	Paston Letters and Papers of the Fifteenth Century, ed. N. Davis (2 vols, Oxford, 1971–6)
Plumpton L & P	Plumpton Letters and Papers, ed. J.L. Kirby (Camden 5th series viii, 1998)
POPC	Proceedings and Ordinances of the Privy Council, ed. N.H. Nicolas, (7 vols, 1834–7)
'Private Indentures'	'Private Indentures for Life Service in Peace and War 1278–1476', ed. M. Jones and S. Walker, Camden Miscellany 32 (1994)
PRO	Public Record Office, London
Revolution and Consumption	Revolution and Consumption in Late Medieval England, ed. M.A. Hicks (Woodbridge, 2001)

RP	*Rolls of Parliament* (6 vols, 1767–77)
Rulers and Ruled	*Rulers and Ruled in Late Medieval England*, ed. R.E. Archer and S.K. Walker (1995)
Stonor L & P	*Stonor Letters and Papers, 1290–1483*, ed. C.L. Kingsford, (Camden 3rd series 29, 30, 1919); *Camden Miscellany* 13 (1924)
TRHS	*Transactions of the Royal Historical Society*
Vale	*The Politics of Fifteenth Century England: John Vale's Book*, ed. M.L. Kekewich, C.F. Richmond, A.F. Sutton, L. Visser-Fuchs and J.L. Watts (Richard III and Yorkist History Trust, Stroud, 1995)
Virgoe	R. Virgoe, *East Anglian Society and the Political Community of Late Medieval England*, ed. C. Rawcliffe, C.M. Barron and J.T. Rosenthal (Norwich, 1997)
Watts, *Henry VI*	J.L. Watts, *Henry VI and the Politics of Kingship* (Cambridge, 1996)

1

PARAMETERS

The Wars of the Roses were the longest military and political upheaval between King Stephen and Charles I. Did the Wars result from fundamental weaknesses in the social and political systems? Or did they mark merely the lowest point in two centuries of under-performance? In actuality they were a wholly exceptional epoch. A deep economic recession ('The Great Slump 1440–1480')[1] and consequent royal impoverishment coincided with unprecedented foreign intervention and popular unrest, which would have strained any political system, however strong and healthy it was. The crisis headlines in the textbooks overlook the underlying harmony and stability. Central government, local government, the judicial system and the economy operated throughout uninterrupted and indeed almost unimpaired. It was not that fifteenth-century England was in turmoil bar a few brief interludes of peace, but that only occasionally and only briefly was normal life disrupted by political crises. It is the systems rather than the events that are the subject of this book.

Behind every system lies the people, perhaps two millions strong, who comprised and contributed to society both individually and in the mass. Society is always shaped by its members, who formulate and constantly modify its rules, which in turn shape, channel and eventually constrain human energies. Such structures are themselves slowly modified in arrears to fit contemporary realities as society gradually evolves. When any society outgrows the rules, the rules have to be altered. Such was the case in fifteenth-century England.

Any political system is a facet of society. Although ostensibly authoritarian and hierarchical, the English monarchy depended on the consent both of its greatest subjects – the magnates, aristocracy and urban oligarchies that comprised the politically active nation – and increasingly of the commons as well. No English king could outrage the values and expectations of these groups and survive. Royal government and

1

royal laws evolved alongside society, more frequently through agreement in parliament and through the actual practice of enforcement and neglect than through violence and revolution.

The fifteenth century in England was a phase within long-lived political and social systems that lasted for many centuries, that already existed by the twelfth century and continued into the seventeenth and even beyond. 'Relatively little structural change took place in English society between the fourteenth and the nineteenth centuries', wrote Professor Stone long ago. Even the English Revolution, Professor Laslett implied, marked no serious break: 'a national social revolution' was 'not in question in the seventeenth century'.[2] It makes sense to consider the central social organisation of bastard feudalism over the five centuries 1150–1650 and to argue that the boundaries at each end are artificial and could be extended.[3] The pre-industrial economy and its attendant society make sense up to the Industrial Revolution of the mid-eighteenth century. No sharp or permanent changes in social and political systems within these centuries were more significant than the continuities uniting them. This is not to say that the Wars of the Roses or the mid-fifteenth-century slump did not matter, but that they failed to break the mould and to institute long-term fundamental change. Neither politics nor society could be static. The structures inherited in 1399 were transmitted to Tudor historians somewhat modified, yet remained familiar enough to Shakespeare and the audiences of his history plays. Contained within this book, therefore, there is a concept of progress, as what was inherited very slowly alters, but not a notion of progress with a moral component, a defined ending, determined theme, or inevitable objective. The present is not better than the past. Even our own present is being rapidly superseded.

The terminal dates that this book observes are 1399 and 1509. These mark important political events, not structures, for which relevant timespans are longer and merge gradually into something else rather than change sharply at precise moments. Historians, however, need definitions and boundaries if they are to understand the past and to communicate that understanding to others. They have to impose limits to their discussions if they are not to become too broad to be meaningful. Hence the dates to which this book is confined, the long fifteenth century that has become hallowed by custom, at least for late medieval historians.

2

POLITICAL CULTURE

Past political cultures

Late medieval people were like ourselves. We have not evolved. Mankind has undergone no discernible biological change since written history began, let alone over the past five centuries. It follows that we can empathise with our fifteenth-century predecessors, imagine ourselves in their situation, and understand why they acted as they did. We appreciate that the past differs from the present: the circumstances, the context, have changed. It seems much more than a century ago that 'great household was still a most potent force in every aspect of the English life'.[1] If the rural Gloucestershire of his youth in the 1920s had become a lost world to Laurie Lee thirty years on,[2] how much more striking (if gradual) have been the transformations from medieval to modern. Researching past circumstances is what historians and archaeologists are for. Once the facts are established, as they generally are, we can place ourselves in our fifteenth-century predecessors' shoes, we can locate ourselves in their England, we can reconstruct and understand what they were going through, and why they behaved as they did. Professor Richmond's twenty-year immersion in the *Paston Letters* revealed that 'the parameters of the political culture' were 'much the same, resemble closely [and were] more or less synonymous with those of our political culture'.[3] We too can be late medieval magnates. Clad in appropriate armour, bearing bows and arrows, on the correct site and briefed precisely on events, we can re-enact the Wars of the Roses and even improve on the results. Some of us do.

'Here we deceive ourselves. We have fallen into a common fallacy. 'Our characteristic failing ... is the complete inability to meet the past on its own terms and value it for its own sake.'[4] Assuming that medieval notions of contract were like our own 'is extremely dangerous', writes Professor Green. 'The longer I have worked on the Middle Ages the more alien and remote they have come to seem to

3

be.'[5] Even professional historians seldom agree what the facts and events mean. Our subjects did not help us. 'For much of the medieval period', K.B. McFarlane wrote, 'the evidence for motive is almost entirely lacking.' We lack the statements of motive that can be taken for granted even for the Tudor era that immediately follows. We therefore deduce intentions from actions. Such deductions are inevitably crude, over-simplified and reductionist. Too often they are expressed in cynical terms of material self-interest and self-preservation. Rampant individualists, even in our society, are conditioned by values and social norms. Of course such material considerations mattered to fifteenth-century people; but what they saw as materially vital, such as the continuance of their family names and titles or the salvation of their souls, were not necessarily what we expect today. We must not presume that late medieval motives were less complex and late medieval people more consistent than we are today.

The application of third-millennium assumptions or commonsense to past scenarios seldom explains what actually happened. Even commonsense or reason has changed its meaning, so that what our medieval predecessors thought reasonable often appears to us perverse. 'Though to modern minds apparently spurious', their arguments were 'rational in terms of criteria that were familiar to the authors'.[6] The reverse also applies. Twenty-first-century judgements are too often anachronistic. Almost every day politicians and broadcasters denounce some aspect of our present as medieval, usually out of ignorance. Fifteenth-century England, its society and politics, bastard feudalism and the Wars of the Roses, its leaders and people have too often attracted hostile historians whose preconceptions prevent them from understanding the past on its own terms. 'This means that now, as never before' – and how much truer is this now than of 1959! – 'there is a danger of underestimating the importance of aristocratic and hierarchical principles in English history ... of aristocratic leadership and the great household before the twentieth century.'[7] Worse than that, for some 'it is only a matter for indignation' that the great had such thickly staffed households or a reasonable presumption 'that aristocrats were an antipathetic group of superfluous parasites'. Was chivalry more than 'a polite veneer' or 'loyalty chiefly a literary device, only active ... when self-interest (or mutual interest) binds man and lord together'? Most historians approve of Henry VII's despoliation of his nobility and Edward IV's destruction of his brother Clarence. Such prejudices can be multiplied, creeping even into apparently sympathetic histories – for no historian, however hard he tries, can wholly exclude his own age from his work – and get in the way of historical understanding.

Perhaps present-minded assertions that 'gentlemen behave badly' and even 'that dukes will throw their weight about'[8] are relevant to us today – the author knows no dukes – but they are valueless as keys to the cultures of the past. 'We fail to realise that at the time these things seemed both natural and momentous', lamented Professor Myers, and thus 'miss an important element in the spirit of the age and the dynamic forces of its society'.[9] When we deduce from first principles, still more when we resort to modern political prejudices, our assumptions diverge radically from those of the fifteenth century; and so too, consequently, do our conclusions.

The past is not separated from the present merely by physical and material conditions, by facts and figures, but by the whole climate of ideas. We cannot bridge this divide merely by reconstructing the context. We need to enter the spirit of the age: the first principles that operated within the set of circumstances that we have indeed established by our research and which caused our subjects, so often, to act differently from ourselves. 'The first and greatest task of a historian', wrote Namier, revealingly quoted by Carpenter, 'is to understand the terms in which men of a different age thought and spoke and the angle from which they viewed life and society'.[10] We have too easily discounted ideas and principles as primary sources of motivation.

Monty Python's Terry Jones strikingly illustrates the point. Roman attitudes to gladiators contrast with those current today. If 'the idea of killing living creatures for sport horrifies a lot of people today', how much more shocking is gladiatorial combat, which made a public spectacle of murder and which everyone would condemn.

> Go back those 2,000 years and the reverse is true. There is not a single Roman writer who condemns the business of public killing in the gladiatorial games ... The Romans believed that it was beneficial to watch people being killed. Not just good entertainment, but morally valuable. It made people into better Romans.

Today we empathise with hunted foxes and would pity doomed gladiators.

> We think that compassion is one of the noblest human virtues – that, in fact, you can measure the quality of a civilised society by its level of compassion for the weak, the poor, for those who suffer. By that standard, Rome may not deserve to be called civilised at all, because in the ancient city compassion

was regarded as a moral defect. Seneca, the stern voice of Roman republican virtue, said it was an emotion that 'belonged to the worst sort of people – old women and silly females'.

Terry Jones exaggerated,[11] but his point holds good. Between the Romans and ourselves there lie not merely differences in intellectual principles but the values that permeate whole societies and civilisations. There is a cultural gulf. Fifteenth-century England was also a culture quite different from our own.

Direct avowals of motive do matter. There always were political and constitutional principles, convictions and beliefs that were consciously formulated and expressed, that impelled people into action, and for which, in the last resort, they were willing to die, in battle or at the stake. We should not doubt their force because we cannot share them. They are the tip of that iceberg of ideas that make fifteenth-century culture so alien to ourselves. There was an accepted constitutional framework within which politicians thought and acted, but political and constitutional ideas were never the sole source of political motivation or even of primary importance. Self-conscious principles are no more important in determining conduct than the unconscious and even subconscious ideas that condition them or, indeed, combat them or insidiously undermine them. Standards and prejudices instilled in childhood may predispose or even predetermine one's political stance as an adult. Already there was a culture of childhood[12] that may well have underpinned much that followed. We need also to allow for all those values and standards, criteria, assumptions and misconceptions, perceptions, attitudes and prejudices, conventions, customs and manners, myths, expectations and aspirations, sentiments and even instincts across the whole range of human experience from military prowess to potty-training. If human nature remains constant, much that we take to be natural and biological turns out to be culturally engendered. Even emotions and feelings, such as Terry Jones' compassion or love for another human, are shaped by nurture, by formal education, example, social contact and environment. Our sense of humour and our sense of the pathetic are cultural phenomena specific to our own era.

What makes up a culture embraces the whole range of intangible notions that we all carry around in our heads. Some notions have long and learned academic pedigrees, which may well have escaped the majority of users. Most are inchoate and imprecisely formulated, many are potentially contradictory, and all are influenced by circumstances and vary from individual to individual. They certainly go beyond the 'ordering, rationalising, contextualising, and articulating of *conscious* thought'.[13] Fully to comprehend fifteenth-century politics, society and culture, we must assimilate all these notions, which is obviously impossible. We cannot psycho-analyse the dead.

Let us consider as illustration our families, into which we are all born and which we all take for granted. Today we presume a free choice of wedding partner by mature and consenting adults (the love match), monogamous marriage (one wife or one husband at a time), commitment to life-long marriage (until death us do part), the establishment of a separate household on marriage, the nuclear family of conjugal couple and offspring, breeding exclusively within wedlock, and remarriage on the death of a partner. Whilst we are aware of other societies that do things differently, that practise polygamy, child-marriages and arranged marriages, we consider their practices inferior, wrong, sinful or even illegal. Our society and our law discriminates against unmarried cohabitees, incest, bastards, wife-beaters, child-abuse and bigamists. Despite galloping changes, such as divorce on demand, sexual liberation, universal contraception, artificial restraints on family size (2.4 children) and a growing acceptance of gay partnerships, marriage and parenthood, most people still regard our inherited conventions as normal and correct. Yet that is what is being discussed here in a fifteenth-century context: not human nature, biology, hormones or instincts, but conventions, which society once developed and which society can change; conventions that apply to our western society and that interlock. Britain today and fifteenth-century England share the convention of late marriage, normally between mature adults in their twenties and long after puberty, from which most of the other conventions listed above stem and with which they interact, which still differentiate our society from those with different practices elsewhere both now and in the past.[14] Neither we nor fifteenth-century people think or thought about such matters very much. We take them for granted, presume them, infer from them, and act on them.

Conceptions of the family shape most aspects of the lives of its members and their relations with other families, larger units and even the state itself. A monarchical system has the royal family at its centre, is presided over by the head of that family who combines or has combined the roles of husband, father, brother and son (or female equivalent), and imposes administrative, financial and military obligations on the heads of every other family. Within the broad similarities of the families of today and yesteryear, however, there are differences over five centuries. Thus aristocratic marriages, even between mature adults, were normally arranged and teenage marriages were common-place. Child labour was normal and most adolescents were boarded as servants with other families.[15] A lower life-expectancy made for short marriages, many step-parents and orphans, more children per family but a higher wastage among them, relatively few – and younger – old people. There were variations between classes and regions and over time. Similar conventions in different cultures can produce different results.

Whilst the family is a fundamental building block of society, even this brief consideration indicates how extensive were its ramifications and the range of conventions that governed its operation and hence those aspects of society with which it interacted. No consideration has yet been given to the related issues of morality, upbringing and accul-turation, gender, lineage and inheritance. A dozen attitudes were explored by Dr Horrox's team in 1994 – attitudes to government, law, the aristocracy, service, religion, education and advancement, informa-tion and science, women, urban society, rural society, the poor, and death: in each case there was not one attitude to be considered, but many.[16] Yet those examined scarcely scratched the surface. What about attitudes towards children and foreigners, to trade and war, contempo-rary senses of the past and patriotism? If there was indeed 'a culture of childhood',[17] surely there was a culture of old age, a teenaged or adolescent culture too? If the English 'very thoroughly believe in prophecies, phantoms and witchcraft', which seemed at times to provide a rational explanation of the present and a hope for the future, if Chief Justice Fortescue was serious about alchemy's capacity to cure and enrich his king, and if all sorts of things had symbolic meaning as tokens, these are Pandora's boxes not for exploration here.[18] And there was also change over time: not just a state, but a 'growth of "legal consciousness"' which 'shaped people's values, beliefs and aspi-rations and ... [influenced] political attitudes'.[19]

It is probably impracticable to reconstruct the full range of ideas current even today and certainly impossible for the past. This book does not attempt the task. Nor does it attempt to assign ideas to particular pigeonholes, as values, assumptions, prejudices, principles, etc. Our predecessors were not machines, who imbibed a common culture with their mother's milk and applied it the same way. Their responses varied; they even reacted against it, both in identical and contrasting circumstances. No book can analyse a whole culture. This one confines itself to political society and hence a more manageable range of ideas. The total remains impressive nonetheless and only some ideas can be considered, some in what immediately follows, yet others more appropriately in chapters to which they relate.

Categories of ideas

The range of ideas is enormous and beyond satisfactory categorisation, yet arrangement into categories is a necessary preliminary to rational discussion.

The first category can be dismissed summarily. It consists of those ideas that are not political. Most ideas in most periods are not primarily political and hence do not demand extended treatment here. Superstition, a mother's love for her children, fear of darkness, squeamishness, and respect for the aged are obvious examples. However most ideas have the potential to affect political principles and indeed political conduct under certain circumstances, particularly if politicians promoted or offended established norms, as some of the examples in the second category demonstrate.

Second are all those ideas that are not primarily political, but which nevertheless have political implications. Religion, arguably the most important, constitutes a whole system, a framework for everything else, and incorporates many facets that bear not at all on politics. Only parts of it are discussed below. Just as fundamental in quite different ways are attitudes towards women and the concepts of worship and service, which underpinned all areas of life including politics, but only occasionally impinged directly on it and determined political behaviour.

Together these dwarf the third category, those ideas that are overtly political: what are normally categorised as political and constitutional theory. Political historians cannot restrict themselves to these. Several key concepts are discussed below: many others are taken up in subsequent sections.

Religion

Sophisticated modern historians find it hard to engage with medieval religion – its literalness, pervasiveness and immediacy. It is still more difficult for those who are not christian or religious at all. Yet engagement with medieval religion is inescapable. It was pervasive and touched every aspect of social behaviour. Christianity was the principal and perhaps the sole religion in western Europe, otherwise known as Christendom. It was a complex system of beliefs to which everybody subscribed or acquiesced. The christian Church was at one level the congregation of the faithful, the sum total of many millions of christians. At another level, it was a vast multi-national organisation knit together in a complex hierarchy, with its own legislative and regulatory machinery, that united into an authoritarian federation the separate churches in every land, their constituent bishoprics, religious houses, parishes and chantries, and hundreds of thousands of professional clergy. The Church was massively endowed with land which it could not alienate and to which it continued to add throughout the later middle ages, albeit more slowly than if the Statute of Mortmain (1279) had not been passed, and licences had not to be secured and paid for. The Church was therefore the landlord of a high proportion of the population, including many aristocrats, who also feature frequently as its estates officers, lessees and the military commanders of its tenants. The ramifications of Christianity are enormous: whole books have been written not just on these topics, but on particular individuals, on specific institutions and on such phenomena as mysticism, new liturgical feasts, shrines and pilgrimages that the people in this book knew about and cared about, but which have not been selected for discussion here.

All fifteenth-century Englishmen were christians. They had all been exposed to the doctrines and moral teachings of Christianity. They believed that the Bible was literally true: the Genesis story, Noah's Ark, Jesus, the Incarnation and the Virgin Birth, Crucifixion and Resurrection, and a mass of saints' lives. Such events were the key dates each year, conveniently correlated to the seasons, by which they regulated their lives. They believed that the end of the world was nigh, when God would judge the just and unjust and consign them respectively to Heaven and Hell, and their conduct determined both their final judgement and intermediate sufferings in purgatory. Hence their good works: their benefactions, to monasteries, chantries or hospitals, their pilgrimages, their veneration of relics and new cults, their almsgiving and contributions to road-maintenance and other public works, and the constant upgrading of church fabrics and furnishings such as screens, pulpits, bells, images, pews and stained glass. They believed that God still intervened in the world, attributed plague, floods and other natural causes to His displeasure, and conformed to His mandates to assuage His anger. They prayed to Him against their enemies and thanked Him for their victories: 'King Edward, distinguished by the double victory, seemed, in everyone's judgement, to have most adequately demonstrated the justice of his cause'; so too did Henry VII in 1485.[20] Christ and his saints were models of conduct and Christ's teaching shaped their attitudes to the poor, to the state and to nature itself. They knew themselves to be part of an international church headed by St Peter's successor, the pope in Rome, which was engaged in a constant titanic struggle against the forces of evil, the devil, the Avignonese anti-pope, schismatics and Islam alike. They subscribed to and maintained churches wherein God was worshipped, they financed and respected the clergy who promulgated His teaching, and answered bishops and archdeacons on visitations. They attended mass every Sunday, on holy days and often on other days too, and ate fish rather than meat on fastdays. The Church baptised them, married them and regulated whom they might marry, confirmed them and buried them. They confessed, were absolved and made practical recompense (penance). Everyone belonged to a parish and many joined gilds and confraternities, which promoted neighbourliness and co-operation and relieved the unfortunate. Charity and education were facets of religion. The names of God and the saints were constantly on their lips, in their oaths and dates. Christian influences were everywhere, unquestioned, often unthought about, but inescapable.

Christianity was practised, perhaps, rather than understood. The niceties of doctrine escaped most people because they were unknown to the clergy and because definition was unnecessary without sectarian challenge. Lollardy, which denied many catholic beliefs, was difficult to detect because orthodox doctrine was not widely known, because key differences were not recognised,[21] and because its teachings differed in degree rather than kind from the puritanism of Bishop Brinton and William Langland. Lollards were not alone in urging the disendowment of the church by Henry IV's parliaments. The Lollards set an example of dissent. They even rebelled in 1414, 1431 and 1437, in the first instance apparently to overthrow the royal family and established Church. Such conduct discredited reformers and denied Lollardy much influence over the catholic Church. That Henry V and Edward IV persecuted heretics was to their credit.[22] From 1401 Lollards could be burnt at the stake: a handful were, but most of those caught preferred to recant. Lollards were nevertheless a small and geographically dispersed minority. The highly intellectual doctrinal teachings of their founder John Wyclif (d. 1384) and his university followers, who were rooted out in 1410–15, were diluted among their humbler followers, who crudely rejected many of the symbols of official Christianity such as transubstantiation, confession and fastdays. Lollards were detected because they did not fast, they read books, were better informed on doctrine and allowed prominence to women in anticipation of the Reformation itself. Astrology, alchemy, magic and folklore, in contrast, co-existed with the Church.

Heretics were exceptions to the christian ideal of a harmonious society. Christian society, indeed, was Christ's mystical society. Taking the mass was a commitment to peace and unity exemplified by the kiss of peace. Ideally christians should live at peace with one another, co-operating rather than competing, in love and concord. This reality was often formally recognised at such towns as Coventry, Exeter, York and Newcastle, where 'love, concord, and unity', 'unity and concord' and 'good unity, concord and charity' were objectives of governance and gild membership.[23] If rural society lacks such formal minutes and ordinances, its arbiters sought rather to reconcile than judge, to replace acrimony with friendship, and to restore the love, unity, concord, and amity that, by implication, existed before.[24] Parsons refused communion to those not at peace with their neighbours. Peace, quiet, order and harmony were norms broken by conflict, not vice versa. Social harmony need not imply equality: the hierarchy of ranks, inequality of wealth and opportunity, the division between those who commanded and obeyed, were inescapable, inevitable and indeed eternal – part of God's divine plan. Everyone, however humble and exploited, was essential and had a necessary place in this world and the promise of better in the next. A whole series of metaphors of society, such as the human body, the ship, beehive and music, enshrined the notion of variegated contributors to a larger whole to the benefit of all.

Most pervasive of such images throughout the century was the human body, or body politic, in which the king was head, various classes and occupations different limbs and organs, all essential to the operation of the whole. Corpus Christi, the mystical body of Christ, as frequently celebrated in urban processions and places, encapsulated the same notion. It has proved useful to modern historians too: 'the concept of body', wrote M.E. James, 'provided urban societies with a mythology and ritual in terms of which the opposites of social wholeness and social differentiation could be both affirmed and also brought into a creative tension'.[25]

Christianity was hence concerned to prevent breaches of social harmony arising from sin, conflict and mere disregard of the interests of others. It was a moral code that was designed to govern human conduct. The Ten Commandments forbade, among other things, blasphemy, murder, theft and adultery. Such defects as pride, gluttony, sloth, avarice and lechery were categorised as deadly sins. Preachers denounced the defects of each social class. The Church regulated social relations, particularly with the poor and helpless, and taught that society – the commonweal – was for the benefit of all rather than the great. Christianity also underpinned and shaped the aristocratic code of chivalry. Such teachings were enforced: by confession, penances or punishment after death. Those unconfessed and unpenitent were denied the sacrament of the mass, which aristocrats and even kings, with their staff of chaplains and confessors, could scarcely escape. All levels of government and justice, not merely the Church hierarchy and courts, held authority ultimately from God and were concerned to do his will. Manors, towns and gilds, for example, regulated sins and nuisances. Adultery and usury were incompatible with civic office at Coventry (War.), where the mayor was obliged to worship daily. Noblemen not only went to mass daily, but required it of their households. Parliament legislated to stop hunting on Sundays and festivals, when all good christians were at church, and against fairs and markets on feastdays and Sundays because they encouraged covetousness, perjury, drunkenness and strife.

Contracts were commonly made not merely by exchange of written indentures, but of oaths, normally taken on the gospels; so too were appointments to office and testimonies in court. Christianity reinforced the action. Breaking an oath was perjury, which was regarded both as a sin and as dishonourable, the source of 'public disgrace' to the offender and his heirs. It was the greatest of shame for jurors to be attainted. Perjury recurs frequently in the chapters that follow. It dishonoured kings.

> It is not knightly, from an oath to vary;
> A king of trouth ought [to] be exemplary.

There were ten counts of perjury in the parliamentary indictment of Richard II. We should not underestimate the gravity of the perjury charge levelled against the usurping Henry IV by the Percies to justify their insurrection or the damage that it did to the reputation of the usurper and his dynasty.[26] Rulers were liable to all seven of the deadly sins, to divine punishment hereafter and to public condemnation at the time. Christian values were highly relevant politically.

Attitudes to women

One could not deduce from the most familiar sources that women constituted around half the medieval population or that it was their fecundity that ensured the continuation of the human race. One reason they appear less than men is because they spent more of their time within their families and dwellings, which is not documented. Another is that their more public activities are concealed because women were comprehended within the context of their male relatives, whether fathers, brothers or husbands. A wife took her husband's status as well as his name. Women were destined for marriage, childbearing, and homemaking. They dressed to delight men and were disposed of in marriage by men. They were conventionally passive, obedient and deferential to their masculine superiors, who could physically discipline them and who represented them economically, socially and politically. They were ineligible for ordination. Hence formal education was wasted on them. Their husbands administered their property and permitted or refused them permission to make their wills. They were disqualified from taking up trades, holding public office, sitting in parliament as peers or MPs, and from warfare. To depart from such expectations, by rejecting the partner selected for them or choosing their own, remaining single, pursuing careers or speaking out, titivating themselves, walking unaccompanied, gossiping, or even leading an independent social life, was frowned upon and excited defamation. For Englishmen, Joan of Arc was a sorceress and cross-dresser, whose chivalric activities were unwomanly and out of place. Women's reputations were especially fragile. If impugned, it detracted from a spinster's valuation on the marriage market and in a wife threatened the legitimacy of the offspring on which a property-based society depended. The virginity, chastity and hence honour of women was thus a kind of property which men felt obliged to defend or avenge, sometimes violently. The double standard effectively condoned among men, especially aristocrats, was denied to women.

We know of such standards principally from the writing of males, whether theologians, lawyers, preachers or legislators, national and local, and by deduction from what occurred in practice. They were the values of a male-dominated society, widely if not universally shared by men, and often – perhaps normally – accepted by women and internalised. 'There is no doubt', writes Pollard, 'that most women accepted their state as the second sex'.[27] Certain women infringed and even subverted all these conventions. Moreover reality often differed from the ideology. Housewifery involved many skills, including management. Many male occupations required participation by wives. Marriage was a partnership: companionate marriages happened. Most women had at least to supplement family earnings. At all levels widowhood removed women from their spouses' shadows and reveals them as effective managers, as doubtless they were before. The Paston ladies were not helpless innocents, but economically and politically effective, whether married or widowed. A masculine chivalric code in practice admitted them to full participation in the day-to-day establishment, maintenance and estimation of honour of themselves and others.[28]

Whether to marry again and who to marry was a widow's choice, in which she pleased herself, sometimes in defiance of convention. Some trades, for example brewing and silkweaving, were all-female preserves. Women have been revealed as holding land, litigating, trading, taking on apprentices and gild office. Women could express themselves: the pious lady, in and outside the monastery, orthodox or conventional, was a contemporary stereotype particularly accessible to modern study. Outspoken and opinionated women, unruly women, wily women, and women who beat their husbands all occur.

Land law gave priority to men over women, both by consigning females' property to their husbands and by preferential treatment of men in inheritance customs. The latter was strengthened by entails in the male line. Yet women were protected against deprivation and bene-fited from the system. A daughter was supported by her father or brother, a wife by her husband whilst living and after his death by dower from his estates for life and a share of his chattels. It was conventional amongst the propertied to endow their daughters, occa-sionally by placing them in nunneries, never a cheap option, or by paying substantial portions for their marriage. Warwick the Kingmaker was not alone in including a bastard daughter in such arrangements. This investment by the bride's family in her future was commonly matched by the bridegroom's family, who settled land jointly on the married couple and their offspring, who were thus safeguarded in the event of the husband's death. Such jointures became commonplace and have been seen by historians as unduly advantaging mothers at the expense of heirs. Coupled with dower, jointure could place half the estate or more in a dowager's hands, to pass to a succession of husbands to the loss of the heir: most propertied dowagers remarried. The longest-lived like Katherine Duchess of Norfolk, widowed 1432–83 and four times remarried, and multiple dowagers like the three Roos widows in 1436 encumbered and impoverished their heirs.[29] The second marriages of elderly men to much younger women frequently transferred land from the offspring of first to second marriages: Ralph Neville, Earl of Westmorland (d. 1425) and John Talbot, Earl of Shrewsbury (d. 1453) sought deliberately to advantage younger sons over their seniors. All such scenarios were potential sources of conflict. Moreover, whatever the inheritance system, a combination of low fertility and high mortality often did bring inheri-tances to women or through women. Heiresses always had a high marital valuation. Even estates in tail male could devolve on women. Most estates and peerages at some point passed through the female line – female inheritance was the principal source of continuity – and

15

some of the greatest estates, such as the Holland earldom of Kent, were fragmented among co-heiresses. Passage to an heiress commonly advantaged her marital kin over her collateral blood. It was male uncles and nephews, cousins and bastards who might have to fend for themselves.

It was far from unusual, therefore, for women to find themselves landholders, even great landholders over many years, and thus to be propelled into social leadership, political influence and power locally or even nationally. Joan Lady Bergavenny (d. 1435) was an unruly dowager and Margaret Lady Hungerford proved a skilful political operator. Pillow-talk was a fifteenth-century phenomenon. Yet the presumption of incompetence and masculine compassion towards the weaker vessel could protect women against the full penalties for their actions. Four royal women convicted or charged with sorcery escaped the worst consequences.[30] Doubtless there were many women apart from Alice Montagu and Margaret Beaufort, respectively countesses of Salisbury and Richmond, who deserved attainder for treason but escaped it. The slaying of a pregnant woman was a particularly heinous crime which no perpetrator could defend: hence its inclusion alongside treason in Henry VI's proclamation against Jack Cade.[31] Wives and widows of traitors lost their dowers, but retained their inheritances and jointures. Admittedly they were regarded as fifth columnists, potential subsidisers of treacherous spouses, often consigned temporarily to a nunnery or closely supervised, and their estates were taken into custody. Their sufferings could be acute, physical and mental: the future Richard III deprived both his mother-in-law Anne Countess of Warwick and Elizabeth Countess of Oxford of their legitimate estates. Despite her piteous lament to two parliaments, Anne's dispossession was approved by Edward IV and made permanent by Henry VII. The penalties of unsuccessful strife created other less recognisable victims, such as those whose marriage prospects were blighted, who were obliged like Frideswide Hungerford to take the veil,[32] or who suffered bereavements. Three young widows, Eleanor Butler, Elizabeth Lucy and Elizabeth Wydeville, may have bought concrete benefits from Edward IV with their sexual favours.

Male discrimination against women mattered greatly in another area, that of succession to the crown. In 1460 Richard Duke of York lodged a dynastic claim to the crown that had been transmitted via two females. Fortescue argued against it. Many former Yorkists backed Henry Tudor because he committed himself to wedding Elizabeth of York, while his own Lancastrian claim derived through his mother Margaret Beaufort, who was still living, yet no consideration is known to have been given to rule by either lady on her own behalf. Henry IV havered about whether to allow his grand-daughters title to the crown; their right to inherit the duchy of Lancaster was undeniable.

The concept of worship

Fifteenth-century Englishmen constantly alluded to their *worship*. It was evidently a touchstone against which events and actions were judged. Had a lawsuit, marriage or public exchange advanced or detracted from one's worship? Was a proposed action, however desirable otherwise, worshipful or derogatory? Worship in this sense signifies reputation or standing, how one was regarded by others, and the degree of respect one attracted. Richard Duke of York in 1450 was accompanied in as 'worshipful wise' as possible.[33] Worship applied also to institutions and corporations, to monasteries, towns and gilds. Dame Alice Braithwaite saw herself as 'the worshipful prioress of Dartford'. In 1457 the London mercers insisted that members settle their quarrels internally, 'within the fellowship of the mercery', since 'unity, rest, and peace' was conducive to the 'worship and profit of the same' and dissension damaged them all. No doubt this applied also to the city as a whole. At Coventry, gildsmen were enjoined to sit and process in order of seniority, 'for the worship of the city and wealth of the said craft'; their plays contributed also 'to the wealth and worship of the whole body'.[34] The town's reputation could only be enhanced by the sober, dignified and seemly conduct of its citizens. Misbehaviour hurt them all.

A king expected to be treated with most respect. His worshipful household must be run worshipfully to magnify his worship. In pursuance of 'the worship and welfare of the whole household', especially 'to the worship of these v feasts of the year', the treasurer (and other chief officers of the household) undertook 'to be a good, worshipful, [and] true officer to the king your sovereign lord' and comply with the 'good, old, sad, and worshipful and profitable rules'. Among many models, Henry I's 'great hospitality daily stood worshipfully without decay 32 years'. There were things that must not be done 'by right or worship'. When deciding who to employ, officers should be conscious of the 'worship of the court', select the worshipful such as 'young servants' only of 'clean blood, good of conditions, virtuous, and of person likely', and reject those who do not 'execute worship, cunning and profit for the king in his court'. 'Rascals or hangers-on, wasters, quarrelsome, malicious, drunk, dishonest or riotous servants, whose continued service could only detract from the king's own worship, were expelled. So too with guests. No riff-raff were to be admitted, but only the worshipful, 'worshipful lords', 'worshipful strangers', 'worshipful and honest people' or 'worshipful men and gentlewomen'. In marginal cases, officers had discretion 'if it seem worshipful', conducive to 'the king's worship', or to his 'worship and profit'. Worship was itself a short-hand term for such people: ideally the worshipful should be sat with their peers, but sometimes, unavoidably, they 'may be coupled with any worship'.[35]

Even when his dynastic claim was accepted in 1460, York was obliged to promise respect to Henry VI's worship and was assured that his own worship would not thereby suffer. Ten years earlier he had lamented how defeat abroad and rebellion at home had brought 'shameful rebuke in the conceit of strangers that [had] ever come to Christian prince'. In 1455 he promised to live and die at the king's command, 'if it be to the worship of the crown of England and the welfare of this your noble realm'. National pride, national shame, fighting for king and country and patriotism are all encompassed here. What was required once again, the Yorkist earls declared in 1459, was that the king, 'his land and people may grow to as great worship and prosperity as they have been held before amongst all Christian realms'. With their reforms, they claimed next year, 'our sovereign lord shall reign with great worship, love of God and his people' and will be able to conquer wherever he wills. 'Worship of the realm' demanded that embassies should comprise the eminent, well and splendidly accompanied, and should give great gifts to their foreign counterparts. King's councillors should be 'worshipful': worthy of respect and respected. By serving the king, his household, officers, ministers and councillors themselves became worshipful. Henry V's army was a 'right worshipful host' and Edward IV's victorious campaign in 1461 was a 'worshipful journey'.[36]

That the king's worship evolved into national honour was entirely appropriate, for worship and honour, worshipful and honourable, were often used as synonyms. It is also apparent that worship is a socially elastic term, that an understandably elitist king had a high cut-off point for those worshipful enough to be his employees and guests, which frequently excluded many respectable people highly protective of their reputations. Amongst aristocrats worship derived in varying proportions from birth and lineage, rank and standing, probity of character, connections and achievements. It mattered greatly. Its loss signified loss of reputation, standing and respect, and hence of such important attributes as authority, service, even perhaps credit. At the top level York had three times to swear that he would not raise armed protests or rebellion on pain that 'I from that time be unabled [disqualified] from all manner [of] worship, estate or dignity, be it such as I now occupy or any other that might grow unto me in any wise'.[37] Perhaps the notion of chivalric honour really mattered only to the militarily minded and aristocracy – kings, the nobility, perhaps some professional soldiers and gentry. Even for them, worship meant more than this – their precedence, a sufficiently impressive escort, display or rewards.

Worship meant different things in different contexts: it was adapted to the means, lifestyle, locality, rank, aspirations and opportunities of individuals. It meant the integrity of behaviour based on social status.[38] York was a particularly grand aristocrat: at a somewhat lower level, the Pastons – a Norfolk gentry family – were also touchy about their worship. To them (and indeed to all aristocrats), it included the capacity to reward or protect minor servants – patronage and good lordship – or to celebrate a funeral or provide a tomb as one's worship demanded. Not to be able to spend up to one's station or to help one's friends 'causeth men to set the less by us'. To lay off servants, 'like masterless hounds', hurt an employer's reputation: it was far less damaging to place them elsewhere.[39] It required effort (and often expense) to maintain one's worship in the face of direct attacks, slights and setbacks and more insidious detractions, rumours, gossip and innuendo. Worship, meaning standing in society, meant living and behaving at the level appropriate to one's station – with *decorum*: everyone had a different worship to maintain. Yet each social level had its own notions of appropriate conduct. Worship therefore was a term adaptable to almost every individual and applicable certainly to all those with an established place in society, such as tradesmen and free-holders. Were *they* meant in 1469, when the northern rebels complained how 'no man of worship [could be] sure of his life, livelihood or goods'?[40] Below their station, we lack concrete documentary evidence of what constituted worship.

The concept of service

Worship and honour were not incompatible with *service*: service was not demeaning,[41] as it is generally regarded today. Service to the king actually was the best way to transform one's fortunes – to lift the servant from relative obscurity to landed wealth and a title, even to a peerage or an earldom. Service to a king made the rulers of his household worshipful and caused him to esteem them as barons or even earls.[42] Some recorded their services to kings or lords in their epitaphs or the badges they wore on their effigies.[43] Service could itself be honourable or worshipful, if it did not involve disparaging oneself. Well-born aristocrats, noble esquires, helped the king dress and undress. A baron oversaw the king's clothes, beds and service at meal times. The high rank of the king's servants or a duke's servants advanced their masters' worship. Similarly it was worship for a freeborn countryman like Richard Calle, a chaplain like John Gloys, and minor gentry to serve the Pastons, for John Paston III to take service in the duke of Norfolk's household, and for Norfolk himself to hold office of the king in peace and to serve under his command in war. The list of offices held of the king by the great magnates is a long one: often they held offices of others too, Northumberland being steward additionally to the archbishop of York.[44] Everyone served their social superiors. It was actually something to which to aspire: the eminence and authority of the master rubbed off on the servant. The prosperous knight William Stonor, with a century of ancestral leadership of Oxfordshire society behind him, nevertheless formally applied to serve both Lord Strange and the bishop of Lincoln.[45] It was necessary. He had no direct access to royal favour. No lord equalled no backing, implied a low valuation on one's service and a certain lack of respectability. Servants were a mark of status – were multiplied according to status – so that even minor clergy, such as the two elderly cantarists at Bridport, tradesmen and ploughmen had them. Not to have a servant was inferiority indeed. Service was a (or even the) 'dominant ethic of the middle ages'.[46]

All servants were employed to undertake duties specified by their master or mistress in return for reward. Characteristically this entailed full-time living-in service in a household for keep and other emoluments or a paid contract of employment. Many tradesmen and labourers had no single employer, but served by the day or by the task. In the higher echelons, service was less specific. Noble appointments or grants of fees typically speak of service done and to be done without specifying what the previous service was, for how long, or whether it was rewarded elsewhere or unrewarded.[47] Rewards might not be monetary, but comprised rather enhanced status, authority, perquisites and backhanders. Fifteenth-century people took service for their own reasons, normally involving the enhancement of their own interests as well as those of their master, often at his expense, and sometimes beyond acceptable limits. The fee alone was seldom the objective. For lesser men, crumbs from the tables of others were not despised, but they could not be counted on: Wyclif, who wanted a bishopric, and Hoccleve, a privy seal clerk, had their share, but were disappointed nevertheless. Hope was the real incentive. In return they served, performing not according to a job description but whatever they were asked that was not actually derogatory. Such contracts were commonly indefinite, undefined and open-ended, compatible with private affairs and part-time service to others. They might develop, if the lord wished and was satisfied with the service offered, if the servant chose and exerted himself to be useful, but they need not. Some such servants worked themselves into the ground, as William Worcester did for Sir John Fastolf; others more easily dubbed sinecurists did more than might be supposed, yet others are best described as 'on call'.

The slightly outdated formula for ending a letter 'your obedient servant' has fifteenth-century precedent in the recommendation of service that commonly began their letters and was applicable, moreover, not just to inferiors and employees, but to lovers and from children to parents.[48] A wholly unsuitable term, to modern notions, was made appropriate to contemporaries by parallels that they saw between these relationships that we no longer perceive and which prescribed how they conducted themselves. The concept of service embodied a broad set of values applicable at every level and in an enormous range of circumstances. We shall encounter its specific and local expression in reference to patronage – arguably the fundamental means for governments to get things done – and bastard feudalism, that wideranging but nevertheless narrower 'set of relationships ... that provided the English aristocracy with the manpower that they required'.[49] Many specific contexts permeated the whole of society. Without service, society in its distinctive fifteenth-century form could not have existed.[50]

Constitutional ideas

Fifteenth-century England was a *monarchy*. It was contemporary practice for one individual not just to preside or reign over everyone else, as Queen Elizabeth II still does today, but actually to rule – to initiate, act and direct everything from routine appointments to vital decisions of peace and war. Government was the business of the king, not of the aristocracy as a class, not of an oligarchy or patriciate, not of the capitalist bourgeoisie or mercantile class, still less of the people as a democracy, nor even of the constitutional and effectively toothless monarchy of today. Monarchy was a fact of political life. To us, of course, an effective monarchy is an unfamiliar notion that we find difficult to understand, that is alien and self-evidently wrong: it blatantly contradicts our most heartfelt political ideals and convictions – notions of equality, democracy, merit and equal rights – the prejudices and presumptions of another age. But monarchy was not merely the practice in the fifteenth century. It was a principle that was self-evidently right and indeed necessary. It was not the only form of government ordained by God – republics had existed in the classical era and still did in contemporary Italy – but monarchy was preferable. There were no English republicans. Monarchy was a constitutional theory, a whole series of constitutional principles that nobody questioned and to which everyone subscribed, a handful exploring the ramifications in detail, the mass concurring automatically. An acceptance and understanding that monarchy was legitimate and right, natural, inevitable and unquestionable is the greatest and most difficult leap in imagination that twenty-first-century historians must undertake to appreciate English political culture at this time.

So the monarch actually ruled. Moreover he – and it was always *he* – was the *sovereign*. Everyone else in the realm, regardless of rank, was his *subject*. The king's *sovereignty* overrode any reciprocal relationships between his subjects and between particular subjects and himself. Formerly kings did not have direct relationships with all their people, but related instead to a series of groups, each of whom owed services in return for rights and had comparable relations with their own social inferiors. Magna Carta in 1215 had defined what the king was due from his feudal tenants-in-chief and what he owed them; set limits to his rights and defined their ties with their mesne tenants. Each group was separate, defined by its liberties or group-specific privileges, and subject only to the judgements of equals: that is, other members of the same group. By the fifteenth century, every Englishman or Englishwoman was the king's subject, equal in rights and obligations to any other. They were equal under the law: royal ministers and judges characteristically swore to exercise their offices and justice without fear or favour regardless of person or rank. Theoretically their relationship to the king was direct, unmediated by others, and they could turn to him directly for redress of grievances. Reality differed somewhat. By 1399 it was the king's right to command all his subjects. It was his right to receive their obedience, in precedence and in preference over any ties, obligations or loyalties. Royal authority was justified by the king's special relationship with God, as God's lieutenant or as His deputy exercising God's political authority on earth, and effectively wielding God's temporal sword. The king's position was consecrated by his formal coronation by the archbishop of Canterbury, by his anointing with the holy oil, by the crown that he wore on formal occasions, and by the throne on which he sat in parliament and at formal audiences.

Kingship has many ramifications reserved for discussion in later chapters. Kings however did not exist purely for their own benefit, whatever they may have thought and Machiavelli's *The Prince* subsequently taught, but rather they existed for the benefit of their subjects. This was because government had been instituted by God, so theorists said, for the benefit of Man. Government's role was to force mankind to live in harmony. 'Without the royal providence, it is impossible that peace be given', preached Archbishop Kemp in 1427. The king was chief justice and preserver of the law.[51] Monarchs therefore had a social function and a social justification for their rule. This was the concept of the commonweal. It had ancient origins, can indeed be traced back to the Greek philosopher Aristotle, but it was in common, almost short-hand, use among all such classes in the fifteenth century. It was expected of monarchs that their rule should advance the interests of their people, by keeping order amongst them, protecting them from their foes, and advancing their personal prosperity. In its deliberations Richard III's parliament 'ought to refer to one singular point ... the advancing of the commonweal'.[52] 'In salvation of the king's people', fifteenth-century bailiffs of Grimsby (Lincs.) swore 'to do right to every person or persons, as well to the poor as the rich, having no reward of any manner of person or persons'.[53] It was to the common good that conflicting kings and rebels alike appealed. Kings swore oaths at their coronations to do justice and prevent oppression. A king was to be judged by how far his rule was conducive to the public or commonweal – to his subjects' common good. 'Also it is the king's honour and also his office to make his realm rich', declared Fortescue, 'and it is his dishonour when that he hath but a poor realm, of which men will say that he reigneth but upon beggars, yet it were much greater dishonour if he found his realm rich and then made it poor'. A king was failing in his duty whose subjects were reduced to poverty. For a king 'to live upon his commons and upon the Church' was 'to his infamy and the withdrawing from him of the hearts of his subjects, which God willed not'.[54] A king had to satisfy his creditors. He was responsible for his servants, from his chief ministers down to his humblest household caterer, who was bound to operate 'truly, justly and equally, without oppression of the poor or favour of the rich, to the most profit and behoof of the king and eschewing of the hurt of his people'.[55] A king who detracted from his subjects' good, who impoverished or even wasted them, was a tyrant. It was a tyrant who levied unnecessary taxes or changed the coinage. How self-conscious must have felt Edward IV, who did both!

In certain senses, therefore, government was already a *public service*. Its justification was that it served the interests of the community of the realm. A great many of its actions, routine and extraordinary, administrative and judicial, were responses to the requests of its subjects, whether individuals, corporations or local communities. Their growing and evolving demands were constantly reshaping government. The greatest of its subjects, at court and in councils, and the elites of town, country and Church, participated in moulding the decisions, policies and conduct of the regime. They had an interest in its operation and it served their interests at least as much as the king's: not to accept their role, to operate as though government was the king's private business and his interests paramount, breached such expectations, with potentially dangerous effects. The standard applied by each individual, corporation and community was how far the king's rule was conducive to the public good – how far it served their own, often partisan, definition of the commonweal; the same criterion operated collectively in parliament. Good and holy Henry VI may have been, but he was judged by his subjects on how far his rule served their interests. Such practical considerations affected every aspect of government, its *patronage*, its finances and its policies: royal officials who served the king alone and a government that served the king's needs exclusively was liable to override the interests of subjects and their notion of the commonweal. The concept of service was relevant even to kings. This service function of the government and the king cannot be too often emphasised.

Maintaining law and order, keeping the peace and seeing justice for all were key functions of a king: perhaps even *the* key function. Murder, rape, larceny, etc. were crimes not merely against identifiable victims but against the king. They were breaches of the *king's peace*. Remedy rested not with the victim, through revenge or the blood feud, but with the king through the royal criminal justice system. It was for him to exact punishment. It was for him to create and maintain a climate in which lawlessness did not happen, was deterred and was repressed when it did happen. Whilst always reserving the right to intervene in person, kings presided over an elaborate judicial system, headed by the chief justice of king's bench at Westminster and including regular assizes, quarter sessions and many occasional commissions throughout England. He also provided remedies for many private wrongs, through litigation using royal writs in the common law courts and by bill in the prerogative courts; again he – or, by delegation, his councillors – handled cases for which there was no remedy. It was the king's task to see *justice* was done. The laws that were administered, whether the common law based on precedent, statute laws passed by parliament, equity or fairness derived from Roman civil law, were supposedly local expressions of the natural or divine law emanating from God himself. 'What else is the law of human nature', asked Fortescue, but 'the truth of justice, which is capable of being by right reason revealed?'[56] The king's authority applied everywhere: everyone's judgements, even those of marcher lords and earls palatine exempt from royal interference, were subject to review of how they exercised their powers and did indeed suffer such interventions. As fount of justice, the king's relationship to all his subjects was identical, at least theoretically. It was 'to do equal law & execution of right to all the king's subjects rich and poor, without having regard to any person' that royal justices swore on their appointment; most other officers, with verbal variants, swore likewise. They always promised not to be influenced by gifts or connections or to be otherwise partial.[57] It was highly appropriate therefore that Richard III appointed a master of requests and that Henry VII established a court of requests, perhaps initially to have statutory authority, that offered equal remedies to those who could not afford existing tribunals.[58]

The king's government, the king's peace, his laws, and the king's justice were in everybody's interests, even those who were restrained, coerced and punished. Those of rank and property had most to lose from disorder, lawlessness and crime. It was the king's *law* – the king's authority – that guaranteed their rights and possessions. He was their 'good lord', 'good lord' indeed of all 'good lords', responsible for seeing justice was done to and for the great; not infrequently his personal involvement was required to still their conflicts and to impose settlements upon them. Whatever frictions arise on particular issues at particular times and whatever abuses may sometimes have arisen, the aristocracy accepted the king's authority and played a full part in the legal system. All resorted regularly to the king's courts, sued those who had wronged them and often sought their prosecution, used the royal courts to register and enforce settlements of land and arbitrations, and frequently acted as judicial officers. 'In the last resort', Watts says, the king 'enjoyed a monopoly of legitimate power'.[59]

A king was not at fault if his subjects' advantage was beyond his power. The relationship between king and subjects was reciprocal: in return for his rule, he was entitled to the support necessary to advance their good. This took two forms, financial and military, and was due in his necessity. This was the *doctrine of necessity*. Once a king was engaged in war, in defence of all subjects and their rights, he was entitled to the means to prosecute it by drawing on the resources of his subjects. All men between the ages of 16 and 60 could be arrayed against foreign invaders and internal rebels. Kings were also entitled to resources, both monetary and in kind. Thus ships were commonly impressed for naval service. Earlier kings such as Edward I had interpreted this entitlement very liberally by seizing wholesale whatever they needed, to general condemnation. Fifteenth-century kings were more circumspect. Taxation was regularly sought through parliament and was occasionally enthusiastically given. Not infrequently efforts were made to secure the same results by resuming royal grants, by seeking economies, or by shifting the burden elsewhere. What was not possible, once the plea of necessity had been entered by the king, was an outright refusal. Such an act, theoretically, broke the contract between king and subject, and entitled him to take what he required. Such levies might take the form of forced gifts (benevolences) or forced loans, which theoretically should have been repaid, an obligation that was frequently forgiven by parliament.[60]

It was however a *limited monarchy*. The power that God possessed was, by definition, unfettered and undefined: absolute. It was this that He had handed down to His representatives. They however had limited it, by voluntary concessions to their subjects through charters or by their assent to legislation. Subsequent kings succeeded to what their predecessors had left to pass on: not, importantly, to what they had originally received. They were limited by previous concessions, such as Magna Carta or a town charter, and by any that they made themselves. English kings were bound by the law and obliged to implement it, although they were entitled to mitigate it by exercise of their grace or to allow laws to lapse into disuse.

England was also a *mixed monarchy*, in that power was shared between the king and his subjects. No English monarch could rule successfully without carrying his subjects with him. There was no natural opposition between the king and the nobility: conflict was the exception, not the norm. Not only did the nobility accept their social inferiority and the king's right to lead, they had a right to participate in government, a constructive interest in doing so, and were, moreover, the king's natural delegates to rule their home localities. 'Not until recently' have historians distinguished 'between the notorious overmighty and the essential mighty subject'.[61] At first a practical reality, the sharing of power and responsibility was elevated into a political theory by Fortescue, who described England as a *dominium politicum et regale*, and was taken for granted by the Elizabethan Sir Thomas Smith. Society was a group of rational beings seeking rational order, whose collective judgement may have been better than that of any individual and who therefore made a useful contribution towards decision-making. 'Whatever has been rightly decided and approved with the counsel and consent of the magnates and the general agreement of the *res publica*', a thirteenth-century treatise states, 'the authority of the king or prince having first been added to, has the force of law'.[62] The essence of the relationship was captured by the English parliament, which represented everyone – the king himself and the three estates. It was a *representative* assembly. The Lords represented themselves and could bind themselves. The Commons attended not as delegates, but as representatives, with the power to bind their constituents without referring back. They were elected to parliament, although the notion of election before 1406, when statutory rules were first established, may have been closer to our notion of selection. The Latin word *electio*, choice, has no necessary implication of a ballot. Long after 1406, indeed, it seems that Yorkshire county elections were still conducted by the stewards of the principal lordships.[63] Elections were seldom contested, but when they were, the majority was meant to win. Perhaps because this conflicted with earlier notions of the *maior et sanior pars*, the larger and wiser part, efforts were made to ensure that the victors were indeed wiser by the property qualifications, set at 40 s. in the shires and variable in the towns. It may well be that the majority rule within parliament was also slow to catch on. Not until the sixteenth century was majority rule established on York's city corporation. It was in parliament that king, Lords and Commons came together to do things that the king could not do alone. Already by 1399 it was only parliament that could vote taxes and only there that new laws were made. Acts of parliament were the highest of laws, to which all were bound, because all had consented to them. It was in parliament also that the king took counsel of his whole realm.

3

MONARCHY

Monarchy, the rule of a single individual, was not simple. No effective system of government is ever simple. This chapter examines more of its ramifications: the panoply, image and attributes of kingship; further limitations, legitimacy and the succession; and the concept of the king's two bodies. The practical applications are deferred.

The panoply of kingship

Kings stood next to God and exercised God's authority on earth. Even Henry VI was like 'God's son or the emperor or King Emmanuel'. Dread or awe was the proper response. Kings were a separate estate, the highest estate, the royal estate, to which appertained royal dignity, majesty, lordship, power, rule, governance, administration, empire, jurisdiction, regality and highness.[1] With propagandist zeal, kings deliberately stressed the sovereignty and majesty of their unique status. They never dwelt upon its limits. Coronations did not make kings. They were awesomely solemn occasions at which those already kings were acclaimed, consecrated and decked in the insignia of majesty: crown, orb and sceptre. There also they swore the solemn oaths that committed them to good rule, normally in Latin, but from 1483 in English. These ceremonies were progressively enhanced by the addition of holy oil for their anointing and the lauds of majesty.[2] The massive record of Richard III's coronation leaves no doubt about the cost and administrative effort that such ceremonies demanded.[3] Separate coronations were staged additionally for Queens Margaret of Anjou, Elizabeth Wydeville and Elizabeth of York. Both in 1454 and 1471 the Lords recognised an infant prince as heir presumptive, swore allegiance and did homage to him. Richard III's somewhat older son was formally invested as prince of Wales at York in 1483, the king himself wearing his crown. Royal funerals were also sumptuous and symbolic.

As befitted demi-gods, *rex et sacerdos* (king and priest), kings routinely touched for the king's evil, the skin disease scrofula, which a king's touch was believed to cure and which a queen, Fortescue alleged, could not perform.[4] The excessive formality of Richard II's court, too easily associated with an arbitrary king, had lapsed, but the Yorkists regulated the royal household more precisely, elaborated its etiquette on the model of Burgundy, premier court of the century, and thus outdistanced those grandest English households that had rivalled the king's. Special efforts were made on the major feastdays, such as Easter, and a long list of minor ceremonies – royal weddings, christenings, the investiture of princes, and funerals – can be composed. One such, the churching of Elizabeth Wydeville, set the monarchy on a different plane from its most elevated subjects and astonished even a well-informed continental observer.[5] Even Fortescue recognised that kingship was expensive and must not be stinted. Kings must be magnificent and must outshine their greatest subjects:

> Also it shall need that the king have such treasure as he may make new buildings when he will for his pleasure and magnificence, and as he therewith may buy him rich clothes and furs, other than been wont to fall under the yearly charges of his wardrobe: rich stones, baldricks, jewels and other ornaments convenient to his estate royal. And also to buy rich hangings and other apparel for his houses, vessels, vestments and other ornaments for his chapels. Also [to] buy horses of great price, trappings, and do such other noble and great costs as befits his royal majesty.[6]

Kings had to out-consume the most conspicuous consumers. Edward IV's epitaphs document his lavish expenditure in many directions, apparently pointless, but politically essential. His chapel music, his artillery, his fortresses were second to none. His badges were carved on public buildings or embroidered on vestments. His livery was to be seen everywhere.[7] What set a king apart was best stressed by multiplying the status symbols of his greatest subjects.

Nowhere is this more apparent than in the king's household, which existed solely to serve the king's needs. Wherever it was, the immediate hinterland fell within its verge and under the jurisdiction of its chief officers. Suites of impressive rooms staffed with aristocrats separated the outside world from the king, who customarily dined in state on a canopied throne with a mere handful of the most eminent at his table. Several times larger, costlier and more lavish than the grandest establishment of any subject, the royal household also contained more staff of higher ranks. Meals were served to all members of the household and their servants, hospitality was tendered to hordes of guests, their servants and horses, and customary gifts of wine were made to religious houses in perpetual alms and to individuals for life. Yet all had to be recorded, regulated according to entitlement, and accounted for. There were strict limits to perks. 'And if any officer abovesaid do the contrary ... he to lose his office and to be put out of the king's house forever.' However magnificent the king's lifestyle, his household had to be economical, expenditure being strictly supervised to avoid waste and to achieve value for money.[8] Moreover it must not be oppressive towards its involuntary suppliers. Edward IV's successful balancing act, his particular combination of outward magnificence and inward thrift, succeeded also in misleading even a well-informed councillor that unprecedented treasure lay behind his apparent avarice.[9]

Beyond the bounds set by earlier charters and laws, kings had a free hand over what were called regalian rights – regality or royalty – or his *prerogative*. Prerogative was the reserve power of a king that was unfettered and undefined.[10] Tudor commentators had yet to determine that they were conferred by the laws of England. Specific prerogatives were numerous, impressive and apparently growing: 'divers other rights and pre-eminences the prince hath which be called the prerogatives royal' ends an Elizabethan list.[11] Kings conducted their own foreign relations, making decisions about peace and war, and directed the waging of war themselves. The exercise of martial law, even involving the death penalty, was for them and their nominees alone. They made all royal appointments, from councillors, bishops and judges to the most menial household officials and created and promoted peers and knights. It was in this area that Jack Cade had acted 'against the king's regality'.[12] They appointed all bishops and archbishops. They summoned, prorogued and dissolved parliaments, agreed and vetoed acts of parliament, appended provisos of exemption to them and overrode conditions attached to them. They changed the coinage at will: counterfeiting was treason. They enjoyed the wardship and marriage of under-age tenants-in-chief and fools. They had the right to take their subjects' moveables for the supply of their household, purveyance, which could be extended to requisition the supplies to munition a war-effort and to impress ships and crews for a fleet, all of which, however, they were bound eventually to reimburse. All writs ran in the king's name: the king's record alone decided legal cases, as Edward IV's unfortunate brother Clarence found, and sufficed for subjects to forfeit their possessions. The prerogative of mercy entitled them to pardon offences and the consequent penalties. No writs ran against the king, who could not be sued, disseised or required to pay tolls.

Kings summoned subjects to them and their council on pain of punishment, *subpoena*, imprisoned offenders at will and sequestrated their lands, and confiscated the possessions of those in arms against them without further need for parliamentary sanction. They levied arbitrary fines on those guilty of misprision – what we would call accessories before and/or after the fact: Alderman Sir Thomas Cook, who was certainly guilty, was fined the quite excessive sum of £8,000.[13] Recognisances for debt or bonds carrying monetary penalties were freely exacted for good behaviour from those who were guilty of no demonstrable offence. Bonds were elevated into something of a system by Henry VII, who imposed retrospective obligations on his retainers, forbidding them to be retained by anyone else or to wear another's livery in his company, levying a year's income from annuitants and lessees, and imposing military obligations on royal office-holders.[14] Henry IV had also insisted on foreign military service unstated in their patents from duchy annuitants, suspending payment for non-performance, and Henry V imposed additional obligations on grantees of French property.[15] Also nowhere defined was the king's undoubted capacity to bias the machinery of government in his favour, notoriously by ordering a sheriff to empanel a jury to acquit Lord Moleyns, by interfering in legal suits and suspending the courts, by offering preferential treatment to particular individuals at the royal exchequer,[16] by determining who tried particular cases, or by straightforward partiality. If Richard II and Henry VII appear to have enhanced the scope and effectiveness of royal authority, they required no new laws to do so. Government and justice alike were always those of the king.

Kings had *liberty* and *grace*. Liberty signified not arbitrariness, the right to do as they wished, but discretion, to mitigate the operation of law and justice. It was by his grace, usually termed his 'especial grace', that he conceded what they need not. Both Henry IV and Henry V made concessions to the Commons, saving their prerogative. It was by his grace that a king pardoned criminals. The *prerogative of mercy* was an aspect of his royal grace. From at least 1465 the judges held that the king had discretion to apply or not apply statutes expressed in the affirmative.[17]

Sovereignty conferred on kings an overriding right of command over their subjects and *necessity* denied them the right to refuse military support. *Allegiance* to the king overrode all lesser loyalties: to observe one's allegiance was an obligation and a duty, not a merit deserving of praise. 'I become your liegeman of life and limb and of earthly worship', vassals solemnly swore to a new king at his coronation, 'and faith and trouth shall bear unto you for to live and die against all manner of folk. So God help me and all his saints'.[18] There were no qualifications to what was surely the most solemn and absolute of commitments. The elaborate process of Richard II's abdication included his repudiation of homage from his subjects and thus freed peers to transfer their allegiance to Henry IV: henceforth this was their prior obligation and they could legitimately be held to account for any breach. So, too, the Lords hesitated to break their oaths to Henry VI, even though York argued that their oaths were invalid because sworn in error. 'We therefore pray you and also strictly charge you', runs a Lancastrian letter of 13 March 1461 in Henry VI's name to Sir William Plumpton,

> that anon upon the sight hereof you with all such people as you may make defensibly arrayed come unto us in all haste possible wheresoever we shall be within this our realm for to resist the malicious intent and purpose of our said traitor. And fail not hereof as you love the surety of our person, the weal of yourself, and of all our true and faithful subjects.[19]

Allegiance provided a framework in which other relationships could take place – lesser relationships, in the king's eyes, such as those of kinship, neighbourliness, service and lordship to other subjects who were not kings. As long as allegiance was superior and overriding, there could be no conflict with other loyalties: the Wydeville connection in Edward IV's latter years operated within allegiance to the crown.[20] Loyalty to the king was neither deserving, meritorious, nor praiseworthy: it was a duty expected of everyone by everyone, regardless of the pros and cons of the particular king. Until 1459 the aristocracy exhibited, Lander notes, 'a surprising fidelity to a king whose feeble incompetence had been very much inimical to their own interests'.[21] Whatever their deficiencies, kings could count on the allegiance of their subjects to give them a decisive advantage over any rebels. Several times during the Wars of the Roses, retainers refused to join lords who, they suspected, planned action against the king. When promising service to their lord against all men, fifteenth-century retainers almost invariably reserved their allegiance to the king and sometimes also to his heir: in 1464 it was Edward IV's eldest brother and heir presumptive Clarence to whom Lord Grey of Codnor gave priority. There are three surviving indentures of retainer with York in 1460 that make no such exclusion. These are the exceptions that prove the rule, since York was evidently planning already to shrug off his allegiance to Henry VI and assert his own title to the crown. That none of these indentures were actually sealed suggests this was a step too far. Not to reserve one's allegiance was prima facie evidence of treasonable intentions; not to have done so was a treason charge against Clarence in 1478.[22]

The counterpart to allegiance was *treason*. A sovereign was protected by the treason laws; so indeed were his queen and children. Just as today, it was treasonable to adhere to the monarch's foreign enemies; it was treason also to resist, rebel against or seek to destroy the king. Late medieval treason focused on the person of the king and on dissident subjects. The conditional loyalty contracted by feudal vassals, which they could withdraw when defying the king, their suzerain, had been superseded by the overriding concept of sovereignty, which made allegiance obligatory rather than voluntary. Earlier rebels had freely renounced their allegiance by defiance, *diffidatio*, and had suffered no special punishment for doing so. By 1403, however, the Percies' renunciation of homage by itself was treasonable. Treason as defined by statute in 1352 protected the individual sovereign and his family against plots against their lives or war levied against them. Narrow though these limits apparently were, they were made to encompass taking the king's horoscope (imagining his death by necromancy), treasonable words, and even causing the king's subjects to withdraw their love from him. It was this last treason, perhaps, that the miscellaneous charges against Clarence in 1478 were supposed to comprise. Popular rebels, who usually claimed to be loyal, were 'tending to bring about the king's destruction and therefore … imagining and compassing his death'.[23] If in custody, traitors were allowed no copy of the charges and no legal counsel and in certain cases the king's own testimony was sufficient evidence. The penalty was always death – a particularly horrible death – and forfeiture, which the Lancastrians extended from chattels and land in fee simple to trusts on the traitor's behalf. Forfeiture did not cover land in tail, for which the traitor was only tenant for life and in which innocent descendants had an interest, until 1411, when the concept of *attainder* was first applied.

Attainder meant henceforth that traitors were *attainted*: their blood and that of their issue was held to be corrupted by treason, so that their descendants shared their ignominy and could not inherit. As attainder infringed the otherwise sacred principle of inheritance, kings were reluctant to apply it. In practice Henry IV and Henry V restored the heirs of many noble traitors. There were few traitors in the ensuing decades against whom these new penalties could be applied, so the concept was still unfamiliar in 1459 to some chroniclers and, by implication, to the population at large. York himself knew of it and feared it as early as 1450[24] – his own father had been attainted as a traitor in 1415 and perhaps he knew (as we do not) what was in store for Gloucester in 1447. Hence the Wars of the Roses required no extension of the scope of treason. Instead it witnessed the systematic application of attainder: acts of attainder proscribed whole categories of people who were not present to defend themselves. Every parliament from 1459 attainted opponents of the regime then ruling. No doubt it was the disinheritance of a potential traitor's family rather than the supposed corruption that made attainder a more effective deterrent – it was not just one's own life that was being hazarded. That attainder became commonplace does not mean that it was accepted or regarded as right. Whatever the original intention, kings were always prepared to negotiate the restoration of even attainted traitors for their submission and allegiance, and it was commonplace also for aristocratic traitors against Lancastrians and Yorkists alike or their heirs to be restored. Wholesale attainders of 1459, 1470 and 1484 were revoked following dynastic changes in 1460, 1471 and 1485. Every parliament from 1463 additionally witnessed acts reversing the attainders of particular individuals. Edward IV, in retrospect, allowed many offenders or their heirs to recover completely, whereas Henry VII, characteristically, was less generous even to the victims of earlier kings and more rigorous to his own, some never being restored and most suffering some permanent losses.[25] By that time Tudor propagandists had given treason the standing that it holds in Shakespeare's *Richard II* as the most heinous of crimes.

The statute of treason covered more than the king alone: its protection extended to the queen and to the heir. The notion of the royal family was developing in this period. The Black Prince had been the first duke and all the earliest dukes were of royal blood. Richard II had completed the process of elevating all his paternal uncles, Edward III's sons, to ducal status; most of his other ducal promotions were of royal descent, though the sheer number disparaged the rank and many were subsequently demoted. All Henry V's brothers also became dukes and even Henry VI's half-brothers, though of questionable legitimacy, became earls. The precedence awarded to new creations, which elevated them above existing dukes, and the marriage strategies of the magnates, were both informed by a heightened sense of royal blood. The concept of 'great lords of the blood' favoured by York and the commons placed an emphasis on royal descent that was often quite distant and which was not shared by kings themselves. The Nevilles, whose head had been regarded as Henry IV's brother, continued to be termed cousin by subsequent kings, but had moved beyond Henry VI's notion of the inner royal family. It was his immediate family whom Edward IV advanced, not merely his brothers and sons whom he immediately created dukes, but also his prospective son-in-law George whom he promoted to duke of Bedford on his engagement to Elizabeth of York. His brothers were elected knights of the Garter whilst still children. Edward even undertook the elevation of is numerous sisters-in-law to the rank at least of countess by manipulating the marriage market, promoting and endowing their husbands. This process culminated in 1483, when a sumptuary act distinguished between royal dukes, who might wear the grandest garb, and the rest, for whom it was not allowed. Edward's perspective was not shared by Humphrey Stafford (d. 1460), who prided himself on his direct descent from Edward III's youngest son Thomas of Woodstock, assumed from 1441 and gave priority to Woodstock's earlier earldom of Buckingham and chose that title for his subsequent dukedom, nor by Humphrey's grandson Henry 2nd Duke of Buckingham, who adopted Woodstock's arms in 1474.[26]

The monarch was unique. Already superior to his greatest subjects, he was elevated more highly during this century and to some extent carried his family with him. Yet he was still *primus inter pares*, the first among equals. However often deferred and sometimes delegated, all those holding land in chief, that is almost every aristocrat, whether duke or peer, esquire or dowager, did homage and swore fealty to him, some several times; there are dozens of certificates of homage amongst the warrants for the privy seal. 'You shall swear', begins the oath, 'as God and his saints you help',

> that you shall be faithful and true and faith and trouth bear unto the king our sovereign lord and to his heirs kings of England and truly you shall do and truly acknowledge the services due to the lands the which you claim to hold of him and which the king to you doth yield.[27]

Relating to purely feudal obligations, this oath by tenants-in-chief had its counterpart in those oaths sworn to them by their feudal tenants. In so many ways, as the most senior prince, the apex of the feudal pyramid or suzerain, as a great landholder, as chivalric figurehead, fount of justice, and good lord of all good lords, the king was similar to his magnates and needs to be regarded as 'a member of the lay aristocracy'.[28] Their upbringing was the same. Henry IV, Henry V, Edward IV, Richard III and Henry VII were not scheduled to reign and received the same education as any other nobleman. Only Henry VI and the short-reigning Edward V were actually brought up to be kings. A king shared the values of his aristocracy. His relationships with his magnates were often reciprocal and co-operative. They were his kindred, friends and allies. In many ways king and magnates differed in degree rather than in kind. A king lived like an aristocrat, always amongst aristocrats, picked aristocrats as favourites, married aristocratic ladies, pursued aristocratic recreations and shared the virtues and the sins of his aristocracy, not always on a larger or more lavish scale. More opportunities and temptations admittedly came his way. Monarchs were aristocrats – the greatest undoubtedly, but aristocrats nevertheless – as they remain today. That was why they worked so well with their greater subjects. Many aspects of the next chapter, about the aristocracy, apply equally to kings. And yet they stood apart. Henry V reputedly allowed no subject to stare him in the face and the most effective kings overawed even their greatest subjects.

The limits of kingship

A fifteenth-century king was not free to rule as he chose. Henry IV bound himself not to act arbitrarily, at will or at whim, not 'by his own will, nor by his wilful purpose or singular opinion'.[29] Kings were far from absolute, even if sometimes they aspired to be or forgot it. They were limited by the concessions made by their predecessors and themselves, by the law, and by the need to consult in parliament, if they were to exercise their fullest powers and draw on their subjects' resources. They were limited intellectually: by God's will, the constraints of natural law and by the consequent requirement that rule should be rational – 'we wish all men to know', declared Edward III in 1330, ' that in future we will govern our people according to right and reason, as is fitting our royal dignity';[30] and by the concept of the commonweal, the obligation to rule for the benefit of their subjects. This was what their subjects expected of them. Their expectations and their consent were not purely theoretical or nominal, even if often merely latent. At times, as we shall see, kings depended on the fullest co-operation and subjects even exercised a veto. No fifteenth-century king could forget that Richard II had been deposed. Kings could not stand against all their subjects. There were also other theoretical limits to their power that kings ignored at their peril.

Kings were part of the same culture as anyone else. They were subject to the same standards, values, expectations and culture as their subjects. They were *christian* kings subject to the same christian influences, teachings and imperatives as anyone else. There were contemporary standards of how christians, kings, and especially christian kings, should behave. *Mirrors for Princes* penned by Hoccleve, Ashby and others instructed them in traditional christian morality. Just because one was a king was no excuse or protection for sin: in a pre-Machiavellian era kings were accountable to God for their conduct and had no refuge in pragmatism or reason of state. Any king who hoped for salvation – and all kings, by definition, did so – needed to live good christian lives, to practise the christian virtues and avoid the deadly sins. They were exposed to more temptation than their subjects and the christian model often appeared inappropriate for effective rule. They were answerable for what was perpetrated in their names. As king's confessor, Abbot Repingdon blamed Henry IV for all kinds of public sins and held him to his coronation oath and his duties to his people.[31] The Crowland continuator struggled over Edward IV, 'a gross man so addicted to conviviality, vanity, drunkenness, extravagance and passion' that he was surely damned, yet whose rank, wisdom and military prowess he respected, and whose status as 'a catholic of the strongest faith, the sternest enemy of heretics, the kindliest patron of wise and learned men and of clerics, the most devoted venerator of the church's sacraments, the most penitent of men for all his sins', and whose exemplary end, he said, gave 'all his faithful men ... hope that he would not be cheated of his eternal reward'.[32] Edward's sexual adventures were damaging politically. His bastards, the consequences of sin, could not inherit. His brother Richard III invoked universal moral standards against both the innocent (but allegedly illegitimate) princes in the Tower and the personally blameless Henry Tudor son of Edmund Tudor son of Owen Tudor, who was, shockingly, 'of bastard blood both of father's side and of mother's side'.[33] Persecution and patronage, in contrast, were both acts of piety with political implications that contemporaries numbered among Edward's good works. No such sins counterbalanced the priggish rectitude of Henry V, whose defence of the Church and orthodoxy, foundation and reform of monasteries, encouragement of devotions and promotion of a just war undoubtedly earned him divine favour. Not only did pursuit of virtue and avoidance of vice influence Henry's conduct, but it secured him political support, and created a legend and model that no successor could live up to and which constricted future policy-makers.

The notion that kingship existed for the benefit of the subject – the concept of the commonweal – was a christian principle. Tyranny was an offence against God. Kings swore at their coronations to protect the Church and subjects and to do justice to all. Apart from foreign policy and defence, it was law, order and justice that was most expected of them. 'Lo! To fight and to judge is the office of a king' declaimed Chief Justice Fortescue. 'Do law always, that is a king', remarked the poet Gower.[34] Justice was a touchstone of effective governance. Kings were expected to see justice was done, both at a general level that required new remedies to be developed and the law to be enforced, and at a particular level, to respond to many difficult cases. There were standards against which they were measured and conventions to which they had to adhere. The penalties were unspoken and ill-defined: but no king could afford to lose his good name, to lose the love of the people, to excite criticism, condemnation or contempt, for fear of where it would lead. The law of treason was invoked as protection even here.

There were many conventions and procedures about how a king should rule. By 1399, for example, it was expected that kings should use their lands to endow their family, especially queens: 'what such a ruler did with his estates, within certain accepted conventions, was a vital part of his sovereign power'.[35] Of course no king could know about everything, the issues involved in every appointment or decision, and no king could do everything himself. Industry and drudgery beyond any king's capacity was required for truly effective government. Nor indeed did any king wish to undertake it, not even Henry VII: his legendary assiduity focused on a few specific areas that he thought important and that have been recorded. Other kings, such as Edward IV and Henry VI, acted more fitfully, focusing their attention on particular topics and at particular times.

Kings needed *counsel*: men of 'great wisdom, cunning and experience … to whom he must trust and lean'.[36] Advisers informed, advised, co-ordinated and, in many cases, also decided. Kings were free to take counsel wherever they chose and in practice that is what they did. All kings had formal councils made up principally of men called councillors, who were sometimes appointed and paid as such. The privy council of limited size and fixed membership initiated by Henry VIII's Eltham ordnance had several medieval precedents. It appealed to Henry IV's parliaments, which several times insisted on the nomination of such councils in parliament. Such bodies were also instituted for the minority, insanities and perhaps the Readeption of Henry VI. Whenever they could, kings resisted such arrangements, which tied their hands, and supplemented their core councillors with whoever they wished. Most advice to the king probably still came informally, in the relative privacy of his chambers, where it was as likely to come from magnates or attendants as from ministers and councillors. Informal counsel was probably more effective at the level of policy than formal advice. Kings also took counsel more formally in the great council, a body of notables that to some extent he shaped himself, and in parliament.

A king was expected not just to seek advice, but to listen to advice however unpalatable, and to act upon it. It was a charge against Richard II that he had rejected the advice of his great council.[37] Councillors had to be committed to the king's interests: in 1440 'to counsel, prefer, increase and advance the welfare and prosperity of his lord and most especially of his sovereign lord'.[38] Councillors were expected to give advice honestly, without fear of the consequences or partiality, and to accept whatever decision resulted, even if overruled: it was, after all, the king's right to decide. On the other hand, it was a difficult role for both parties. Counselling was a career move. To counsel a monarch was a privileged opportunity offering scope for self-advantage. All councillors expected the legitimate rewards and wanted the rate for the job, at the ducal, comital, baronial or knightly rate.[39] The temptations emerge in the literary stereotype: a councillor/courtier was the flatterer who told the king what he wanted to know and who feathered his own nest.[40] Was it not acting against one's own interests to tell a king what he did not wish to hear? What king can have welcomed critical counsel? Apart from swearing to advise the king and to keep his counsel secret, both chancellor and treasurer swore not to

> know nor suffer the hurt nor disinheritance of the king, nor that the rights of the crown be decreased as far forth as you may let [prevent], and, if you may not let it, you shall make it clearly and expressly known to the king with your true advice and counsel. And that you shall do and purchase the king's profit in all that you may.[41]

Here was the justification for ministers knowing a king's interests better than he did and safeguarding them, if necessary despite him. Several chancellors are known to have refused to seal particular grants, and Fortescue sought to institutionalise such conciliar control over the king's patronage. Elizabeth I, it is reported, took the advice of Vice-Chamberlain Hatton so much amiss that he had to leave court.[42] It was not unheard of for councillors to be punished for their advice. It did not help that such conduct was improper if kings were free to do it and it was the councillor who suffered. If things went wrong, if rule was seen as evil, it was a convention that it was not the king who was blamed – as God's representative, he was above such criticism – but his *evil councillors*. The solution was to substitute good and sufficient councillors: in practical terms, men of substance and experience, his natural councillors. Evil councillors should be punished as traitors, as Suffolk and Say were in 1450 and as Strafford and Laud were to be under Charles I.

Kings were limited by the law. 'By the law', declared Chief Baron Fray in 1441, 'he himself and all his subjects are ruled'. It was only by the law, as expressed in his court of parliament, that he drew revenues from justice, from forfeitures and from taxation.[43] Kings were bound by the acts – and concessions – of their predecessors and succeeded to what the previous king had held net of concessions. In 1461 Edward IV had to accept that the acts of the Lancastrian kings were as valid as if they had been kings of right. The alternative was chaos. Chrimes lists what the king could not do. He could not change the common law, deprive anyone of his common law rights, override negative statutes, or delegate his prerogative.[44] Legally he was far from absolute.

Legitimacy and the succession

There were three rights by which fifteenth-century kings reigned: by conquest, by election and by inheritance. Conquest meant mere possession: it sufficed for Henry VII, said the judges when asked, for the king's victory at Bosworth and his accession rendered any early attainder obsolete. A king could not be attainted. Election was normally a formality, part of the service of coronation long after the accession, but it mattered and was carefully orchestrated at usurpations, in 1399, 1461 and 1483, when kings *de facto* secured approval by parliaments or pseudo-representative assemblies. On all three occasions it was the power, veiled or naked, of the usurpers' adherents that prevailed. Who succeeded was decided by the candidates already in control. They were in control for other political reasons, the deficiencies or defeat of the previous incumbent, rather than their claim to the crown, although proximity to the crown largely explained who led the winning side. Dynasticism was a means to an end, not the end in itself.

Hereditary right determined the choice of successor. Never before, from 1216 to 1399, was there an option, as each father was succeeded by his eldest son or his eldest son's son. The king was the king. There was no need to debate how he came to be there. Even in 1327 the accession of Edward III, eldest son of Edward II, had merely been advanced. Until 1399 there was no call for rules. Insofar as any serious thought was given to the topic by Edward III, his claim in 1340 to the crown of France suggests that he thought inheritance could be transmitted *through* a female – his mother Queen Isabella of France – who was still living – but not *to* a female. He himself was the intended beneficiary, as Isabella's son. He thus elevated a king's sister above a king's daughters. He rejected for France both English primogeniture, which allowed daughters to succeed, and the newly devised French Salic law (entail in tail male). In 1376 he may also have advanced his eldest surviving son John of Gaunt, Duke of Lancaster, and his male issue over a senior female line, represented by his Mortimer great-grandson Roger by Philippa, the daughter of an elder son Lionel Duke of Clarence. His daughters may have been induced publicly to renounce any hereditary rights they possessed. If so (and the evidence is slight),[45] it was not widely known and was of dubious validity. Could a king entail the crown? This entail foreshadows both the choice with which England was faced in 1399 and the succession then of Gaunt's son.

Richard II, unlike Edward II, had no son to be enthroned. Besides Henry Duke of Lancaster, Gaunt's son and Richard's male heir, there might have stood the heir general Edmund Mortimer, Earl of March, had he not been a child and thus not credible in a revolutionary situation. Henry duly acceded as King Henry IV. Well aware of weaknesses in his claim, he buttressed them by fudging his lineage, but not by citing the supposed entail of 1376. The Lancastrian title was reinforced by parliamentary acts in two charters and two acts of 1404 and 1406, which indicate some understandable indecision on Henry's part. None of his sons were yet married nor could he know whether they would bear only daughters. First of all he settled the crown on his four sons in turn in tail general, so that a daughter of an elder son would take preference over a younger son; next he settled it on his sons in tail male, thus excluding female issue; finally and definitively, in a statute, he opted for tail general again.[46] These fine distinctions proved superfluous. What actually happened – the untroubled recognition of Henry V in 1413, Henry VI in 1422 and of Edward of Lancaster in 1454 – was valid, whichever settlement had been in force. Strangely Henry IV showed no urgency in ennobling and endowing the three younger sons, nor did they hasten to marry or to father sons. Whilst Thomas, the second son, married relatively early, his brothers postponed their weddings until they were well into their twenties and even thirties.

What Henry IV did not foresee was that three sons died without legitimate issue and that from 1447–54 only one life – that of Henry

VI – continued his line. Henry IV's settlements of the crown did not look beyond his sons and their issue. Both his daughters had married foreign princes and their issue may have been disqualified from inheritance. So were two of his sisters. There remained only two other sisters and three brothers by his father's first and third duchesses. Elizabeth was Henry's only sister of the whole blood by Blanche of Lancaster. Henry was prepared for his duchy to descend by primogeniture and thus devolve differently from the crown. It was Elizabeth's grandson Henry Duke of Exeter who in 1454 laid claim to the duchy of Lancaster and probably also to the protectorate during Henry VI's insanity and her great-grandson Ralph Earl of Westmorland, who may have speculated about it in 1484.[47] Henry IV's three half-brothers and his half-sister Joan were Beauforts, the bastard progeny of John of Gaunt by his mistress Katherine Swynford, ultimately his third duchess. The Beauforts had been legitimated in 1397 and therefore logically took precedence over Elizabeth as male heirs of Henry IV and Edward III. When confirming their patent in 1407, Henry excluded them from the crown, to the advantage of Elizabeth,[48] but without thereby impugning the legality of their original patent, which surely remained valid. Strangely nobody seems to have considered legitimising the bastards of the Lancastrian dukes of Clarence, Bedford and Gloucester on the precedent of the Beauforts, not even their fathers.

The Lancastrian succession was not universally accepted. There was a rebellion on behalf of Richard II in 1400 and a number of other treasonable utterances and conspiracies built around him after he was certainly dead. A pseudo-Richard masqueraded as the king until 1417. When they rebelled in 1403, the Percies claimed that Henry IV was disqualified by perjury, because he had sworn in 1399 that his intention was to recover his dukedom and not to take the crown. Nor was the Mortimer claim forgotten. Several plots were woven around it and the Lancastrian regime jittered even at the name.[49] Following Edmund Mortimer's childless death in 1425, his earldom and his claim to the crown descended via his late sister Anne to his nephew Richard Duke of York. Attention was drawn to Richard's claim even in 1450, perhaps without his knowledge or consent.[50] To contest the title of the king was obviously treasonable; so indeed would have been parading the arms of his great-great-grandfather Lionel Duke of Clarence. When Richard at last did so in 1460, it was Lionel's title he asserted, tracing his descent by a line senior to the king's to the Lords, who ultimately found it irrefutable. Lancastrian entails and their own oaths of allegiance to Henry VI, York argued, were defeated by his undeniable hereditary right. The oaths were made on false pretences and could not prevail against God's will.[51] That he had not asserted the claim before or used the arms of Clarence did not cause his title to expire. The resultant *Accord* maintained Henry as king, but elevated York to his heir. Next year Edward IV's parliament had merely to reiterate the Yorkists' hereditary claim.

The Yorkist title continued to be rejected by Henry VI, his family and, surprisingly, many others for the next decade. Popular support for the Lancastrian Readeption in 1470–1 indicates how many continued to regard Henry VI as king. Why cannot be divined: Fortescue's pamphlets promoting Henry's rights may be a factor. Fortescue rejected the notion of female succession at great length and also questioned the legitimacy of Philippa herself, from whom the Yorkist title derived, whom he alleged was 'conceived in adultery' by Sir James Audley and was not therefore the grand-daughter of Edward III.[52] Most likely the Readeption parliament recognised Edward IV's brother George Duke of Clarence as next heir to Henry VI and his son, to the understandable dissatisfaction of returning Lancastrians, some of whom – Exeter and the last Beauforts – surely nourished hopes themselves.[53] On returning to England in 1471, Edward IV – like Henry IV before him – found support for his irrefutable right to his dukedom from those who opposed his title as king.[54] Following his victory and recovery of his crown, he made Fortescue refute his own pamphlets.

When Richard III deposed his nephew Edward V, he diverted his brother's Yorkist title to himself by disqualifying rivals. He had no Lancastrian contender to fear. His claims in the petition *Titulus Regius* were later enacted as law. Richard's nephews were bastards, because Edward IV and his queen were not legally married, and the legitimacy of Edward IV himself was questioned. Hereditary right was thus elevated above other elements of title: deposition became 'the weapon of first resort'.[55] Yet Edward IV was undoubtedly king, by conquest, election and coronation. His son Edward V had been acknowledged by the royal council, universally accepted, and had been recipient of oaths of allegiance not just from his uncle Richard, but from all those whom Richard had required to swear. The offspring of Richard's elder brother Clarence were supposedly excluded by their father's attainder. More pertinently, they were children. It was not legitimacy, in fact, but might – conquest – that was decisive.

Richard's heir was his son Prince Edward (d. 1484). His title may also have been even weaker, because his parents too may not have been legally married, but that, if true, was not widely known and did not make it into contemporary sources. Apparently he contemplated wedding his niece Elizabeth of York, Edward IV's daughter, who was young, fertile and could have strengthened his title. Had he done so, the match would have been a long-term investment. In the meantime, he looked to his nephews to head his regional government and perhaps also as heirs: Clarence's son Edward Earl of Warwick and the son of his sister Elizabeth Duchess of Suffolk, John de la Pole, Earl of Lincoln. To promote the former or indeed marry Elizabeth implicitly denied Richard's own title. Richard's accession and his subsequent manoeuvres indicate that kingship, rather than legitimacy, preoccupied him.

Conspirators against Richard initially sought to restore Edward V, but on his disappearance turned to Henry Tudor, the future Henry VII. Henry later claimed to have been king the day before Bosworth. His first parliament simply declared him to be king. Whilst undoubtedly a member of the Lancastrian royal family – his father Edmund was maternal half-brother of Henry VI – any claim to the crown derived from his mother Margaret Beaufort, who outlived him. Given that the Lancastrian title was as heir male to Edward III, a claim founded through a female from a legitimated branch that had been explicitly excluded was not compelling. It was more important that he was royal, adult, male and single, for the other essential component to his title was his commitment to marrying Elizabeth of York. It was as king by conquest and election that he married her. This marriage, so Tudor propaganda claimed and was immediately believed, united the lines of Lancaster and York. The immediate blessing of a son postponed discussion of female succession for thirty years.

Henry VII's rivals, the two pretenders, Lambert Simnel and Perkin Warbeck, who posed in turn as Clarence's son Warwick and as Edward IV's younger son Richard, and the two de la Pole princelings, John (d. 1487) and Edmund (d. 1513), all failed to secure the crown and (bar Simnel) consequently perished. Before 1399 there had only ever been one possible recipient of allegiance. Later, after the revolution of 1399 and especially from the 1460s, the king's title was opened to debate. Conspirators could justify their disloyalty to the monarch *de facto* to themselves, if never to the current authorities, by an alternative allegiance. The crown became the object of individual aspiration. The overriding bond of allegiance was diluted by alternative claimants. By 1483, for Richard III, if not by 1470 for Clarence, dynasticism had become an issue in its own right, rather than merely a means to achieve the reforms that Henry IV, York and Edward IV, the Kingmaker, and even Henry VII had sought.

King and crown

A king was the current representative of an enduring institution or corporation, the *crown*. Distinctions were made between succession to the crown, for which inheritance by females was not permissible, and succession to a king's private estates, for which it was allowed. Kings had both a public and a private person. These correspond to what Elizabethan lawyers and more modern historians have called the *king's two bodies*. Kings had two bodies, a body politic and a body natural. 'His Body natural', the Elizabethan Plowden explained, is

> mortal, subject to the Infirmities that come by Nature or Accident ... But his Body politic ... consisting of Policy and Government, and constituted for the Direction of the People, and the Management of the public weal ... is utterly void of Infancy, and old Age, and other natural Defects and Imbecilities, which the body natural is subject to ... What the King does in his Body politic, cannot be invalidated or frustrated by any Disability in his natural Body.[56]

Hence it was not the person of any particular king to whom fidelity and obedience was due, but to the office of king that an individual temporarily held. However exalted royal estate was, kingship 'is an office in which he ministers in his realm defence and justice'.[57] What was due to him was not dependent on his individual personality, capacity or fitness as a king. The concept had been developed by the Church and continued to be influenced by canon law and ecclesiastical parallels. The efficacy of the sacraments could not be allowed to depend on the state of grace of the individual priest or bishop, since the whole system could unravel because the ordinations of some earlier bishop – from whom derived the power that enabled the Holy Spirit to be invoked now – were invalidated by his past defects. Under-age kings, wicked kings and even usurpers were all kings, all God's representatives, and all entitled to the obedience due to God. Subjects could not be allowed to pick and choose which to obey. The loyalty and obedience due to a king in fact (*de facto*) who was not a king by right (*de iure*) was a live issue. Attainting as traitors those who observed their duty to one king was bound to weaken the appeal of allegiance to his successor, as Henry VII found. The *de facto* act of 1495, which declared that obedience to a king *de facto* was not treason, could have been repealed by any future usurper. The Tudor solution, undoubtedly influenced by Henry VII's questionable title and publicised through official Tudor propaganda, was expressed in the twin doctrines of *order*

45

and *non-resistance*. A king, just or not, was God's representative. There was an obligation of obedience to him. However evil he was, even if he was a tyrant, his rule must be suffered patiently, judgement and punishment being reserved to God. A tyrant could be God's punishment for sin. All the elements of this theory were current in the fifteenth century, during which the underlying issues became acute, but it was not until the reign of Henry VIII that it was fully developed, most succinctly and elegantly in the 1547 homily on obedience. It was internalised in future generations.[58] It was propaganda that worked.

Kings were people. Away from their thrones and public venues, they had private lives, private interests, private tastes and private recreations. They were accountable for their private vices. Every king had a soul, about which he cared and on which he lavished money. If kings were expected to patronise the Church, each had his own taste, in the latest fashion and indeed shaping contemporary devotions. Already the residual heirs of their predecessors and ever more defunct families, each was by inheritance the patron of literally hundreds of abbeys, priories, friaries, colleges, hospitals and chantries, yet no adult king was content with these or even to adopt the mausolea of his forebears. Where John of Gaunt, like former dukes of Lancaster, was interred at Leicester, his son Henry IV chose Canterbury cathedral. Henry V founded two new monasteries, his Bridgettine abbey of Syon and his charterhouse at Sheen, yet was buried in his chantry at Westminster Abbey. Henry VI, in contrast, established the twin educational colleges of Eton and King's, Cambridge, modelled both upon William of Wykeham's Winchester College and New College, Oxford and upon the triple foundation of chantry, school and almshouse of Archbishop Chichele. Although the family college at Fotheringhay was good enough for his father and next brother, Edward IV effectively re-founded St George's College at Windsor for himself, whilst Richard III planned the largest-ever chantry of a hundred priests at York minster. After dallying with Windsor, Henry VII created the most lavish of chantry chapels for himself at Westminster. Kings devoted to their private foundations resources that we regard as public: the resources of suppressed alien priories, of the crown lands and their private estates, of escheats, forfeitures and resumptions. The contents of the exchequer formed part of their estates. Its emptiness and the late king's obligations caused Edward IV's executors to renounce their role.[59] Like any other noblemen, Henry V and Edward IV earmarked private estates for performance of their last wills.

The character and capacity of our six adult kings varied, but the quality was generally high. Strength and personality counted for much.

The military leadership of Henry IV in 1403, Edward IV, and Richard III in 1483, Henry V's capacity to reconcile erstwhile traitors and Edward IV's to face down magnates, could not be delegated to a committee or bureaucrats. By fifteenth-century standards, Henry V was a model of what a king should be. He was a military leader – strategist, tactician, fighter and logistician; an able administrator, decisive and effective; a lion of justice and the most orthodox of Christians; able to mix with the aristocracy and to coerce them; vigorous and untiring, ruthless and relentless, yet also gracious and forgiving. He coerced where other kings patronised. Henry's victories made him into the legend consecrated both by Shakespeare and McFarlane, who thought him one of the greatest of English kings. It was thus that contemporaries regarded him, not merely those he led and inspired, but even those Yorkists who presented themselves as his true heirs when opposing and eventually unseating his successor.

Four other kings approached Henry's model. His father Henry IV, a knight of great renown, established his dynasty against overwhelming odds. The strictures of uncomprehending parliaments, rebels, and his impatient son, combined with his own ill-health, have clouded him with mediocrity. The teenage Edward IV had to grow up on the throne. His aristocratic upbringing and outlook, his towering physique, martial skills and genial charm made him a king for the nobility. He was as well the most successful soldier of the Wars of the Roses, the monarch who rebuilt royal solvency and, at times, an assiduous and effective administrator. Over-inclined to free-wheel and to decentralise, disinclined to impose his will or to still faction, a poor predictor and a vacillator, he was decisively outmanoeuvred by a full-time professional in Louis XI. To blame Edward for both the revolutions of 1469 and 1483 is unduly harsh – he was a usurper, after all, who died in bed – yet he falls well short of the greatness recently attributed to him.[60] His less physically imposing brother Richard III was perhaps the more cunning politician, the more ruthless egotist and manipulator, a king of undoubted courage and administrative capacity and possessed of all the necessary qualities of leadership and interpersonal skills, yet unable to persuade even Yorkists and the Yorkist establishment of his right to rule. Henry VII's supreme attribute was not to be Richard III: a master of detail, an economist first and a general very much second, he preferred coercion to patronage and rigour to conciliation. He was fortunate, perhaps, that his opponents were individually less formidable, had less popular appeal and had to contend with renewed prosperity. In contrast, Edward V was a two-month interlude. It was the longest reigning king, Henry VI, who fell most short, and whose personal deficiencies have obscured the intractable problems that brought down his successors.

Besides personalities, kings had life cycles. Starting like everyone else as babies, they passed through childhood and adolescence to maturity and perhaps senility. They were not always at their best. It is perhaps no accident that the five who best fitted the role acceded as experienced adults. Two fifteenth-century kings succeeded as minors, Henry VI as a baby and Edward V at the age of twelve. Self-evidently they could not rule, but they could reign. 'Even though ... he may not as yet have executive powers', the chancellor declared in 1427, yet 'as great an authority in government is now in the person of our said sovereign lord during his tender age as shall ever reside hereafter'. 'God hath called me in my tender age to be your king and sovereign' was the text for the opening sermon at Edward V's abortive parliament.[61] Both boys succeeded their fathers without question: the political establishment faced up to the interim arrangements until they came of age. Nonage was a frailty of the body natural, but the body politic endured. An infant prince's right eventually to protect his mad father was recognised in 1454.[62] When the unfortunate Henry IV was prostrated by chronic ill-health, there was talk of abdication, but he refused and imposed his will at the end. Strangely this was never proposed publicly for Henry VI until 1460, when even the most committed Yorkists failed to back it; perhaps, however, York did not intend the *Accord* to last and perhaps meant to make Henry VI abdicate.

Kings had their own private possessions separate from those of the crown. The Lancastrian kings held the duchy of Lancaster, their private inheritance, in their capacities as private individuals, their bodies natural, separate from the crown. It had its own chancellor, seal, chancery rolls, estate management and – in Lancashire – its own palatine administration where the king's writ did not run. Henry IV could contemplate it devolving through the female line and perhaps being separated from the crown. The prospect indeed became a reality under Richard III, who authorised the restoration of the former Bohun lands to Henry Duke of Buckingham and may have anticipated a claim to the duchy itself from Ralph Earl of Westmorland. An act of parliament was necessary, since one had been required to enable Edward IV to keep it as an appurtenance of his body natural rather than by forfeiture of his body politic.[63] Though much less formal, Edward IV also maintained the separateness of his earldom of March under a chancellor. Outside England, kings always had possessions separate from their English crown: Ireland, Aquitaine and the Channel Isles. English chancery rolls record some dealings of the English government with Ireland, just as the French rolls record dealings with Aquitaine and the Channel Isles, internal records being kept on the spot. Calais, in contrast, and occupied territory in Scotland, were part of the crown of England. The greatest such properties were the English conquests in France, held by English monarchs as kings of France: a topic beyond the scope of this book.

The reign of Henry VI, minor and lunatic in turn, is a series of case studies of the king's two bodies. His long minority forced the nobility to rule on his behalf. An appointed council led by the king's uncle Gloucester as protector, a title denoting no right to rule, was sanctioned by parliament. Their brief was to keep government operating and to hand it over intact to the king on his majority. They declined in 1434 to grant lands even to the Regent Bedford. It was not open to English negotiators at the Congress of Arras in 1435 to renounce the crown of France on Henry VI's behalf, nor was his minority government entitled to dispose of lands at home or even to license alienations in mortmain. The minority council fulfilled their charge, subject to serious disagreements in 1426 and 1433 between Gloucester and Beaufort that were resolved by the king's eldest uncle Bedford. The year 1422 was the model when Henry VI went mad in 1453–5, although this was a time of faction rather than common purpose and the remedy was partisan and authoritarian. In 1454 and 1455 York had insisted on sharing responsibility with a council nominated by parliament. Though already in control, his son Gloucester owed his protectorship in 1483 to appointment by the council. Councillors trespassed only reluctantly on royal prerogatives in 1446 and in 1453, when they undertook only the minimum essential and what would cause unbearable inconvenience if left undone.[64] In 1440 Gloucester charged Beaufort with taking powers 'which none of your true liegemen ought to usurp'. York wisely denied 'any presumption on my part' in 1456.[65]

Henry VI failed to fulfil the military expectations of a king when they were especially required. It is even questionable when he came of age. Relevant political theories were not fully developed. Coronation, it appears, was regarded as the key moment: in that case, his coronation in 1429 in England and in 1431 in France should have brought about his majority. It was of course a polite fiction: no 9-year old could rule effectively and Richard II, in practice, had to wait until he was 21. The protectorate ended and a chief councillor, still Gloucester, was installed. There is surprisingly little sign that Henry's majority commenced in 1437, as it should have done, and evidence indeed of a conciliar attempt to restrain his patronage.[66] Three times power was

WITHDRAWN

taken out of his hands and protectorates were established, twice apparently when he was not incapacitated by madness, and during the Readeption, most tellingly, it was the Lancastrians who sought to control his liberality through an appointed council. Fortescue did not then recommend taking decisions out of Henry's hands – he was, after all, king – but instead that decision should be deferred until council had debated and advised on it, which (he asserted ingenuously) 'may in no way restrain his power, liberty and prerogative'. These articles were not fully implemented and Henry made numerous decisions, though admittedly in minor matters, principally ecclesiastical.[67] If even Henry's most committed partisans wanted him excluded from decision-making, he was indeed a hopeless king.

Alternative interpretations are possible. If all agree that he was incompetent, they disagree why. Did he degenerate progressively, as Griffiths argues, or was he always inane? Was he uninterested in rule, by preference 'a model of new devotional piety', or sporadically wilful and malicious as Wolffe supposed, or was he a complete nothing? The latter proposition, that Henry was a vacuum at the centre filled by others and that even his pious foundations were the work of others, has been forcefully argued recently,[68] but goes too far. There is too much evidence of Henry's obstinacy, his refusal to concede to overwhelming odds as in 1450–1 and in 1460, his consistent peace-making and his over-indulgent forgiveness, repeatedly unrequited by York.[69] Not frequently, but on occasion, Henry did intervene in politics, sometimes decisively, often counter-productively. That is what incompetence entails. Henry may indeed have been too willing formally to delegate or to allow others to subvert his kingly functions and his personal interventions were seldom constructive or judicious, but his kingship was nevertheless a reality, to which everyone at times had to bow, and without which his reign would have been very different from what it was. Effective rule was possible – the late 1450s witnessed the resolution of the more serious aristocratic feuds! – and his deficiencies alone did not cause the Wars of the Roses.

If loyalty and obedience was due to the office and not the individual, a king's personal defects were not material. It should not matter that people said that Henry VI was simple and compared him with a child, because his authority did not depend on his mentality or capacity – theoretically. It was because it did matter in practice that the slanderers were prosecuted. The argument that Richard III need not fear his nephews, because he was king and they were bastards, fails because many rejected the pre-contract story and saw him as a usurper and tyrant. However often theory and practice coincided, they sometimes parted company.

4

ARISTOCRACY

The aristocracy was the ruling class. A minority were pre-selected by birth and inherited wealth to social eminence, plutocracy and power, and were predestined to life-long respect, deference and obedience. Such notions are hard to stomach today. They offend our most heart-felt principles and preconceptions. In an age founded on merit and equal opportunities, means tests and the redistribution of wealth, already committed to universal access and inclined increasingly towards positive discrimination, they are literally incomprehensible. Private health-care and public schools advantaging individuals are deplored alongside anything harking of privilege, elitism, inheritance or wealth. We don't kowtow to anyone, tug the forelock, or say 'sir'. Nobody condescends to us or patronises us. Relegating the majority 'to the permanent disdain of their more honourable superiors' is no longer acceptable.[1] How then can we today engage with a culture where such wrongs were not merely tolerated, but were valued, prioritised and, indeed, were unquestionable? We misunderstand that culture whenever we allude to the 'simple if vicious purpose' behind the aristocratic monopoly of hunting, presume that 'members of the ruling class were *in general* men of arrested intellectual development', or assert that 'upper class brutality ... is what defines the upper class'.[2] We accept that aristocrats believed their 'social advantages were rightfully imparted by inheritance rather than performance' only on the cynical basis that they had an eye for the main chance and wished to maintain the system that privileged them.[3] But such values were not confined to the aristocracy. They were widely held. Bishop Russell, who rose from obscurity on intellectual merit, agreed with Aristotle that 'noblesse is virtue and ancient riches' and that 'the politic rule of every region well ordered stands in the nobles'.[4] As in so many cultures 'leadership properly lies with those who enjoy an innate, special claim to it'.[5] The term aristocracy originally denoted not merely an elite, but the rule of

51

the best. Copious fifteenth-century evidence located the aristocracy within the *maior et sanior pars* (greater and wiser part). Aristocracy is another concept to which we must acclimatise ourselves. It was a fact of life – a natural fact of life – as beyond question as the God-given social hierarchy itself.

The aristocracy was a class comprising the titled nobility and the gentry. They were distinguished from their social inferiors by privilege. To the jurisdiction and authority bestowed over others as householders and landholders, which included the penalty of petty treason against their murderers, were added titles demanding deference and marked by distinctive dress denied to their social inferiors. County office was theirs alone and hunting was an aristocratic privilege. Aristocrats were almost the sole licensees for private chapels, free-warren and crenellation. Modest pedigrees sufficed for popes and bishops to dispense aristocrats from the criteria of age, legitimacy and incompatibility applicable to church livings, to authorise portable altars, earlier morning masses and a choice of confessor, to allow entrance to the most enclosed nunneries, to stay overnight and to eat meat there. Household chaplains were dispensed from residence in their parishes. High-born students secured graces expediting their university studies and graduation and became university chancellors very young. Yet such privileges were more limited than those of their continental counterparts. English aristocrats had no exemption from taxation, no closed offices restricted to them, and their titles and privileges devolved only on the heir. Younger sons tumbled down the hierarchy: from the nobility into the gentry and from the gentry even beyond. Noble paternity conferred no noble status, nor was gentility guaranteed to the offspring of the gentry. Great weight was attached to seniority, but high mortality and a fairly active land market meant that *ancient* might prove quite recent, merely one generation.

However the aristocracy were not uniform. They varied greatly in wealth and had their own hierarchy, which after 1440 comprised eight ranks, each marked by different standards of dress prescribed in the sumptuary acts. The graduated poll tax of 1379 broke down them down as is shown in Table 4.1.

Differentiation by rank was not exact, some knights being worth as much as a baron – the distinction was somewhat artificial outside parliament – and three levels of esquire were recognised, the third – in the era before gentlemen (1410) – being landless. The list resembles the tables of precedence like those in John Russell's *Book of Nurture* and those actually implemented for Archbishop Neville's enthronement feast in 1465. Different rates of pay were set for different ranks

Table 4.1 Graduated tax assessments of the aristocracy, 1379

The Dukes of Lancaster and Brittany	10 marks
Each Earl and widowed countess	£4
Each Baron and knight who can spend as much as a Baron; each baroness	£2
Each knight and each esquire who ought to be a knight [£20 a year]; each widowed lady, whether wife of a knight or esquire, by assessment	£1
Each esquire of lesser estate; each lady, widow of such an esquire	6s. 8d.
Each esquire not owning lands, rents or castles, who is in service or arms[6]	3s. 4d.

for royal service at arms – dukes were paid 6s. 8d a day – and on the royal council. Kings graduated the hospitality they offered according to rank: thus about 1445 a duke was entitled to a chaplain, four esquires and three yeomen, who dined in hall, two liveries in his chamber and, at night, to a loaf, a pitcher of wine and a gallon of ale. Much more elaborate regulations around 1475 set out entitlements to breakfast and supper, to faggots, candles and rushes to be strewn on the floor, and differentiated meticulously the smaller allowances for marquises, earl, viscounts and barons.

Table 4.2 Entertainment entitlements in the royal household, 1475

	Knight	Chaplain	Esquires	Gentleman	Yeomen
Duke	1	1	3	—	4
Marquis	1	1	3	—	2
Earl	1	1	2	—	2
Viscount	—	1	1	1	1
Baron	—	—	—	1	1

All peers normally dined in the king's chamber, though mere barons could be sat in the hall: dukes, marquises, earls and bishops sat at one table and earls normally together, though earls could be put with barons. Their goods could not be taken for royal use (purveyance) without their permission.[7]

Similar distinctions were made with their inferiors. Surviving indentures of retainer specify conditions of service 'as other of his degree shall have', such others ranging from esquires to barons. Not infrequently provision was made for a change of degree, such as succession to a barony for Sir Thomas Dacre (1435) and Sir Edward Grey of Groby (Leic.) in 1440 or to an inheritance for Richard Musgrave (1456), in which case the fee would be increased. So, too, in Grey's case, would be his entourage at his lord's expense, from an esquire, three yeomen, a groom, a page, and seven horses appropriate for a knight to two esquires, four yeomen, one groom, two pages and ten horses as a baron.[8]

> It were great shame
> A knight alone to ride,
> Without squire, yeoman, or page,
> To walk by his side.[9]

Knighthood conferred precedence over esquires and gentlemen, yet many chose to pay a fine – to be distrained for knighthood – rather than to take on such honour, probably because they wished to avoid the extra expense involved – the extra show expected of them. Moderation and prudence rather than competitive assertiveness was often urged in housekeeping: spending 'in measure ... each man after his estate' was Peter Idley's recommendation.[10] Refusers of routine promotion often accepted as far more honourable the order of the Bath at the king's hands on royal ceremonial occasions or promotion on campaign, like the fifty-two knighted and thirty-seven made bannerets by Northumberland and Gloucester in Scotland in 1481–2.[11] The tomb of Sir Reginald Cobham of Sterborough (Surrey), a lapsed peer, displayed the banner that distinguished him from his neighbours.[12]

McFarlane and other modern historians have over-stressed the distinction between the parliamentary peerage – the Lords – and the gentry.[13] They too were lords. A peerage was crucial in some specific contexts, but not others: in some counties and parliamentary elections it mattered not at all. Yet the Lords were a privileged minority. By 1399 their personnel was fixed and hereditary: kings could only influence membership by new creations, forfeitures, or where succession was through the female line or disputed. There was some discretion in which titles to assign to which co-heir, but the husband of a sole heiress was usually allowed her family's peerage. Demotions were rare. George Duke of Bedford was forcibly degraded from the peerage altogether in 1478 and two dukes of Suffolk, primarily for financial reasons, took earldoms instead. Descendants of some erstwhile barons, such as Hilton, Camoys, St Amand and FitzWalter, continued to exercise the title and hankered after parliamentary peerages, only the last with success. The Lords were an elite with greater wealth and bluer blood. They were summoned in person to counsel the king, who debated with them in the parliament chamber and their views were requested individually. They (and, from 1442, their consorts) were entitled to trial by peers in parliament and by the high steward outside and qualified for more dignified execution, with the axe rather than the rope. Their incomes were assessed individually rather than under counties in 1436. From 1390 only they could retain or give livery outside their households or to non-officers and then solely to gentry. They were immune from arrest except for treasons and serious felonies, exempt from outlawry in civil suits and from imprisonment for debt, and were protected against defamation by the action of *scandalum magnatum*.

Distinctions within the peerage mattered more as old families were replaced by new and as higher titles were created. Dukes were granted annuities of £40, marquises £30, earls £20 and viscounts £13 6s. 8d. The peers processed and sat in the parliament chamber in order of rank, wearing splendid parliamentary caps and robes of scarlet with ermine bars: in 1399 four for dukes, three for earls and two for barons, and by 1447 four for dukes, three and one-half for a marquis, three for an earl and two for a baron. Such distinctions came to matter. Henry VI promoted his friend Henry Beauchamp in 1444–5 first to premier earl, 'prime count', with precedence over all earls and the right to wear a coronet even in the king's presence, and then to duke of Warwick, with precedence over Buckingham. John Viscount Beaumont, whose viscountcy in 1440 had elevated him above all barons, secured a grant of precedence over all future viscounts in 1445. William Lord Berkeley resented the devaluation of his ancient barony by the importation of exotic viscountcies (but later accepted one for himself). There were a series of precedence disputes from 1405, notably the twice-contested dispute of the earl marshal vs earl of Warwick 1405–25, and between the earls of Northumberland and Salisbury. These were fought because they were of importance. Mere precedence was but one aspect of 'the name state honour and dignity' of the earldom of Salisbury. It threatened the earl's right to the title, which could have escheated in 1428, and the battle honours that went with it. The earldom of Arundel, similarly, could have been terminated in 1433.[14] It was the higher ranks, the magnates, and especially the great lords of the blood, who counted for most. The greatest honorific offices, commands in chief and, increasingly, the treasurership of England, chamberlainship and stewardship of the household were reserved for them. Far from all being equal, York enjoyed revenues equivalent to 600 mere gentlemen or 300 knights.

That the Lords were special was most obvious in times of minority. In 1422 they asserted their authority even over the king's uncle Gloucester, denied him a regency, and devised the form of the minority government, to which the Commons then assented. In 1427 royal authority to rule, govern and keep the laws belonged 'to the lords spiritual and temporal of his land ... assembled in parliament or in great council' and, when not assembled, 'unto the lords chosen and named to be of his continual council'. It was they who delegated power to the protector, just as in 1422 they had insisted that Gloucester's commission to open and close parliament was by their counsel and consent. It was to them – the lords of the king's blood and peerage – to whom discussion of York's title in 1460 pertained.[15]

Yawning though the gulf was from courtiers and commanders to attorneys and backwoods squires, there was nevertheless a common aristocratic identity. 'A complex web of habits, traditions, relationships, behaviours, assumptions and beliefs', says Dr Mertes, 'gave them a common world and enables us to talk about them as a unit'. They were well-to-do and hence leisured: any who were not dropped out of the class. They constituted Peter Laslett's 'one-class society':[16] the only class, even 200 years later, with a national identity and national horizons. They counted individually in national politics, comprising indeed most of the political nation, and supplied an entourage, commanders, councillors and even ministers to every king. They were a rural elite, who lived predominantly in the countryside in castles and manor houses and indulged in country sports. They were a hereditary aristocracy, proudly aware of ancestral pedigrees, coats of arms and connections, and of a host of genteel cousins. They were managing directors of family concerns – the family estates, large or small – which had to be run, generally by delegation: decision-making, policies and allowances, and the buck, stopped with the lord. However tempted by self-indulgent idleness and inevitably sometimes irresponsible or incompetent, they could evade neither the demands of rank, patronage, nor affairs. Competence was as essential for them as it was for a king. The aristocracy was a military caste, trained up in arms and athletic pursuits, and expected to participate in the monarch's wars. Service to those greater than themselves added to their renown. They were local elites and natural rulers everywhere, on whom every king relied for local government and whose pre-existing authority he recruited to his own service. Government rather than warfare had become the main route to royal favour, power and the peerage.

The aristocratic ethos

Both William Worcester and William Caxton deplored the decline in martial spirit of the aristocracy.[17] Increasingly a nobility of service, rather than a military cadre, they nevertheless subscribed to a military code of conduct. Chivalry was 'an ethos, in which martial, aristocratic and Christian elements are merged'. It was an international code respected and approved by monarchs everywhere. Five principal values were stressed: *largesse; franchise; loyalty, prowess,* and *honour. Trouth* and *courtesy* were scarcely less important.[18] *Franchise* relates to the frank and open bearing expected of an aristocrat. Loyalty, trouth and worship are discussed elsewhere. Actually honour was their natural state – the state into which they grew up. Even chivalry itself, to Edmund Dudley in 1509, was a pseudonym for the nobility and gentry.[19]

Prowess reminds us of the military origins of the elite and the military justifications for its continuance, to protect the helpless in society and to protect society itself against foreign enemies. It was certainly not then accepted that 'a violent man is a bad man'.[20] Knighthood was a military rank: all peers became knights. The far more numerous esquires were also aristocrats eligible for knighthood. Aristocrats were prepared physically and intellectually for their military calling. An armoured knight required the physical fitness and stamina, skills in horsemanship and in weaponry, instilled from formal training, much practice, mock combat, and what we would regard as sport: the hunting, hawking and jousting that kept him fit and militarily adept into middle age and beyond. Familiarity with heraldry and the law of arms guided conduct in the field. Just as important, however, were intellectual qualities: belligerence, raw courage, obduracy, leadership, the urge to excel, pride in performance and the thirst for renown that matched the model heroes of contemporary romance. The greatest of magnates was flattered by comparison with the nine worthies and such antique heroes as Hector and Roland. Much of the reputation, worship and honour to which all aspired was accessible also through everyday activities closer to home.

Arms was a dignified profession that was itself honourable and ennobling. The qualities it required blended with those of hereditary nobility itself, for which arrogance, a sense of natural superiority, pride in lineage and family honour, and the appropriation for oneself of achievements inherited from past generations, dovetailed with the values of chivalry itself. Lineal and personal honour forced men to expose themselves to danger, to persevere against superior odds, and conform to christian principles, the laws of war, contemporary conventions, manners and etiquette (courtesy).

Courtesy was no frill: it was a code of conduct designed to instil 'virtue' in preparation for a life 'of honour'. It was formally taught in 'schools of urbanity and nurture' in line with contemporary courtesy books. Besides the physical attributes listed above, gentlemen had need of book learning, the 'learnings virtuous', and of such accomplishments as harping, piping, singing and dancing that enabled them to hold their own in polite society. Polite knowledge, such as 'the arcane mysteries of venery', and polite skills, such as meat-carving, were marks of the born aristocrat.[21] Self-discipline, frankness, openness and 'other honest and temperate behaving and patience', whereby polite society regulated its behaviour, were inculcated. A master directed genteel children (the king's henxmen) on 'their demeanings [at table], how mannerly they eat and drink, and on their conversation and other courtly matters (forms curial)'. Regular participation in religious services was prescribed. All aristocrats learnt how to speak and act in polite company, and about the degrees, orders of precedence and seating at table which they would need 'after they be of honour': after they had grown up and entered their designated station.[22] All these were achieved to the fullest degree by one chivalric hero of the fifteenth century, Richard Beauchamp, Earl of Warwick (d. 1439), who was allegedly 'called the father of courtesy [by] the emperor [Sigismund], for if all courtesy were lost, he said it might be found in his person'.[23]

How exceptional Beauchamp was we cannot tell. Aristocratic upbringings still strove for that effect. Good manners leave few records. The forms or 'polite veneer' of courtly love, challenge and tournaments still emerge from the *Paston Letters*. Positive evidence of compliance with the chivalric code, on the battlefield or elsewhere, is confined to the exceptions and the extremes. There were indeed rude rustic boors for courtesy books to denounce.[24] Deduction from silence suggests that most aristocrats conformed. A stronger motive for such a supposition emerges from the negative evidence, from those slurs on an individual's honour, reputation or worship that impelled him to resist, not least because of the undesirable practical repercussions.

These fall into several categories. Marrying beneath oneself and poverty could detract from one's honour and might even result in demotion. So, more strikingly, could breach of faith, which was a sin that was taken very seriously: for example non-payment of a ransom once released on parole. 'Hold thy peace, Michael', a former chancellor was told in 1387, 'it becometh thee right evil to say such words, though that art damned for thy falsehood both by the lords and parliament'. It was perjury, his promise to content himself with his duchy of Lancaster, that the Percies alleged against Henry IV and used to justify their insurrection in 1403. A promise of security 'on the faith and fealty by which I am bound to God and as I am a gentleman and faithful knight' emboldened Nicholas Radford to surrender himself in 1456 into the hands of Sir Thomas Courtenay, a knight and heir to an earldom, shockingly also his murderer. Far from redeeming his reputation, George Duke of Clarence's rapprochement with Edward IV in 1471 perjured himself once more. Not to relieve the siege of Caister Castle by the duke of Norfolk, Margaret Paston warned her son, 'shall be to you a great disworship, and look never to have favour of your neighbours and friends but if this speed it'.[25] The charge of cowardice at the battle of Pataye laid against Sir John Fastolf, for which he was suspended from the Garter, threatened his career as well as his honour, and demanded the most vigorous rebuttal. The perjured traitor Sir Ralph Grey was ceremonially degraded from knighthood in 1464 before his execution.[26] *Scrope* v *Grosvenor* and *Hastings* v *Grey*, two cases in the court of chivalry, turned on defence of the family coat of arms, symbolising a family's whole identity, its lineage, renown and honour, against an interloper. Precedence disputes were similar. No peer would willingly abandon the status, rank or precedence that they held in trust for their heirs.

Such litigation could be acrimonious – Henry Percy cannot have liked being addressed as 'Henry pretending [to be] earl of Northumberland'[27] – but no violence ensued. To our thinking, such disputes did not touch on essential interests and were not worth risking everything. We are therefore amazed that in 1399, charged with the murder of his uncle Gloucester, the earl of Rutland not only denied it, but threw down his gauntlet before his accuser, committing himself thereby to a duel that hazarded his life to protect his reputation and honour; many other peers followed suit. Lord Morley, for instance, declared Salisbury to be a false traitor to the king and offered to prove it in person by force of arms.[28] The king, who forbade prosecution of these quarrels, had been earlier prepared to risk his own life, to our notions *unnecessarily*, against the duke of Norfolk at Coventry.

Yet more striking to us are surviving written challenges in the Courtenay–Bonville and Berkeley–Lisle disputes. These were open letters, directed to more than the nominal recipient, and were designed to provoke a duel as much by public shame as by casting private aspersions on the recipient's honour. That they were written to a formula, in 'chivalric mode', according to a standard ritual, suggests that they were two of many. Such trials by battle had no status at English law – although Henry IV, at least, was inclined to respect them – and could not settle titles to land. Participants moreover were liable like any other violent criminals to prosecution, although those who were peers, as in these cases, were protected from more serious penalties. Undeterred by such disadvantages, and indeed pleading that their actions prevented rather than caused the shedding of christian blood, all four gave precedence to their honour over the law and presented themselves as operating with God's approval, within their allegiance, in accordance with the chivalric code, and in pursuit of their just causes. In both these cases, however, the exchange of challenges were followed by trials by battle – the fight at Clyst (1455) and the battle of Nibley Green (1470) – and in the latter instance one of the principals, Viscount Lisle, did indeed lose his life. These were the denouements that the letters sought to provoke: an examination of the letters, therefore, reveals what slurs could not be overlooked.

Unable to achieve his objectives by conventional political means, it was the weaker party, William Lord Bonville, who issued a challenge designed to bring Devon out into the open on as equal terms as possible. Taking the moral high ground, he claimed the backing of God, the law, and the commonweal, declared himself to be both a true liegeman acting like a true liegeman and a true knight behaving as a knight should in pursuit of his just quarrel, and denounced the evil conduct of his rival Thomas Earl of Devon who, he claimed, was guilty of a host of crimes: ambush, murder, unlawful assembly, the harbouring of criminals, perversion of justice, the ransoming and impediment of the king's subjects. Furthermore, Devon had committed such offences, so Bonville said, falsely, cowardly and traitorously, in breach of his faith as a knight, his prowess and honour, his allegiance, the common good, and the standards 'that should pertain to thy estate' as an earl. So damaging were these charges to the earl's good name and standing that they could not be ignored. Accordingly he took up Bonville's gauntlet to 'save such worship as is in you', denying the charges and proclaiming his intention to appear in person to vindicate himself as a true knight and true liegeman and to prove Bonville false and untrue. Devon won: victory confirmed his pre-eminence. Bonville escaped alive. He had lost the feud and failed to overturn the Courtenay ascendancy: what derogation of his honour, if any, followed his escape unharmed is not recorded.

The second dispute was merely an episode in two centuries of the Berkeley–Lisle dispute. Immediately following his majority, Thomas Viscount Lisle took up his family feud against Berkeley, who occupied estates that were properly, he felt, his own. Berkeley was challenged to combat on his knighthood, his manhood, and on the honour and order of knighthood, all of which would be tarnished by a refusal. Such considerations outweighed Berkeley's advantage, as the actual possessor, in avoiding conflict. He accepted Lisle's challenge, justifying himself with God's backing and a plea of self-defence. He denounced Lisle for his 'malicious and mischievous purpose'; for his reliance on false advisers, of whom Mulle was 'attaint of falseness and erasing of the king's records' and Holt had perjured himself, so that 'every worshipful man should refuse to have [either of them] in his fellowship'; and for his own personal lack of judgement. Not only would the battle vindicate Berkeley and confirm his honour and standing, but it would prove 'thy great shame and disworship'.[29] Berkeley won, his honour purged, and Lisle was slain, but the dispute rolled on for another century. The verdict of battle in a dispute of honour did not bind the common law of inheritance.

Such extreme charges brought both parties to the field. Did they have to be so extreme? Would anything else have failed? Devon and Berkeley were in possession, in the ascendant, and content to leave matters to the established channels which served them well. Serious though the fundamental issues were, they need not have risked their lives; others did not. Only the most wholehearted and damning slurs could force them out in battle. When Clarence challenged his accusers to combat in 1478, he was bereft of any other defence.[30] It was formal charges, of perjury, cowardice and treason, that invoked the operation of the machinery of the chivalric code. Sir John Fastolf took great pains to clear himself of the charge of cowardice at the battle of Pataye. The quarrels of the dukes of York and Somerset in 1450–5, it has been argued, arose from the former's outrage at the latter's betrayal of Lancastrian Normandy.[31] 'What is a man but his promise?' asked the septuagenerian Lord Darcy in 1536,[32] thereby consigning himself to a shameful death and his house to ruin. Although constantly in dispute, aristocrats seldom fought about such issues because other channels for resolution existed. Only occasionally when everything was hazarded did they demonstrate the compulsion of the honour code.

Largesse, in contrast, was an open-handed generosity without regard to cost. A lavish tip was what the heralds expected when they called on the largesse of newly promoted knights or peers. Generosity was peculiarly an aristocratic quality: the word generosity itself derives from the Latin *generosus*, denoting a gentleman. It was ingrained. 'The prime test of rank was liberality, the pagan virtue of open-handedness. "A Gentleman (if he will be so accounted) must go like a Gentleman"'.

Other expressions were open-house hospitality. The keeping of a good household, according to Caxton's *Book of Chivalry*, was 'an essential attribute of knighthood', and the exchange of hospitality additionally expressed both courtesy and franchise. The epitaphs of two Cobhams in 1355 and 1403 specifically remembered them as 'a courteous host' and for a 'sumptuous table'. Contemporaries were awed by 'the exceeding household' which Warwick 'daily kept in all countries where ever he sojourned or lay'; the enthronement feast of his brother Archbishop Neville was legendary.[33] Sir Thomas More prevented his readers from approving Richard III's liberality by converting it into extravagance.[34] Largesse, in short, was an aspect of the conspicuous consumption that medieval people valued so highly and expected of the great.[35]

Aristocrats had to accept all kinds of obligations. Providing for their siblings and marrying off their sisters and daughters was expensive, especially if it was done properly and without disparaging them with low-ranking but cheaper spouses. Rejecting mere barons for his sisters-in-law was burdensome even for a king, as Edward IV found. To be without a portion and obliged to take the veil was not just a personal tragedy, but a considerable blot on the family's escutcheon. Living up to one's rank, in the style expected of them, demanded a relatively large household, a lavish meat-based diet, up-to-date residences and mausolea, furnishings and decoration, monuments and chapel equipment, dress, plate, jewellery, and horses, and an escort ideally of the tall, well-born and liveried wherever one went. They had to emulate, or at least equal, their peers. It helps explain why so many declined to take up knighthood – it demanded a higher cost of living – and why it was those on the margins, the poor duke or poor baron, who found it hardest to keep up. It was better not to attend parliament at all, so John Duke of Suffolk felt in 1470,[36] than to come with an entourage unworthy of a duke. It may explain why three financially embarrassed dukes – Exeter in the 1450s and Norfolk and Suffolk thereafter – pursued the main chance so aggressively. A combination of impressive public display and decorum with an economical avoidance of waste and rigid discipline was the ideal sought by the household ordinances. Largesse had to be carefully calculated.[37]

Pedigree, lineage and inheritance

An aristocrat was a stage on a continuing family tree. His *lineage* had a future as well as a past. Because of entails, he was often merely a tenant for life, guarding what later generations also had rights to. Aristocrats

ARISTOCRACY

were conscious whence they and their inheritances came, of the need to protect their heritage, and, if possible, to augment it. Muniment rooms were stuffed with deeds and cartularies were composed from them. Dozens of contemporary genealogies and family histories focus on the direct line of descent, each faithfully identifying the family of each lord's spouse. The quarterings of coats of arms recorded past marriages: they could be read on banners and shields, and were chiselled into houses, churches and monuments, painted on stained glass, stamped on to dinner and communion plate, and embroidered on vestments, hangings and beds. Aristocrats maximised their antecedents, stressed the antiquity of their lines, rejoiced in past glories, minimised disasters and extolled noble and royal connections. Costly royal genealogies were repeatedly customised to intertwine the royally connected families that had commissioned them. Parvenus like the Pastons invented noble forebears. Even magnates extended their pedigrees back first to the Norman Conquest and then beyond. The Beauchamps of Warwick reclaimed from the romances the legendary giant Guy of Warwick, naming sons after him, and refounding the chapel at Guys Cliff near Warwick, complete with Guy's huge statue. It was pride of lineage that prompted so many old men like William Lord Botreaux (d. 1462) to remarry in the hope of a son, to the understandable offence of middle-aged daughters like Margaret Lady Hungerford (d. 1478). Earl Richard Beauchamp remarried to keep his line going and enjoined his son to keep the title of Warwick if ever promoted: Duke Henry obeyed.[38] Not only did the potential for inheritance determine many a marriage, but careful track was kept of properties yet to fall in and of claims, hitherto disappointed, and yet to be realised.

An *inheritance* was controlled by the current head of the family, but was the endowment of the whole family. It provided for them all. Direct descents in pedigrees changed sharply at the present day, at which point all siblings and children and their marriages were recorded, sometimes including even those who died in infancy. Provision for cadets was an accepted obligation on fathers and brothers: the marriage of a daughter or her consignment to a nunnery, in each case with a dowry, terminated her entitlement. Once married, she joined another lineage, which took priority – although her mother's and maternal kin were not uncommonly remembered in her will or chantry. Out of each nuclear family there evolved a series of different nuclear families, each with their own distinct pedigree and membership: priority within the lineage always rested with one's own spouse and offspring over collaterals, even brothers and sisters. Hence such pedigrees quickly went out of date and had to be constantly extended or otherwise adapted for future generations. Those proud genealogies that culminated in the 1st earl of Westmorland were subsequently extended and adapted for his Latimer, Bergavenny, Middleham and Westmorland descendants, who each required different slants on the same material.

Inheritance was the foundation of the aristocracy and of each family within it. It came in two forms: land and moveable goods or chattels. Chattels could be bequeathed within strict rules; some at least usually for pious purposes. Debts died with the debtor: a disincentive to creditors to over-lend. Since this system dispersed chattels in each generation, even the greatest fortunes in liquid assets – such as the £6,000 of Richard Whittington (d. 1423) and the £7,000 of John Earl of Oxford in 1513 – could have bought only a modest baronial estate. There are no parallels for the £76,000 of the earl of Arundel in 1376 or Cardinal Beaufort's vast loans to the crown. Land was much more important. The aristocracy were above all landholders, often of substantial or extensive estates, and land was the most visible form of wealth and the most secure form in which wealth could be held. There was no danger of it suffering shipwreck or embezzlement. Land bestowed status and authority on its holders. A family estate underpinned an aristocrat's whole lifestyle, standing and career, and those of future generations also. Landholding was what contemporaries meant when they talked about inheritance. Inheritance was a sacred right.

If inheritance was the sacred right that Lander and others have made of it,[39] this arose not from any explicitly christian sanction, but because of its worldly significance. Inheritance was the means whereby status and wealth could be transmitted. The greatest families were those that had accumulated many inheritances, always taking as foundation what had been passed down to them by their predecessors. To deny someone his just inheritance, as Richard II sought to do to his cousin Henry of Lancaster, was an irredeemable wrong. Even those hostile to Henry IV and Edward IV as kings could not deny their rights to their dukedoms. Everyone knew their own claims to inherit and asserted them vigorously. Inheritance was fundamental – so important that nobody could afford to concede it – but regrettably contemporary land law had not kept up with the practice of contemporary conveyancing. It was because their titles were so often ambiguous or conflicted that inheritances were so commonly in dispute, with serious implications for family harmony, law and order, and indeed public peace.

Primogeniture was the system of inheritance used for land held by knight service and serjeanty, as most manors were. It applied originally to peerage titles too. This was the system that mattered to the politically important. The direct line took priority, whether male or female, males of the same generation being preferred to females. Sisters inherited equally. Only when the direct line was exhausted did collateral heirs enter the reckoning. It was a winner-takes-all arrangement in which the heir took everything and junior or collateral relatives nothing. It ensured that the holder's son succeeded first, thus keeping the estate together, but allowed women to inherit also. Should there be more than one heiress, the estate was broken up. Since the later medieval ages was an era of high mortality and gentle population decline, failure in the direct male line was commonplace. It was a reality for more than a quarter of noble families every quarter century.[40] There were thus many heiresses, often unforeseen. Even where the male line continued, the heir often found himself in possession of only a portion of his inheritance, as his predecessor's widow enjoyed a third of the estate in dower and perhaps some more in jointure. Thomas Lord Roos was burdened in 1436 by three dowagers who left him hardly anything. Not surprisingly many heirs and heiresses resented stepmothers, often younger than themselves, who had reduced their expectations. Margaret Lady Hungerford's distaste for her young stepmother Margaret Lady Botreaux is well-attested. Some dowagers long outlived their first husbands: Joan Countess of Hereford (d. 1419) and her grand-daughter Anne Countess of Stafford (d. 1438) held much of the Bohun and Stafford jointures and dowers for 46 and 35 years respectively.

Such temporary interruptions to the orderly process of descent, which must sometimes have appeared everlasting, could have advantages, mitigating the effects of minorities and even (as the Percies and Hungerfords found) forfeiture. Theoretically primogeniture should have kept estates intact in the direct line to support the whole range of family interests at the not inconsiderable cost of disinheriting younger sons and females. Reality was somewhat different. Relatively low fertility, high mortality and low life expectancy meant that many families failed in the male line. This must not be equated with failure of heirs. McFarlane's definition of failure was unduly strict and included the succession of a male collateral, such as a brother, uncle, nephew or cousin, who continued the family name, kept the estate intact, and perhaps took on all the family burdens. Even when the male line failed completely, it was more common to have one heiress than several, like Sir Thomas Chaucer's daughter Alice or Sir Thomas Hungerford's daughter Anne, and many co-heiresses – like the Stanhope nieces of Ralph Lord Cromwell or the daughters of the Kingmaker – sustained only one enduring line. In an era of low replacement rates, when each generation was failing to reproduce itself, there was a tendency towards accumulation in the same hands through marriage and inheritance rather than dispersal via partition amongst heiresses. Passage intact via an heiress to her husband's family, however, was liable to end the performance of any pre-existing obligations to her family of origin.

From different points of view, the system had other disadvantages. First, it was a system of feudal tenure, in which the current holder was a tenant if his feudal lord, who took the lands into *wardship* and wasted the capital assets, became guardian of the person of the heir and married him off at will, and trafficked in any of these commodities, to the loss of any other family dependants. Secondly, the current tenant had unfettered possession and, subject to legal restrictions, could do what he liked with the land, including selling it or giving it away, again to the loss of the heir. Thirdly, the tenant-for-life had no control over what happened after his death, so that it was difficult to provide for younger children, to raise money on the security of land (the equivalent of the modern mortgage), or to devote the income to pious dispositions after his death. This applied particularly to those gentry of modest means, who divided their estates. Such considerations gave rise to *trusts* and *entails*, which meant that much land had ceased to be held in fee simple by the fifteenth century, and in particular very little of the land of the high nobility.

Enfeoffments to use enabled a tenant to settle land on feoffees (trustees) in trust for purposes that he designated or could subsequently amend in his will. This was used to perpetuate his authority beyond death, avoiding wardship, enabling annuities to be paid to junior relatives, monies to be raised on what were effectively mortgages or towards the marriage portions of daughters, and religious foundations to be financed.

The loser might often be the heir. Fulk Lord FitzWarren, for instance, used lands in trust to enlarge his wife's jointure, whilst Gill Thame appropriated the revenues of her manor of East Thorpe (Hants.) for the twenty years after her death to endow a chantry for the good of her own soul. It was for such a purpose that Sir William Moleyns was sold a manor of his own inheritance. Two generations of Beauchamp heirs were deprived of the lands of the Beauchamp trust.[41]

The second device, the *entail*, often settled lands merely on the descendants of the feoffor, thus rendering alienation much more difficult. Frequently lands were entailed on the male line only, to the exclusion of women, thus ensuring that land and family name descended together. Tenants frequently placed a high valuation on continuation of the family name, the lineage or pedigree. Female heirs and their spouses often disagreed. It was normal by the fifteenth century to settle lands at marriage on a couple and their issue, the jointure, which ensured that the surviving spouse and any offspring were provided for. The diversion of lands to the issue of second marriages caused the Neville–Neville and Talbot–Lisle feuds.

Each variation in inheritance was devised with particular ends in mind, but was adaptable to other circumstances. They gave control to the current landholder. They enabled him to postpone descent to the next generation, to appropriate revenues to other purposes, and to prescribe or even change an inheritance's subsequent devolution. Every settlement reflected the landholder's sense of family, enshrined particular circumstances and family relationships which often passed unexplained, and ascribed alternative valuations for the interest of spouses, direct issue and collateral heirs, male and female lines, the good of the donor's soul, his extravagance and the financial pressures to which he was subjected. Not infrequently, it was pressure from creditors for reimbursement and from the fathers of prospective brides for jointures that caused new trusts and entails to be created. Such motives can often be difficult to gauge because premature deaths revised the circumstances. Trusts could be revised by the feoffor, up to death, but entails (until 1473) could not be broken. What originally liberated a landholder might tie his hands. Entails often produced unpredictable results and constrained future generations. Inheritances accumulated in the same hands might have different titles: thus the earldoms of Arundel and Warenne, united in 1347, were divided again in 1417: the Arundel patrimony continued with the male heir and the Warenne estate was partitioned among heiresses. The most famous instance, the four great inheritances of Warwick the Kingmaker, should have passed to a male heir and two heiresses. Not uncommonly grantors over-stretched themselves, seeking to over-ride reversionary rights by new enfeoffments and entails. The Beauchamp estate included many properties that had been assigned as jointures and entailed more than once: presumably the later settlements were actually invalid?[42] Sometimes, perhaps commonly, grantors got away with it. We know most about those who did not. When donors re-entailed lands already entailed, as James Earl of Wiltshire did in 1458, created trusts out of entailed land, sought to create estates for cadets such as Leonard Hungerford or bastards such as John Hopton, or sought to sell lands the heir for whom was a distant cousin, as Sir John Clifton did with Buckenham Castle (Norf.),[43] the law was far from clear and there were conflicts of title with no correct answer. Distant relatives had residual titles that needed to be bought out if they were not to upset whatever arrangements had been made. Thus in 1469, following the death of her elder brother, Frideswide Hungerford acknowledged in chancery twenty quitclaims to Hungerford and Botreaux lands,[44] even though she had a grandmother, two brothers and a niece with better claims. One could not be too sure.

We should not exaggerate. All church land was undisputed. Three-quarters of all aristocratic inheritances descended to the direct male heir. Most of those that did not descended to a single heir, male or female. Co-heiresses seldom posed problems. Most inquisitions post mortem are unambiguous about who was the heir. Few inquisitions were traversed or overthrown. Normal succession was the norm. There was no anarchy. Disputes most commonly arose where titles had been challenged or changed, by resettlement or sale. When Robert Armburgh claimed that his nieces were bastards, no jury was prepared to believe him.[45] It is unfortunate that it is only his partial version which we can consult. We may also be misled by the survival of the Paston letters – always the Pastons' version[46] – and by the archives of Sir John Fastolf, not those of their opponents. Perhaps East Anglia and the Pastons were exceptional. Land in East Anglia may have been particularly negotiable; an especially active land market is suggested by the substantial estates purchased by the Pastons, Townshends and Fastolf. Titles based on purchase were often, perhaps always, less than watertight and overrode the reversionary rights of others. Whatever the Pastons themselves thought, their rights to East Beckham, Gresham and Caister did not extinguish the titles of others.

Inheritance was not a small matter for anyone. Inheritance disputes were serious for all involved. On an inheritance depended a whole lifestyle, its acquisition or its loss.[47] When magnates were involved and what was at stake was a great inheritance, the effects could have major social and political implications that could impinge on or dominate national politics, as the Warwick inheritance did both in the 1450s and the 1470s. Inheritance was the expectation on which many aristocrats built their lives. Holders of land spent much time and effort in planning its subsequent devolution. Inheritance caused them to take the long view, to calculate, and to invest for the distant future. It was not just their own interest that concerned them, but the fortune of their lineage, which inheritance underpinned.

Making choices

It is not difficult to demonstrate that particular aristocrats were influenced by rank, by inheritance and by honour on specific occasions, but it is important to recall that all such considerations and many others were shared by all aristocrats in varying proportions and with differing priorities at all times. Sometimes, perhaps normally, there was no conflict: the dictates of honour conveniently conformed to those of rank and class or allegiance self-evidently took priority. Sometimes, however, a choice needed to be made: it was not possible to sustain both family rights *and* honour, both lineage *and* religion, both good lordship *and* respect for the law. Maintaining a retainer in his just cause did not necessarily involve backing him up to the hilt against all-comers, whatever the retainer might suppose. In the many cases in which contemporaries were faced with choices, conscious or unconscious, that they may well have found difficult to resolve, historians are unaware of it or have great difficulty in disentangling their motives, and probably, generally, fail. This applies even when some of the simpler, more straightforward and commonplace, motives are considered.

How far pedigree, family and inheritance motivated individuals and in what ways was governed by a range of other considerations. It depended where one stood upon the family tree. Heirs presumptive, younger sons and collaterals understandably viewed the estate as the *family* inheritance, which existed for the benefit of them all; heirs additionally regarded it as *their* inheritance, to accrue in the future. Actually it was the possession solely of the current holder, who might or might not acknowledge moral obligations to his kin, heirs and dependants. Notions of kinship and family changed over time, as the original nuclear family evolved into a series of separate nuclear families, as brothers were replaced by cousins, as the tenant's own offspring took familial priority over his siblings and collaterals. Whereas Ralph Earl of Westmorland (d. 1425) provided for all his children, mostly via good marriages, increasingly they distinguished the interests of their branch of the family from others, so that, for instance, Salisbury participated in the killing of his brother-in-law Northumberland at St Albans in 1455. The 2nd earl of Northumberland supported his younger sons, including Thomas Lord Egremont, but his grandson the 4th earl showed less favour to Egremont's son, his Percy cousin, than to his sister Margaret's husband Sir William Gascoigne, in contemporary parlance his brother [-in-law]. There was a natural growing apart of aristocratic families, as the component members grew up, married, bred and accrued their own interests and priorities, which might indeed clash.[48] The sense of obligation of even the most family-minded and responsible head to his kin declined as each left the nest and was provided for. Receipt of a marriage portion, for instance, ended obligations to daughters, who might receive only a token in their parents' wills if indeed they were mentioned at all.

Continued descent was not inevitable. Many a landholder died childless or without sons. Landholders, in McFarlane's words,

> rarely if ever died without heirs. Without issue, yes, often enough; but without any blood relations, virtually never. And the longer the Conqueror's followers were established in England, the wider the network of their blood-ties spread.[49]

The longer a family had held an estate, the more certain there was an heir somewhere on the family tree emanating from the original tenant. Failure to produce children or sons, in short, meant not escheats, but the devolution of the estate on daughters, brothers, nephews and nieces, and cousins, to whom the current tenant perhaps felt no obligation. Many tenants who wanted a male heir to continue the family name, such as Earl Richard Beauchamp, the last Lord Botreaux, and perhaps Sir William Plumpton, remarried to bear the son who would cut out their daughters. Almost invariably jointures were settled on the new brides to provide for them and any offspring, inevitably at the expense of the next heir: fathers-in-law paying substantial marriage portions ensured such deals were watertight. Sometimes moreover efforts were made afterwards to transfer the main estates from the offspring of the first marriage bed to those of the second marriage bed. 'Such power have young wives over old husbands', observed John Smyth of Nibley (Glos.) much later.[50] Hence Clifton sold Buckenham Castle to Sir Andrew Ogard away from his Knyvet heirs and Fastolf, like so many others, gave more generously to the Church than he might have done had he possessed a son to succeed him.

What emerges from this, of course, is that a landholder himself viewed his estate with reference first to himself and only thereafter with regard to his heirs and wider kin. He might have very distinct views about preserving the direct line and/or family name.

Sometimes other obligations, to spouse and mistress, bastards, favoured kin and servants, mattered more to him. These were met by the dower and jointure of the widow, by estates for life or annuities for younger sons, from the landholder's chattels and, increasingly, from trusts created to raise money towards marriage portions for daughters and other purposes. Amongst these were the needs of his soul, such as the payment of debts, endowment of the masses and the foundation of chantries. Some such duties were discharged in life but many others, such as support of a dowager and the fulfilment of trusts, were inescapably at the expense of the next generation, as the following instances illustrate. Before dying in 1443, Elena Armburgh resettled her inheritance in trust, to the lifetime benefit of her husband Robert, thus postponing the entry of her heirs. For almost fifty years, £325-worth of annual revenues were diverted from several generations of heirs to fulfil the bequests of Earl Richard Beauchamp. East Beckham (Norf.) was sold by the executors of William Winter (d. 1415) to fulfil his will. Trustees holding the manor of East Thorpe by Basingstoke and advowson of Hackwood (Hants.) were directed in 1472 by Gill Thame to hold them for her life and twenty years afterwards to pay her debts and found a chantry. They were to lease the property to her daughter Katherine, her husband John Whitehead and their heirs for rent towards these objectives and thereafter to release the properties to the Whiteheads provided they had made the chantry perpetual; and, if they had not, not. Not dissimilar was the direction of Margery Moleyns (née Bacon) to her executors to sell Gresham (Norf.) for the good of her soul, offering first refusal to her grandson; when he could not keep up the payments, they foreclosed and sold the manor elsewhere.[51] Both Whitehead and Moleyns were obliged to buy their own inheritance: or else.

Not all landholders were free to act in this way, their hands being tied by earlier entails. It was to prevent his grand-daughters from inheriting at the expense of his sons that Thomas Earl of Warwick (d. 1369) resettled the inheritance in tail male and tied the hands of his successors, who were merely tenants-for-life. They did not, however, behave as such, freely re-entailing portions of the settled lands in jointures and enfeoffing them to the use of their wills: most of lands of the Beauchamp trust were entailed. The estates late of Sir Guy de Brian were settled in jointure on Avice Stafford, her husband James later earl of Wiltshire, and their issue around 1439, and following her death were resettled by James on his Ormond kinsmen.[52] If the former transaction was valid, which it may not have been, the latter certainly was not.

The Hungerford family illustrates many of these points and some others. Each landholder settled jointure on his spouse, endowed chantries – sometimes after death – and provided estates for sons and dowries for daughters. Kinship and family honour in 1458–9 prompted Robert Lord Hungerford (d. 1459) and his wife Margaret

(d. 1478) to borrow £2,000 towards the ransom of their son Robert Lord Moleyns and to secure its repayment from the enfeoffed family estates, effectively a mortgage. Moleyns' wife Eleanor mortgaged her inheritance for a further £3,000. Following Moleyns' treason, forfeiture and death, the now widowed Margaret maintained the payments and planned for the estate to devolve on Moleyns' eldest son Thomas; when he was executed in 1469, leaving only an infant daughter, she worked instead for the succession of his brother Walter, her grandson and heir male. She chose to honour the debt, no longer a legal requirement, to fulfil the will of her father-in-law, and to found a chantry for herself, at the price of closing her father's new hospital, selling lands and impoverishing the family, even though she herself strongly resented her own father's attempts to settle her Botreaux estates away from her and his incumbrance of them with a youthful dowager who outlived her. The similarity of her situation vis-à-vis her father and that of her grandchildren's relationship to her apparently escaped her. Evidently her grandchildren criticised her, esteeming their interests more highly than the debts burdening the soul of their late father Moleyns, so she appended a lengthy autobiographical justification to successive wills to induce them to leave her dispositions undisturbed. Her soul would suffer if her land-sales were reversed. Her pious objective no doubt justified to Margaret herself the exaggerations and half-truths in her account. We can imagine what inducements persuaded Frideswide Hungerford, with virtually no hereditary expectations, to agree; those with greater claims, understandably, gave no such assurances. In contrast Margaret's daughter-in-law Lady Moleyns, once widowed, wriggled out of her mortgage – the soul of her last husband but one mattered less than her own well-being – and planned to provide for her soul and all her children, including her daughter. When her second husband was accused of treason, however, all such provisions were forgotten – her daughter Frideswide, now portionless, became a nun – as she released properties in perpetuity to save his life.

Moleyns was destined to unite the three Hungerford, Botreaux and Moleyns inheritances as the greatest magnate in Somerset and Wiltshire. He served the king at court and at war, being captured at Châtillon, whence he was ransomed. Personal liberty and honour necessitated the mortgages that sacrificed his future and that of his parents, siblings, spouse and children. Sent out of harm's way to Italy, he returned in time to embroil himself in civil war. Careerism and ambition, dynasticism, allegiance, sense of duty, friendship and collegiality may all have played their part. Perhaps Moleyns had no choice but to hold the Tower against the Yorkists in 1460, but throwing in his

lot with Queen Margaret, fighting on the Lancastrian side at Towton
(1461) and prolonging his resistance till his death at Hexham (1464)
were all choices, ever more reckless.[53] He could have made his peace
and recovered everything in 1461, he could have saved his life in
1462–3 and worked his way back, as other Lancastrian peers did, but
he chose not to do so. He was committed and irreconcilable, to the
destruction of himself and his house. Why we cannot tell. We know
little of his contacts and relations with either side. To Henry VI he was
loyal: a passive term that in his case *impelled* him forward regardless.
Others with more obvious Lancastrian ties wavered: Henry Duke of
Somerset and Sir Henry Lewis made their peace. It was a painful
choice, damaging perhaps to their worship and service, yet much the
safer course and to their material advantage. It was a realistic assessment of the odds. All these calculations were upset by Somerset's
reversion to his Lancastrian allegiance. Like Moleyns he perished in a
doomed cause. For both, allegiance ultimately prevailed over all other
more reasonable considerations: comfort, security, family, reputation,
self-interest and self-preservation.

Both are extreme cases. Many Yorkists at Ludford in 1459 chose
not to follow York into exile but submitted, accepting fines, humilia-
tion, perhaps confinement and temporary forfeiture, as the necessary
price of forgiveness and restoration. The two Wydeville peers were not
alone in early accepting that their cause was irretrievably lost. The
Calais garrison in 1483 were persuaded that Richard III's accession
superseded their oaths to Edward V.[54] The strength of such motives
should not necessarily be exaggerated and did not affect everyone
equally. Self-interest and self-preservation had their place and are
culturally engendered, not necessarily leading to conclusions that we
expect today. Just as the Lollards unheroically avoided courting
martyrdom, so medieval aristocrats were apparently more pragmatic
and flexible than some of their successors. This capacity to compromise
is relevant in many other contexts.

5

CLASS PERSPECTIVES

Perhaps only the aristocracy operated as a self-conscious national class: the ruling class. Their superiority was no accident. It had been ordained by God. Society was equated with the christian community. It had been created by God for the benefit of the individuals within it. Society was a mechanism designed to serve the interests of all, in which each invested his or her labour or skills in exchange for the benefits that accrued in return. Everybody's role was essential: without the contribution of each individual, something would be lacking and all needs would not be met. Whereas the peasants supplied their labour and food, the clergy prayed for all and aristocrats protected all. Here we have the notion of the *three estates*, to which some contemporaries made reference. To achieve these ends, God had organised society in a *hierarchy* of ranks, each individual in their place. Employment law, tax assessment and wages varied with rank. So too did dress, manners and speech. Almost everyone had inferiors. The greatest men, earls and dukes, also had superiors to whom they were subordinated and for whom they performed services. It was the top ranks of society whose role it was, as God's representatives and his natural councillors, to exercise that rule through government, which was God's instrument. Superiors commanded inferiors. They acted on their behalf in parliament, when they spoke for all. Let 'the commonalty ... nor presume above their own degree', enjoined Edmund Dudley in 1509, 'not let any of them presume or counterfeit the state of his betters'.[1]

Politics, national and local, was therefore the business of the ruling class, but it was no longer solely their preserve nor entirely under their control. To king and magnates had been added rural and urban elites, who had forced themselves to political attention and who had secured a right to attendance as elected representatives at parliament, where many important decisions were made or approved. Churchmen had key roles in central government, parliament and even the house of

Lords. Townsfolk directed their own communities. In the shires officers and jurors from below provided assistance indispensable to the county elites. The 40s. freeholders voted in parliamentary elections. In abnormal times the aristocracy could not exclude their inferiors, who intervened in politics more often than in past centuries and in the next and much more decisively. Numbers counted.

This chapter will discuss these other social groups.

The clergy

The second estate is by far the best documented. The clergy were a professional cadre comprised principally of men: nuns could not celebrate the sacraments and were generally strictly enclosed. Of distinctive appearance, with special haircuts (tonsures) and clerical dress, invariably literate and often educated, the clergy were required to be legitimate and celibate, were debarred from shedding blood violently or judicially, and were bound to more disciplined private lives than mere laymen. If infringements were not unusual, they were regulated by their own disciplinary code, and their sins were never admitted to invalidate their spiritual functions. If they committed offences against the criminal law, benefit of clergy protected them from the full weight of secular justice. Secure in their own privileges, which every king swore to uphold at his coronation and avoided thereafter,[2] they negotiated their financial support to the king separately from the laity.

The privileges of the clergy derived from their orders and consequent education, which gave them a monopoly over the sacraments and religious services, which they conducted in Latin, a language incomprehensible to most worshippers. They were a self-perpetuating cartel, who did not doubt or question either the justice of their lot or the manner in which they operated. Thus the increase of divine worship, through the employment of further clergy to say mass, was supremely good in itself and was frequently accepted as the justification for appropriating benefices. Religion, the Church and the faithful were viewed by the clergy from their own perspective. Emma Mason has indicated how uneven was their relationship with their parishioners. They emphasised their rights and obligations and conceded relatively little in return. Parishioners were bound to render tithes – a 10 per cent levy on their production – and many dues, to maintain most of the church fabric and bear many running costs. Defaulters were routinely excommunicated and sued for fulfilment in the church courts. The full round of services was not infrequently neglected by clergy who were non-resident, pluralists, on temporary leave of absence or too old and infirm, or was delegated to stipendiary curates of little learning or commitment.[3] Expectations of almsgiving and hospitality were often evaded, often allegedly deliberately. The poets Langland and Chaucer considered that monetary gain – 'Lady Meed' – too often shaped clerical behaviour.

Admittedly the Church authorities disapproved of abuse and denounced it vigorously, but counted few of those problems cited as cases of abuse: for example, pluralism being limited and often dispensed, and temporary absences from livings for a few years at a time were often allowed. The hierarchy repeatedly sanctioned the diversion of parish revenues to objectives they saw as desirable that scarcely benefited tithe-payers. Pluralism and non-residence were routinely permitted for clerics in service to the Church, crown and aristocracy or in academic training at the universities. Revenues surplus to the maintenance of the parson were permanently appropriated to support 'the increase of divine worship' at monasteries and chantries, university colleges and almshouses, and even for senior ecclesiastics: the rich bishop of Winchester and the distant vicars-choral of York minster were rectors respectively of the Hampshire parishes of East Meon and Nether Wallop. Several thousand parishes had been appropriated by the Reformation. Surely it was not only Chaucer who judged his parson by his commitment to his flock?

Such ecclesiastical offices and institutions, moreover, never died. They never forgot past rights and regarded their safeguard as holy charges. They were guardians of the rights of St Alban, St Cuthbert, St Edmund, St Guthlac, St Swithun or St Osmund. All compromises were rejected and all rights maintained. It was a pious duty not to concede, even in disputes between religious corporations, for which papal confirmation was required. Hence the struggles over so many generations of the bishop of Salisbury, abbeys of St Albans and Bury St Edmunds to maintain the subjection of their county towns when many inferior ones were already enfranchised. Cathedral franchises impeded city governments, profiting from the unfair competition of unlicensed and unregulated traders, generally resisting negotiation and coercion and jealously holding on to their rights.[4] Hence the strife and litigation, which takes up so much of their chronicle, between Crowland Abbey and its neighbours, including Peterborough Abbey, whom their chroniclers denounced in the strongest terms and against whom they invoked the support of God. Infringing Crowland's property rights incurred the strongest religious censures.[5] It was against such 'tyranny' that the people of East Meon petitioned against Bishop Waynflete in parliament in 1461.[6] Hence the attitudes also of the clergy towards

infringements of their liberties – which kings made use of to seek
support, as in 1399 and 1461, without actually remedying the
supposed wrong – and clerical taxation. 'O what a servile and perni-
cious ruin of the Church!' exclaimed the Crowland continuator in
1483.

> May God turn away the minds of succeeding kings from
> following up, in any way, an action like this, lest perchance
> they should be afflicted by these misfortunes, or worse if they
> can be imagined, which unhappily soon afflicted this king and
> his noble descendants.[7]

It was for despoiling the Church that the Yorkist dynasty was
destroyed!

Such attitudes were epitomised by the religious orders, to which
monastic chronicles provide a revealing insight. They were written for
internal audiences of monks who would understand. They reveal the
priority given to the prestige of the house (and to its patron saint) and
how much this depended on material considerations. Leading abbots
wanted exemption from their local bishop and the right to wear mitres,
to avoid royal custody and waste during vacancies (knowing well how
to pull strings and secure privileges from pope and king), yet they
often failed to attend the house of Lords.[8] Running a late medieval
monastery required confronting the real world. Officers frequently had
to be outside the cloister and it was administrative rather than spiritual
skills that were most sought after in abbots. Abbot Thomas of
Crowland did not neglect

> works of goodness; for he was always strenuously exerting
> himself in increasing the possessions of his church, by means
> of which he might more abundantly promote the worship of
> God, and more readily perform the duties of hospitality.

In particular he enhanced the choir with new forms and the bell-
tower with four new bells, 'to the glory of the house of God', and the
precinct with 'those extremely handsome buildings … a brew-house
and bake-house, built in the most expensive manner'. Contrary to
modern expectations, these were pious acts: devotion of St Guthlac
was sufficiently genuine for one particular monk to have prayed to die
on St Guthlac's day, a request that was fulfilled. It was to the glory of
St Guthlac and the enhancement of monastic observance that hospitality should be encouraged, even domestic buildings enhanced, and

that everything should be as splendid and elegant as possible. Similarly the abbey kitcheners gave money saved from the abbey's own revenues towards the cloister, endowed provision of almond-milk for service to the monks on fastdays, and commissioned an entire set of vestments in black with letters of gold. Apart from massive building works in the cloisters, aisles and nave, the relevant obedientary erected a lady chapel 'of the most elegant workmanship with a vast outlay of money' and a new refectory 'with artistic elegance and the greatest magnificence'. Note the superlatives: the status of monasteries and their patron saints, like others, was measured by their spending – the more ostentatious and more fashionable the better! It was the great value of the books added to the library, the cost of the vestments and the superior manner of the new abbot's hall that earned the chronicler's praise for Abbot Richard.[9]

Even though a century or centuries old and representing religious ideals no longer current, monks believed their professions still to be relevant and repeatedly updated their practices. They went to university. The eating of meat, banned by the Benedictine rule, became commonplace. The communal life was fractured, as the refectory and dormitory were abandoned for private rooms and alternative dining arrangements, and as monks were issued with pocket money and clothes allowances. To outsiders, such changes were degenerations from the rule, but to monks they were sensible reforms that had been sanctioned by their general chapters. Undoubtedly there was a communication problem, that meant critics did not understand, but it is nevertheless obvious that the old communal life was being deliberately abandoned as out of date.

This is not to say that the clergy or specifically monks were corrupt. The Crowland chroniclers were concerned about the execution of Franciscans and Archbishop Scrope by Henry IV, the rebellion 'of a profane multitude of Lollards' and their just incineration.[10] No doubt most performed their functions scrupulously. Singing the canonical hours daily was both arduous and repetitive. Monks in the greatest religious houses were able to dine lavishly and had staff to perform their menial services. Their calorie intake was excessive and their servants numerous: situations that they wished to maintain. Declining numbers of the religious after the Black Death arose not merely from mortality and adjustment to a lower population, but from the deliberate restriction of numbers to maintain standards of living at houses both great and small. Bishop Oliver King was able to rebuild Bath cathedral by restricting the diet of its monks. Nor were monks alone guilty of such calculations. The obstacles posed to canons wishing to take up residence in secular cathedrals were designed to deter newcomers from sharing in the common fund and successfully reduced the residentiary body at York minster to one.[11] The movement of the beneficed clergy from living to living, from prebend to prebend, and even from diocese to diocese, was often primarily motivated by money. Clerics lived in the real world. Entering the church did not mean abandoning the ties of family, neighbourhood or patron. The successful often promoted related clerics, endowed lay kinsmen or were interred near those who had patronised them.

The clergy was not a uniform estate. Enormous differences in wealth and lifestyle separated the hierarchy of bishops and cathedral chapters, the beneficed clergy of the parishes, the uncountable proletariat of chaplains and mass-priests salaried or on piece-rates, those merely in minor orders and often married such as the poets Hoccleve and Langland, and those whose only claim to clerical status was when their literacy enabled them to escape the rope. The secular clergy fell from first tonsure into two groups – the select few destined for benefices, in particular the better ones, dignities and even bishoprics, and a clerical proletariat who would be lucky ever to hold a benefice at all. The former, commonly better-born and university educated, staffed the administrations of Church and state and exercised their livings by deputy. If easily caricatured as laymen in clerical disguise, they were nevertheless normally celibate, and, on the evidence available to us, genuinely interested in religion. Dr Jewell has demonstrated how crucial fifteenth-century bishops were as benefactors of education.[12] That such foundations were fashionable and sophisticated indicates that the founders understood and were in tune with best practice in the contemporary Church. They sincerely believed that they were serving the Church better in high and/or administrative office than in the parishes. Their livings were run for them by the clerical proletariat, who served as curates, parish, gild and private chaplains, chantry priests, anniversarians, and evidently in many roles currently concealed from us. Ordinations far exceeded known employment opportunities. Even at Farleigh Hungerford on the Somerset–Wiltshire border and decidedly out in the sticks, ninety-three priests were paid for attending the obit of Sir Thomas Hungerford (d. 1398) in 1429 and another forty-three in 1430.[13] Since most were predestined to penurious lives, scraping a living from a succession of short-term contracts, it is difficult to escape the conclusion that the 'floods' of ordinands had genuine vocations – 'a concept of service in, and to, the church, which they were keen to fulfil, even if wealth, riches and security were not to follow'.[14]

All these, moreover, were secular clergy: the monks, nuns and friars, arranged in thirty different orders, were as different from one another – and often mutually hostile – as the rest. Disendowment of the clergy found support not merely from Lollard heretics, but from friars who opposed monastic wealth and others who thought it could better be used to pious ends. The parliamentary Commons felt that the clergy needed to be induced to perform their charitable duties and often took the lead in moral reform. It is no wonder that parliament felt able to decide the legitimacy of Edward V. Clergy inevitably partook of the attitudes of their fellow ministers, politicians, judges, officials and peasants whose lives they shared. They participated in the political movements and insurrections of others, but never, it appears, did they initiate their own.

Townspeople

By European standards, only London was a city of the front rank, but there were nevertheless 600–800 settlements with claims to be classed as towns, ranging from single streets of a few hundred inhabitants up to half a dozen walled cities with 10,000 inhabitants or more. If some were royal boroughs or even county boroughs, many others were managed by manorial courts. Towns provided services to surrounding rural society and were coloured by the character of local husbandry. Whatever their scale, economic function, or political constitution, all towns were societies apart from the countryside and its aristocracy. Towns had their own hierarchies, from mercantile elite to artisans, retailers, professionals and poor labourers, often hailing from diverse locations and backgrounds. Generally they governed themselves and had their own corporate interests. Mutual interest bound such varied populations against outsiders: against oppression by their lords and against rival franchises, such as the cathedral liberties at Norwich and York. They pressured king and parliament for corporate patronage, such as reduced fee-farms and trading privileges to advance themselves, often at the expense of neighbours and rivals. The communal solidarity displayed to outsiders could be reinforced internally by cycles of play- such as, which can be interpreted as justifying the authority of the town rulers.[15]

Towns were too big for cosy day-to-day interchange and contained within themselves disparate societies. The range of origins, occupations, wealth and lifestyle fostered many potential divisions. Freemen were united by participation in town government, often on outer councils, but only theoretically, since power and decision-making were normally confined to the elite. Instead townsmen grouped themselves in smaller organisations, in gilds, parishes and fraternities, which served social, religious and representative functions, and offered scope for personal fulfilment through office-holding and the management of their own affairs. Such bodies met together, dined and worshipped together, attended one another's funerals, performed together and sometimes cared for members and their dependants who had fallen on hard times. Often gilds had their own liveries, built corporate chantries, as at Cirencester (Glos.) and Coventry, employed their own gild chaplains and erected common halls. Already responsible for trading standards by delegation from the town government, gilds additionally regulated the moral conduct of their members, imposing standards of morality and even etiquette. That they were concerned particularly about how members behaved when wearing gild liveries demonstrates pride in their gild and concern for its reputation, ultimately *their* reputation. Some gilds banned gambling and sexual adventures on pain of expulsion. Mutual interests demanded that differences were settled amicably and internally, not in the royal or even urban courts. Mediation and then arbitration should precede litigation. The Wymondham gild of the light ordained that 'none of the brothers and sisters shall plead with [one an]other ... till the rulers and their counsel hath attempted to make an end and unity and love between [the] parties'. The brethren and sisters of the Lincoln gild swore to support (maintain?) fellow-members as guarantors and witnesses 'as though they were children of the same parents'.[16]

Such bonds were stronger than those exerted by the towns themselves. At Walsall (Staffs.), Coventry, Stratford-upon-Avon (War.), York and Norwich gild membership reveals ties with outsiders as strong as those with fellow townsmen. If the city rulers were convinced of the merits of their rule, this could not be taken for granted and had to be asserted.[17] Rivals, even rival gilds, were suppressed. Ceremonies and plays such as Corpus Christi, in which gilds attended in order of gild and within gilds in their uniforms, stressed both the unity of the whole city and the interdependence within it of the particular gilds, whose dependent role was displayed for all to see. Hence they reinforced the status quo.[18] Civic buildings and institutions, halls and chantries, civic officers and liveries, elaborate regalia and ceremonial, consecrated the rule of the elite. Aldermen and councillors were distinguished, so ordinances required, by their sober and respectful conduct, their respectable occupations – inn-keeping was discriminated against – and by their morality. Adulterers were penalised. In practice they were not above prejudice and profiteering. Mayors were monarchs more absolute than the king, able to act almost without restraint, albeit without much power of enforcement and only for a year, after which time they became accountable.[19]

In their own eyes, oligarchs were the better sort, most suited to rule, and they ruled in the interests of all. They swore oaths of office to put their urban commonweal first. They campaigned against public sin, evil customs and public nuisances.[20] The privileges they sought from the crown were on behalf of all. Or so their civic ordinances, memoranda and minutes tell us. The daily audience of the mayor and sheriff for settling amicably the many disputes of a trading community, we are told, was 'greatest preservation of peace and good rule to be had within the town and shire of Bristol that can be imagined'. The occasional rebel was corrected and humiliated.[21] That oligarchy continued and controlled the historical record cannot conceal widespread friction. It was the majority who were excluded, not just from rule but from the freedom and the gilds and, generally, it appears, made their livings free of regulation. There are indicators at times that even masters were difficult to control. Demagogues like Lawrence Saunders at Coventry and rival mayoral candidates at York – themselves symptoms of rifts within the oligarchy – excited support below those theoretically entitled to govern. If there existed class-consciousness and class conflict, therefore, its leaders were freemen. Factions of burgesses were certainly involved. Origin myths and indeed plays reinforcing rule were open to alternative interpretations by the ruled. If conflicts focused on the defects of particular individuals, such as the king's evil councillors, hostility to the whole oligarchy could lie beneath. Experiments with democracy did not last; perhaps because central governments consistently supported authority and because livelihoods had to come first.[22] Since townsmen lived busy lives, it was speed and certainty above all that was most required.

The peasantry

Most fifteenth-century Englishmen were neither aristocrats, clerics nor townsmen, but rustics: artisans and agriculturists. We conveniently label them peasants. There were actually as many gradations of function, wealth and status among the peasantry as the rest of society, but they are far less easily perceived. An unknown percentage of people were excluded from office-holding. Most probably these included, as in post-medieval times, unmarried living-in servants in their teens and twenties as well as the lowest labourers and wage-earners, cottagers, petty husbandmen and unenfranchised tradesmen. They combated the

harsh realities of an underdeveloped economy, which related production closely to the input of labour and meant that productivity and
yields were hard to improve. That does not mean that peasants and
artisans were unskilled or inexpert or that their occupations did not
have to be learnt – by nurture and example, admittedly, via living-in
service and apprenticeship, rather than book-learning. To succeed,
cope or merely survive, an agriculturist had to know about crops and
their cultivation, the climate and the seasons, the rearing, the care and
slaughtering of stock and the marketing of produce. He needed to buy
his seed and whatever he did not produce, as well as to maintain his
equipment and buildings, support himself and dependants, fulfil
customary obligations and pay tithes, rent and taxes. He needed to be
aware what opportunities for innovation and adaptation the fifteenth
century offered and could not be isolated from external influences. He
might be both employer and employee. Even the rural craftsmen
possessed unusual skills, premises, tools, materials and customers. Such
rustics had to exploit the distinctive soils, customs and markets of their
locality and to survive in an economy that fluctuated from season to
season, year to year, and decade to decade. The mid-fifteenth-century
slump lasted forty years: more than many a lifetime.

Such rustics were not on their own. Their tenancies and some
protection were offered by their lords, to whom they were bound by
contract and who had an investment in their success, to whom they
could look for justice and favour and to whom they owed not just
formal agricultural, but informal military and political services. The
peasant unit of production was the family. Peasants operated within a
wider co-operative framework, in which field systems and commons,
frequently decisions, equipment and draught animals were shared.
Community seasonal celebrations of the christian and farming year,
drinkings, meals and team-games dimly reconstitute recreational
aspects of peasant culture. The resultant wealth, easily measured by
size of holding, number of stock and living conditions, determined an
individual's ranking within his particular community, as modified by
status – freedom or villeinage – and inheritance, seniority, marital
status, kindred, office-holding, responsibilities and obligations to lord,
neighbours and kin. A healthy young man, recently out of service and
married, aspired to expand his income, holdings and stock in line with
or ahead of the growth in his family; a veteran, in contrast, was more
probably realising his capital by land sales to maintain himself.

Seniority brought with it public service, a say in local affairs,
perhaps personal profit and practical advantage, and inevitably respect.
Some extended it beyond their immediate community 'to the political

advantage of their own families'. Much routine administration, within and outside the village, such as tax collection, the assize of arms, enforcement of the statute of labourers and policing, fell to social inferiors of the gentry. 'The logic of a family's village politics', writes Goheen, 'became the logic of jury service beyond the village'.[23] Hence perhaps the substantial turnout of 40s. freeholders, on occasions hundreds strong, at shire elections. Such conduct was expected. Peasants had positions to maintain. Standards of living, dowries for daughters, regularity at mass, legacies to the Church and tenure of office needed to correspond to station within the community. Not to conform, to flout custom or convention, to work during service-time, shed blood or otherwise breach bye-laws or ecclesiastical laws, was derogatory, shameful, sometimes carried penalties, and was therefore to be eschewed. Such considerations have aristocratic and bourgeois counterparts. Whilst distinctive in many ways and with marked local variations, peasant culture was actually a variant of contemporary English culture.

Low though they were in rank, such property-holders were too inextricably enmeshed by a web of interests, assumptions, attitudes, aspirations and concomitant values, standards, conventions and mutual obligations to be activated by mere emotions or impulses. Their intellectual paraphernalia was no less complex than that of their aristocratic betters, if, perhaps, somewhat less sophisticated. Immediately before the Peasants' Revolt at least forty rural communities applied for exemplifications of their entries in the Domesday Book in the belief that the status of ancient demesne would exempt them from villeinage (the 'Great Rumour').[24] Though mistaken, their supplications demonstrate resentment at their inferior condition, a legalistic respect for precedent, a sense of community and a capacity for common action, and a self-interested willingness to use whatever weapon came to hand. Custom and precedent were rejected by those Sussex peasants about 1450 who withheld rent and services.[25] We may presume that notions of what was fair, reasonable, just and the market-rate opposed exactions that they considered unreasonable, unjust, coercive and exploitative. Such frictions were compatible with existing relations – the landlord–tenant contract endured – and did not endanger participants' holdings, livelihoods or status. Protesters never acted alone. Their conduct was acceptable and respectable within their communities: co-operation was the norm.

The hypothesis that peasant involvement in county politics arose naturally from village politics can be extended to parliamentary elections. Jurors were required at county courts, where parliamentary elections were held. By 1429–30 so many commons were attending parliamentary elections that the franchise was restricted to the 40s. freeholders – quite a low level of eligibility, well below the gentry, that qualified as many as 600, or 5 per cent, of the male population of Nottinghamshire. More than that and less propertied, by implication, had been attending before. If they caused disorder, it shows that they cared about the result, that they had made a real contest of the election, and perhaps also had over-ruled or at least disputed the stance of their superiors. More contested elections have been deduced than can actually be shown, in which the 'one-man, one-vote' principle prevailed, enabling for instance sheer numbers to override quality. Whilst evidently they knew who they were voting for and discriminated accordingly, it was as likely due to local cross-class loyalties, to their wapentake or part of Lincolnshire, as to their lords' command, or even because they were paid. 'They must often have followed the lead of their greater gentry neighbours', writes Payling,[26] but they had to be managed. Their role could be decisive. Complaints in 1450 indicate how much Kentish voters valued the franchise and that they could not be taken for granted. Practical administrative experience informed the politics of the peasantry.

The commons in national politics.

The fifteenth-century commons repeatedly moved beyond the local political spheres assigned to them. In 1399 the future Henry IV was joined by tenants of his duchy and by hordes of commoners who saw in him their salvation. In 1470 commoners supported Warwick's invasion in overwhelming numbers, variously estimated at from 30 to 60,000 men, and altogether deserted the incumbent king, Edward IV, who was obliged to flee abroad. Edward admitted that his victory next year flew in the face of popular opinion: an additional reason for attributing it to divine intervention![27] The events of 1470 were not the only occasion when 'the people' mattered. The victory of the Yorkist earls in 1460 owed little to their retainers. Recruitment took place far from their home countries, which were cut off by the king's army and most probably obedient to royal authority. 'You have many prayers of the poor people that God shall speed you at this parliament', wrote Margaret Paston to John Paston I, MP. To the Calais garrison, the crews of Warwick's ships and their fellow exiles were added principally commoners from Kent and London, who sufficed both for the delivery of the City and the victory at Northampton.[28] The quality of such recruits, their equipment and training may have been no better than in the Barons' Wars, when they were slaughtered *en masse* by armoured cavalry, and certainly they sometimes under-performed,[29] but it was their sheer numbers that enabled returning exiles twice to overthrow governments and to initiate dynastic revolutions. If these were the most dramatic and most decisive interventions by the people in the fifteenth century during the Wars, they were far from unique. Mobs lynched Richard II's half-brother at Cirencester (Glos.) and another earl at Pleshey (Essex) in 1400, the duke of Suffolk at sea and other ministers in London, Portsmouth and Potterne (Wilts.) in 1450, Lord Scales in London and the earl of Salisbury in Yorkshire in 1460, and the earl of Devon at Bridgewater (Som.) in 1469; others had tried to eliminate Suffolk earlier in 1450 and the duke of Somerset at Northampton in 1463.[30]

We know very few of the commoners by name. Snobbish chroniclers thought them unworthy of attention. The few exceptions were those prosecuted for misconduct in times of peace. Hundreds were indicted from the losing sides in the Percy–Neville and Courtenay–Bonville feuds.[31] Known participants in Cade's Rebellion in 1450 are mainly substantial peasants and artisans, officeholders and leaders of their communities. Jurors of presentment were acquainted with men of standing and means and not with the rabble, whose lack of property made their forfeiture unprofitable and prevented them from buying pardons. Generally we cannot tell how many commoners from how far across the social spectrum were involved. Those pardoned in 1450 do not equate to Cade's rebels.[32] Rebels also were fined in 1459, 1471 and 1497.[33] From Fauconberg's rising in 1471, we know of 'well over 200 citizens of Canterbury', several jurats from the Cinque Ports, and seventy-nine sample individuals from sixty different hundreds (out of sixty-five in total) who were fined. Apart from Mayor Faunt and parish clerks, we know chiefly of 'working men' from a variety of trades and perhaps from all social classes. Fauconberg's countrymen, in contrast, were merely a selection, comprising thirty-five gentry, twenty-one yeomen and eleven husbandmen. We are ignorant of their social inferiors – the cottagers, labourers and servants – and unclear how general was insurgency in the area that rebelled. Only the fines of the Cornish Rising of 1497 are recorded adequately: 4,000 in number. That rising embraced 'the entire community of the west', from Cornwall to Somerset. Those fined ranged socially from 'the natural leaders of the community, the gentry and clergy', to urban merchants and artisans, rural craftsmen and peasants down to a single bondman. Though the rural elite are thus well-represented, the sheer numbers and the absence of occupational titles consign many of the payers to the lowest level of rural society, and thus indicate that the Rising of 1497 did indeed encompass a genuine cross-section of regional society.[34] Regrettably there were never any lists of the victorious commons of 1460 or 1470 or for protests where threats alone sufficed.

The 'common people' were engaging in national politics in response to national issues. Account had to be taken of them. Government abstinence from poll taxes was insufficient to stop them. There was a new political audience to be addressed and controlled. A series of reforming demagogues demanded their political attention, directed their propaganda to them, and encouraged the commons actively to support their programmes. 'Their influence in political life', observes Dr Harvey, 'should be measured less in the incidence of popular revolt than in the attention given to popular opinion by those who governed and the volume of political propaganda produced'.[35]

A literate society is not a society in which everyone can read, but in which all rely on and have access to the written word; people did not have to have read it all themselves. Since every copy had to be written separately by hand, even short bills and poems could not be mass-produced so that every place in Kent had one, let alone every village in the home counties or every literate villager! In practice few 'literate individuals' outside London could obtain 'considerably more detailed information about persons or political issues ... from reading the hand-bills and schedules of articles posted on doors, windows and town crosses'. Bills posted in public places could be read aloud publicly; bills scattered may have passed from hand to hand. Jack Cade's second manifesto in 1450 requested royal 'letters patent to all his people there openly to be read and cried'. Verses may have circulated by word of mouth, by recitation, repetition and singing rather than reading. 'Such rhymes about Suffolk and his circle', asserts Harvey, 'would be on doors and windows around the south-east for passers-by to read and some men and women may have been signing or dancing to these refrains'. The 'common voice', by which John Paston was informed, was oral. So too was 'the common fame' upon which chroniclers relied, and the oral notoriety that Cade cited: 'it is openly noised', 'it is noted by the common voice', that Suffolk's men 'be openly known traitors'.[36] General literacy was not a pre-requisite for Cade's Rebellion. There were other routes for popular access to elite culture.

Political propaganda was directed at the commons, sometimes at particular groups. The target audience can be deduced from what is written. If a manifesto tackles the grievances of a particular group, then logically that group was the intended target, the author shared the grievance, the message was designed to arouse their support, and any support can be attributed to the success of the appeal to these grievances. This is a circular argument with weak links at every point. But such arguments are inescapable. Thus Harvey ascribes the complaints of Cade's rebels to property-holding people familiar with the machinery of local government and interested in elections, those well-to-do peasants and artisans who were 40s. freeholders, who acted as jurors and electors and who staffed the bottom echelons of local government. They were responsible citizens with a stake in their communities, not the impoverished and dispossessed; serfdom and other ills of 1381 pass unmentioned, perhaps unsurprisingly. There was no serfdom in Kent, plenty in Sussex, for which no manifestos survive. 'The voice of this county community', Harvey boldly asserts, 'can be heard in the rebels' bills'.[37] Similarly we may presume that the anonymous supporters of Robin of Holderness in Yorkshire in 1469 were settled holders of agricultural property, liable to payments of petercorn to St Leonard's Hospital at York, adherents of the Percies whose restoration they demanded, and natural village elders.[38] Responsible community leaders were unlikely to have been the only audience, susceptible or not, in 1469 or at other times.

Sometimes those addressed by propaganda were rural, sometimes urban, sometimes shipmen, sometimes doubtless mere *canaille*. Different social groups were tackled and the same ones did not always respond in the same way. York's hopes in 1452 to revive Cade's insurgents of 1450 conspicuously failed. Most probably Cade's first manifesto assembles the grievances of different groups, which were not necessarily compatible, and these were ironed into the generalisations of the latter manifestos to which all Kentishmen and recruits from further afield could subscribe. A fear of forest law, presumably in the Weald, should not have alarmed those around the Cinque Ports oppressed by the court of Dover. In 1459, when Warwick's supporters actually hailed from the Cinque Ports, he appealed to maritime and commercial interests instead.[39] It was the Calais staplers and the anti-Genoese, not licensed traders, who were then his backers and it was the mob that forced the city corporation to admit him. Only Kentish grievances were specifically addressed by Cade's manifestos, which do not altogether express or represent the sentiments of rebels in Sussex and Wiltshire, still less those unpaid and defeated veterans who lynched Bishop Moleyns at Portsmouth. Scales' slayers in 1460 were retaliating to his bombardment of the environs of the Tower. The enthusiasm for Warwick in the south-east in 1460 contrasts sharply with the hostility of some northern commons towards his father.[40]

Rejected as a tyrant by southerners, Richard III's death was notoriously regretted in York, and northerners resisted the Tudor regime after his death. If there were specifically local causes for Cade's Rebellion, so there were on the Robertsbridge and Battle abbey estates,[41] and so too were there for the Yorkshire uprisings of 1469 and 1489 and the Cornish Rising of 1497. There was 'a significant regional dimension' to public opinion, Pollard has argued,[42] which may have left the north unmoved.

The grievances set out in the commons' lists of complaints, such as those of Cade's Rebellion (1450) or the Pilgrimage of Grace (1536), show that they responded to wrongs that had affected them in their everyday lives and that could not be resolved within their own communities. What specifically aggrieved the (evidently rural) people of Kent takes up most of Cade's first manifesto. The protesters may not always have liked the law that protected their titles and punished criminals, the structure and machinery of local government, the judicial system and management of parliamentary elections, royal taxation and dues such as the green wax, but they accepted them and did not object to them. Current institutions and processes may have been less than ideal and may sometimes have needed reform, so that men of Kent should no longer be dragged across the whole county for quarter sessions and to Westminster to the central courts, but together they constituted a system to which they were accustomed, with which they could live, which perhaps they knew how to work. What the rebels hated was abuse: the application of forest laws to 'simple people that useth not hunting'; the operation of the warden's court of Dover beyond its liberty; the denial of free election for MPs and tax collectors; the misappropriation of taxation for purposes other than that for which it was granted; the farming of office, that prompted farmers to maximise revenues from their bailiwicks; the collection of more tax and more fines than were due to the crown for private gain; and the manipulation of justice, so that titles to land were undermined and legal owners dispossessed, the innocent convicted to secure their lands while notorious criminals escaped punishment. Cumulatively such abuses threatened that the king 'would battle in his own realm to the destruction of all his people': a result that was not merely against his own interests but which was also sinful. 'Kent should be destroyed with a royal power & made [into] a wild forest', they feared.[43] Existing and accustomed property, rights, customs and liberties, so they supposed, were to be subsumed in a more intrusive, unpredictable, harsh and costly judicial system. Their articles presume notions of right and wrong, of justice, fairness and equity. So clearly was the line perceived between the legitimate and the corrupt, and so outraged were the petitioners by transgressions, that they denounced the offenders as criminals deserving of death, even of the full penalties of treason.

This summary reveals how government impacted even on peasants, directly or at one remove. Their particular oppressors may have been local, but the root causes were national – what the rebels perceived as 'widespread government corruption' – and the solutions were therefore national also. Action within local communities was not enough. Protest and violence born of discontent within a myriad communities 'drove thousands … to rise up'.[44] That the movement has become known as Cade's *Rebellion* was the one achievement of a beleaguered regime. Insurgents did not regard themselves as rebels. They were subjects engaged in legitimate protests. We are not 'risers and traitors and the king's enemies', declared Cade's second manifesto, but 'his true liege men and best friends', 'your true liegemen of Kent': 'by our writings you may conceive we be the king's friends not his enemies'. They professed loyalty and commitment to the king: '[we] desireth the welfare of our sovereign lord the king and of all his true lords spiritual and temporal'. They were operating within their allegiance, the law, and the constitution and were engaged in legitimate protest. They wanted the system to work properly. Theirs was a peaceful and loyal uprising of limited duration: their protest completed, they would resume their roles as loyal subjects, prepared not only 'to defend our country from all nations', but even 'to go with our sovereign lord where he will command us'. They requested the remedy of grievances on grounds of reason, divine law and their own cogent arguments. Jesus was begged 'that God of his righteousness shall take vengeance on the false traitors of his royal realm that have brought us in this mischief and misery'. The insurgents themselves would not rob, steal, nor take the law into their own hands, though 'we will mark him [any opponent], for he is not the king's true liege man'.[45] Should wrongs not be redressed, they would right them themselves. All they wanted was the trial of the guilty by due process of law and, on conviction, that they be punished and not pardoned. New rules could prevent any recurrence of malpractice.

It is striking how specific, restrained and limited in scope and objectives were the numerous refusals of peasants to pay rent or render services. They did not steal, vandalise, murder or wreak vengeance on their lords. They posed no threat to the political and social status quo even within their own communities. Robin Hood's fictional outlaws showed 'deep respect for a good knight' by assuring him his appropriate accoutrements of dress, mount, and attendance.[46] They accepted that aristocrats had a role to play. Though unfamiliar to medievalists, this kind of loyal rebellion and riot is commonplace to early modernists.

Cade's complaints presuppose a model or models of how society ought to operate, which must certainly have foregrounded what suited or benefited the rebels and protesters themselves. Notions of government were not couched in airy-fairy theory, but rather, says Harvey, 'took the form of certain long-held assumptions ... that probably appeared to them to be common sense'.[47] Their criticism of local landholders and governors may sometimes reveal elements of class hatred. Hostility to one's social superiors among the populace, however, is less easily demonstrated than fear of what the commons might do and class-consciousness among the political elite. On occasion the commons' recorded statements are distinctively treasonable, envisaging the destruction of king and peerage alike, but such sentiments, if not mere drunken ramblings, had little currency. 'If the commons were well-advised', one dissident reportedly said, 'they should arise and destroy him [Henry VI] and all his council that is about him'.[48] The populace were not so enlightened. Reform was what they sought and what they felt justified in urging. They had no intention of overthrowing a system in which the king, the Lords and parliament worked together for the common good. Their lists of wrongs could be formulated in terms of abstract principles, such as the self-justification of Suffolk's plebeian assassins. 'The Wars of the Roses', Watts remarks, 'began with a series of statements of constitutional principle'. Commoners 'made a point of drawing attention to the ideas and principles which underpinned their actions',[49] which often coincided with the constitutionalism of the elite. It is not the case, as alleged by Professor Richmond, that constititional principles were confined to the elite.[50]

6

GOVERNMENT

Central government

All actions and decisions of the government were made on royal authority. It was the king's policies that were formulated and implemented, his peace that was maintained, his writs that ran, and his law that applied. All crimes were offences against him and his peace. A host of suitors petitioned him and thousands of warrants came to him for approval each year. His hands could not be tied. Yet much was delegated. Some matters were decided in council and others by heads of departments, who presented to lesser ecclesiastical livings, issued protections, appointed customs officers and leased estates. The household chamberlain 'presenteth, appointeth and dischargeth' and punished staff as 'chief head of rulers in the king's chamber', whilst the 'secondary estate and rule under the king of all the excellent household is wholly committed [to the steward] to be ruled and guided by his reason'.[1] The senior officers of the palatinate of Chester, duchies of Cornwall and Lancaster filled junior offices, made grants and leased property, in short managed the king's estates, exercised his patronage and wielded his authority.[2] No king could know of many practical decisions made by his government departments, courts of law and estate officials. For most people, most of the time, it was the king's officials – his clerks – who were the public face of monarchy. Their conduct was identified with their master – any malpractice actually detracted from the king's own worship. His esteem conferred status on them – generally above their natural rank: it was the king himself who handed the chamberlain and steward their staffs of office and tendered their oaths.[3] It was his authority that they exercised and that guaranteed them respect. Only he could intervene, override, pardon or mitigate their actions.

Central government was highly visible and, by fifteenth-century standards, huge. It was always several times larger than the biggest noble or monastic establishment or even the most awesome noble

92

entourage in times of crisis. The royal household alone, *reduced* to perhaps 550 individuals at Edward IV's accession, grew inexorably back to 800 by his death *en route* for the 1,500 of the early seventeenth century.[4] Add to that the permanent staff of chancery,[5] the exchequer, the privy seal office and the central courts, totalling in all at least 200, and allow under-clerks for every tenured clerk. There were as well suitors, litigants, attornies, creditors, sheriffs and other debtors, who used the government's services or were engaged there involuntarily. All the inmates of all the inns of court dealt in the king's law through the king's courts. How much of London's trade – food, drink, buildings, clothing, luxuries – was supported by all this demand? Allow a further 80 lords spiritual and temporal with their households and 296 MPs (in 1485) with their servants in time of parliament, and one can see that the king's establishment, like the city of London itself, was without compare for anyone whose experience was confined to England. Only Westminster and London could cater comfortably for parliaments. No wonder that provincial backwoodsmen so often regarded the king's household as overgrown, too extravagant, too far beyond what they should reasonably finance, and in urgent need of pruning, economy, retrenchment, curtailment and resumption of grants. Parliaments however occurred infrequently, the royal household was often elsewhere, and the law terms were brief (only twenty weeks a year), so there normally remained at Westminster only the central departments. They, however, were the largest institutions most subjects ever encountered.

The central administration and judiciary had settled at the palace of Westminster. It was there that the king's ministers and justices presided, where the courts met, and where the royal council routinely sat several times a week. The palace possessed all the state rooms, private suites of king and queen, chapel royal and menial departments necessary for royal residence. The ceremonial heart of the monarchy, Westminster Abbey, lay just across the road. It was there that kings were crowned, the accompanying banquet being in Westminster Hall, and there that they were normally buried: a tradition strangely dishonoured by most fifteenth-century monarchs. Westminster was the preferred location for parliaments. At such times the white chamber housed the king and Lords, whilst the Commons were accommodated in the abbey refectory. It was thus at Westminster that changes in power were regularly sanctioned, by due succession, in minorities, or by usurpation, and that the major contests between king and subjects and the state trials took place. Parliaments could be held in other cities, at Coventry, Leicester, Shrewsbury, Winchester and York, but the central machine was always at Westminster.

Government touched on the whole range of activities that it covers today, much of it infrequently. Before the 1530s governments had little interest in charity or social welfare, education or employment, agriculture or industry, except in response to pressures: resistance to heresy, to forestall or frustrate revolt, and to maintain essential supplies. The customs and the mint sometimes embroiled governments in foreign trade and exchange rates. They had no desire to improve or change the world: to keep things running was sufficiently ambitious.[6] Governments needed to *do* nothing. Their essential functions were the maintenance of law, order and justice at home, and diplomacy and the waging of war abroad. Law and order required relations with local leaders everywhere, who were commissioned to exercise royal authority, with hierarchies of police and courts, and the central courts themselves. Foreign affairs entailed embassies, permanent garrisons and short-term armies, the maintenance of royal ships or impressments of merchantmen, an ordnance train, munitions, supplies, musters, billeting and much else. To fund all these functions, the king needed revenues – from the farms of the shires, the crown lands, the customs, the aulnage, the profits of justice, taxation and much else – each with its machinery for local collection and each audited by the massive bureaucracy of the exchequer. He also needed somewhere to live – a court, a home and a household. His court must deliver regal splendour at all times. His home must allow him safely to live, relax, decide and rule. His household must routinely feed, dress, accommodate and transport the king himself, hundreds of inmates of varying status and wildly fluctuating numbers of guests. It must also organise, regulate and pay for itself. Its staff must be available for random and unpredictable services. The household was the equivalent of the great spending departments of today.

All these structures existed to fulfil the king's needs and to carry out his commands. He needed letters written for him of all kinds: hence the writing departments – the chancery, the privy seal office, the signet office. He needed money to keep himself and his household, and to finance his activities: hence the exchequer, such revenue-raising devices as wardship and the customs, and the duchy of Lancaster. It was through such king-oriented structures that vacancies were filled, patronage was dispensed, law and order was enforced, trade was regulated, diplomacy was conducted, treaties concluded, and wars were organised and financed. The division of the sweep of government into departments organised by function as familiar today had scarcely commenced. Impressive though these requirements were and the corresponding structures, staff and premises that they entailed, they alone could have generated only an inward-looking bureaucracy. That fifteenth-century government was more than that was largely because of the demand from subjects for its services – demand that increased incrementally and into ever more areas. The twelfth-century call for justice had prompted the creation of the central courts. Ever-burgeoning demands for justice from royal subjects now led to a proliferation of writs, actions, and cases and further delegations of new grievances for the chancellor and groups of councillors to remedy. Enforcement required networks of administration and justice throughout the realm.

Sometimes the king intervened locally on his own initiative. Normally the government became involved in the provinces on the invitation of local individuals – because local people wanted appointments, favours granted, wrongs righted and crime curbed. It was the king's subjects, his customers, who sought the appointments, grants, leases and licences that pack the chancery rolls, the writs of all kinds that initiated inquisitions and civil lawsuits, who reported the crimes and sought the repayment of royal debts for services supplied that comprised most of the routine business of the central machine. Decade after decade demand for central intervention grew. It was channelled through existing, often archaic structures, the tenured staff and time-honoured procedures, compulsive record-keeping and fail-safe mechanisms. Suitors, customers and litigants purchased the necessary guidance and expertise with fees and *douceurs* at every stage from first initiative to triumphant conclusion. Royal appointments, paid or unpaid, grants of property and presentations to livings, leases, trading licences and protection required patronage. Patronage involved the favour of the appointing minister or perhaps even of the king, access to them directly or through intermediaries with the right connections, and sometimes introductions to those intermediaries. It had to be made worth all their whiles. Once successful, if successful, it was only the beginning. A formal instrument needed to be drawn up, from king or treasurer (perhaps indirectly) to chancery, engrossed, enrolled, checked and sealed, ideally this year rather than next, once the formal royal fees and the informal clerical ones were paid. Some final documents still remain in the archives, uncollected because the fees were never paid. Nor was enforcement always easy. A writ might cost only 6s. 8d, but it had to be purchased at Westminster from the correct clerk, and, required writing, recording, sealing, transmission to the sheriff, serving and returning. Every stage had to be watched through the weary process by an attorney, on retainer and expenses. To provide such guidance and expertise there emerged whole professions, of scriveners and lawyers, many of whom made comfortable livings and some of whom were enriched. Hence the understandable complaints about costs and delays which, at times, became cries of corruption and prompted calls for reform.

Chancery, exchequer, the privy seal office and the central courts routinely transacted masses of business, generating endless rolls and writs. Their labours were exhaustive, hidebound, and administratively correct. They were not exciting and could be counter-productive. Kings resisted red tape. They tried to keep new sources of revenue to themselves, away from exchequer processes, whether the Lancastrians' duchy revenues or Edward IV's French pension, and the Yorkist kings and Henry VII preferred to handle their finances themselves in their chambers. Up-to-date estate administration was preferred to low-yielding exchequer farms.[7] Exchequer data was nevertheless good enough to allow estimates of income, expenditure and the king's financial state to be produced, although only the 1433 budget survives from the fifteenth century.[8] The common law courts were also out of date. Their actions were antique, irrelevant to modern fifteenth-century concerns and incapable of resolving disputes.[9] Such strictures need to be seen in the context of booming business and the development of new forms of writ and action to right new wrongs. Chancery was burgeoning, perhaps to equality with the central courts by the Yorkist era, and new prerogative courts emerged, requests under Richard III and the star chamber under Henry VII. Many cases – perhaps ever more – were resolved informally by arbitration.[10] The king's courts deserve some credit that a law-minded population was choosing increasingly to resolve its disputes through peaceful litigation and mediation.

The king was chief executive of his kingdom. He could make no permanent laws by himself. He could and did issue proclamations and summonses on his own authority, with penalties attached for non-compliance. He could determine whether laws were to be implemented or not and could pardon offenders both their offences and penalties. More importantly, he was still the fount of justice, with the right, if he so desired, to sit in on any case, as Edward IV symbolically did. The justices were his men, he called the serjeants-at-law to the coif, it was his law that was administered, and his writs that ran. Courts acted in his name: *Rex* v *Cook* in 1468. He could not be sued or convicted. His interests were treated sympathetically, for example in his court of the exchequer. He was free to interrupt proceedings by writs to the justices, by ordering sheriffs to empanel favourable juries and, most frequently, by pardoning defendants and convicts their offences.

Parliament

'The development of the representative parliament with so many of its classic rights and procedures', Professor Brown observes, 'was one of the greatest and probably the greatest governmental achievement of this period'.[11] Parliament was the king's highest court, his principal council, his legislature and the source of additional revenue. Its inexorable advance was marked by a series of landmark judgements.[12] Parliament enabled kings to do what they could not achieve alone. Parliament was theirs to direct: 'the royal prerogative was always in command'.[13] Kings summoned, prorogued and dissolved parliaments as they chose. They determined when it met, where it met and for how long it met. They had tasks for parliament to undertake and drafted legislation that they wanted enacted. From 1461 kings were preparing bills in the form of the ultimate act in order to ensure the desired wording in advance.[14] Kings had the final say on all bills, giving or withholding their assent to legislation which normally they had encountered before, adding whatever provisos they chose after the bills had passed and recasting enactments into a more acceptable form. The government revised bills into acts, wrote the formal record, chose which acts were enrolled and selected those to be further revised and enrolled as statutes. The chancellor set the tone, the king's nominee as speaker presided over the Commons, and royal clerks managed proceedings and composed the formal record, the parliament roll. Royal judges sat amongst the Lords, at least some of whom were recent royal creations. Many courtiers, councillors and other servants sat in the Commons. Few in either house did not serve the king in some national or local capacity. Unsurprisingly, most parliaments did the king's will; sometimes they were quite subservient.

The upper house, the Lords, was a relatively small body of men, never many more than a hundred in number, made up of two archbishops and eighteen bishops, between twenty-six and twenty-seven abbots and priors, a dozen dukes, marquises and earls and forty or less barons. All were great men, the heads of noble families, religious houses and/or administrative organisations, each a monarch within his limited compass, accustomed to making decisions, to respect and to having his way. From the late fourteenth century at least parliament channelled them into estates, lords spiritual to the king's right hand and temporal on his left, and into hierarchies. They sat in order of precedence distinguished by their parliamentary robes, none being at the apex and many relatively junior. Not all attended, the abbots being particularly slack and probably also relatively silent. In 1454 only 48 out of 105 peers attended, and even in 1461, when 67 attended altogether, a fifth absented themselves.[15] Justices and serjeants-at-law sat with the Lords, but were not full members. From at least 1449, the clerk of parliament kept a working record of Lords attendance, which was enforced in 1454 by fines. It was the higher ranks, the magnates and the ministers, who attended most assiduously.[16]

The Commons were an essential part of parliament. They made it into a representative assembly that could bind everyone. Their presence made parliament sovereign. MPs were either gentry or members of the highly select urban oligarchies. The thirty-seven shires each elected two knights of shire and the boroughs about 200 burgesses, who should have represented respectively the rural and urban elites. By 1399 the gentry had invaded the boroughs. Whereas there should have been three townsmen to every aristocrat in 1422, in fact there were two gentry to every townsman.[17] The new boroughs elevated from 1447 were generally small seigneurial towns that returned gentlemen and lawyers. Merchants and tradesmen were few in number and almost confined to the greater towns, such as London, York, Colchester and Grimsby. They were rated lower than knights of the shire, from whom the speaker and Commons deputations were selected. It may have been for this reason that many towns appointed gentlemen to office and elected them as their representatives. Genuine burgesses had specific interests and expertise, which may sometimes have proven of value in parliament and that perhaps gave them interests different to the gentry. It may be significant that it was the gentlemen who objected to the 1485 act of attainder, not the burgesses, and that it nevertheless passed because it was the king's will.[18] Townsmen leavened an overwhelmingly aristocratic assembly. Bishops and abbots were landholders who shared aristocratic tastes and lifestyles. The theory that parliament represented all was a fiction necessary to bind everybody. No commoners sat in parliament. Even allowing for genuine townsmen, parliament consisted of the privileged, propertied and aristocratic, who had much in common with one another. Shared outlook and interests did not preclude divisions, but made them much less likely.

What happened in parliament emerges only fitfully from the formal parliament roll composed retrospectively from the vantage of the

Lords and from surviving original bills. Few of the notes necessary for day-to-day management have survived. Chance survivals, of parts of a Lords journal of 1461 and a Commons diary of 1485, reveal much otherwise concealed: intercommuning, committee work, external consultation and debates that produced no legislation.[19] The laws enacted – the results – and the major crises were only part of the business and not perhaps what the government valued. Kings seldom had legislative programmes. It was petitioning, consultation and state trials that mattered to them. Individuals and vested interests valued parliament's guarantee of answers to petitions, which increasingly were channelled *through* the Commons rather than via the receivers and triers. Such bills cannot safely be presumed to emanate *from* the Commons: noblemen were often behind them. Bills may not have been closely scrutinised by the Commons: indeed this may be why the Commons route was preferred. On one embarrassing occasion the early Lancastrian Commons had to repudiate a Commons petition before the Lords that they had not seen – an incentive, surely, to tighten procedures – yet clerical practice did not record all eventualities even in 1455 and Commons petitions were receiving only one reading and Lords bills perhaps none at all as late as 1485. At least they were coming to the Commons: only one bill under Henry V and another two in 1429 are known to have proceeded from Lords to Commons. Three readings are first mentioned in 1495. Moreover, if an attainder was rejected by judges in 1489 because it had not been passed by the Commons, one wonders what other legislation escaped their scrutiny. It may be significant that from 1452 the formula 'by assent of the Commons' was sometimes substituted for 'at the request of the Commons'.[20] 'The formation and formulation of policies were above the heads of the commons and to all seeming, above their desires'.[21] Study is not helped by the moving target, as procedures and privileges were consolidated and formalised, but the inferiority of the Commons to king and Lords seems as pronounced under Henry VII – who never faced a parliamentary crisis – as under his Lancastrian predecessors.[22]

Parliaments were enormous set-piece occasions that needed a great deal of preparation and management before and during the actual sessions. Meeting six days a week, perhaps already only in the morning, they preoccupied the government. King, ministers, councillors and many others were involved and deferred their normal duties. Moreover parliament could spin out of control. Kings therefore needed good reasons to conjure it into existence. It was normal to summon parliament at the start of a new reign, in recognition of the new regime and to secure a grant of customs, at the beginning of wars and to vote taxes, and for state trials. The chancellor's opening sermon set out parliament's charge. Presumably parliaments were prorogued (adjourned) rather than dissolved because business remained to be transacted: the convenience of a parliament in being, especially if compliant, may explain the seven sessions of the parliament of 1472–5. Sessions, especially prorogued sessions, were often put off, as circumstances and royal priorities changed: three times in 1464 Edward IV further prorogued sessions summoned to York. Parliamentary sessions guaranteed an impressive context for state ceremonial, which itself ensured a good turnout in parliament. It was at parliament time that Edward IV organised the tournament of Lord Scales and the bastard of Burgundy (1467), and the marriages of his sister Margaret (1468) and of his son Richard (1478). It was also in 1467 that he replaced Archbishop Neville as chancellor.

Parliament was much more than the king's instrument. The Lords concentrated the independence, expertise and power of the king's greatest subjects, without whose counsel and support major initiatives could not proceed. They alone acted as the judges in state trials, both impeachments – in which the Commons were petitioners – and in attainders, in which before 1489 the Commons did not necessarily participate. Stewards of England appointed for the occasion pronounced sentence in the Lords at Yorkist parliaments.[23] Sometimes the Lords agreed with or protected the accused. From 1407 the Commons alone could vote taxation.[24] Each house discussed, approved, amended, stalled and rejected legislation. The Commons handled not merely what was passed down to them by king and Lords and such official bills as were introduced to the Commons, but they also raised many other issues, local, private and 'commonweal', grievances that cried out for remedy. They were the mouthpiece of all kinds of individuals, communities and pressure groups with complaints, grievances to remedy and hobby-horses to promote, which the king's agents could not always steer or stifle to their master's advantage. Parliament had a role as safety valve for thwarted and potentially explosive aspirations and energies to which every king must sometimes defer. 'By the end of Edward III's reign', writes Harriss, 'it could authoritatively voice the interests of the whole political community'.[25] Parliament as a point of political contact, of interaction between ruler and ruled, centre and peripheries, and between the ruled, is discussed in Chapter 10.

Decision-making, co-ordination and direction

The central machine routinely implemented decisions taken elsewhere. It did not decide itself, nor did it reconcile the competing demands of the king and his subjects. It responded to initiatives from above, as directed by king and council, who were themselves influenced by outside events, persuasion, inducements and coercion. Since the king, household and court were usually at a distance from Westminster, decision-making was separated from implementation. We know that ministers constantly corresponded with the king, were not infrequently at court and had a right of access. Edward IV was visited by his chancellor at Westminster at least twenty times over four weeks in 1465. Lord Treasurer Essex, admittedly the king's uncle, had an audience every day.[26] Decisions were made in contexts from the most private and intimate to the most public and formal. It was not necessarily the latter that mattered most.

The royal household was the king's natural environment. It fulfilled the functions both of public and ceremonial state rooms and private and intimate living quarters, what Edward IV's black book called the magnificent household (*domus magnificencie*), and the menial service departments (*domus providencie*). 'Upstairs' aristocrats – the king's carvers, knights and esquires of the body, ushers and sewers of the chamber, yeomen of the crown – staffed a suite of interconnected rooms, served, conversed, entertained and inevitably influenced the king. They were commanded by the steward of the household, by the 1460s commonly an earl, and by the chamberlain of the household, who certified when homages had been received and sometimes also royal warrants. The chamberlain controlled access to the monarch. Here was where most decisions were made and policies initiated: policies rarely, patronage constantly.

Patronage consisted of the rewards and favours in a king's gift: a vast array of appointments in central and local government, in the household, on estates and in forests, in garrisons and the Church, even as almsmen; grants and leases of land; wardships, custodies and marriage of wards; licences to trade, alienate or convey; pardons; cash; and much else. Of course such offices needed to be filled, functions performed, meals served, estates run, masses celebrated, messages delivered and policies devised. Patronage was also a key instrument of political management for governments that lacked much power to compel. Royal office conferred status and authority on royal servants, which was often what they actually sought. It was in the hope of such rewards that men served, through such rewards that the politically influential were persuaded to co-operate and from such rewards that courtiers and administrators were financed. Patronage was essential to government. All kings needed staff they could rely upon. Weak kings, especially usurpers, tried to strengthen themselves by using patronage to buy service, generate gratitude and create vested interests in their continued rule. Confronted by a succession of rebellions, Henry IV added substantially to the heavy load of annuities charged to his patrimony; Edward IV dissipated the enormous forfeitures of 1461 within three years and Richard III those from Buckingham's Rebellion on his northerners. Patronage needed to be distributed skilfully, in a balanced fashion, so that no group felt excluded, cliques were not created and the king was not isolated.

There were applicants for everything that a king had to give and bounty suitable for every suitor, though never enough for all. Discussions of patronage normally confine themselves to what is and was quantifiable: formal grants under the great seal, which was only the tip of the iceberg. Household office in particular may not have required formal appointment. Less permanent rewards – of cash or jewels – or favours not at the royal expense are largely concealed from us. A few surviving letters or copies of letters record gifts of deer, licences to hunt in royal forests, the recommendation of potential husbands to widows and of clerics to the patrons of benefices. Intervention from the king could even secure preference over equally deserving creditors in payments at the exchequer.[27]

The basis of all patronage was the petition. The first request might be oral, which might occasionally be conceded. Then or soon after it was set down in the appropriate written form, the humble supplication preceding a draft letter patent setting out precisely what was sought. Once initialled, this became a signed bill, or was recast into a signet warrant. Fifteenth-century kings were always accompanied by secretaries (the signet office), household or chamber accountants, and their records. Within his household Richard III accessed information sufficient to list all those holding annuities and offices from him, to calculate the values of his largesse to his favourites, to know what suitors had already received and to establish what remained unallocated. This was no innovation. From 1450 every beneficiary of royal largesse needed the king's approval for a proviso of exemption from each act of resumption. It had to be drafted in correct form, presented (perhaps via intermediaries) to the king, initialled, passed to the clerk of parliament, enrolled and writs of *mittimus* sent to appropriate officers: a costly and time-consuming process. In 1467 each supplicant had an interview with Edward IV, at which he was obliged to reveal what royal favours he enjoyed and what they were worth, in the light of which the king stated what might be kept. Edward kept his own independent record. When the proviso was submitted in appropriate form and as agreed, it was checked against the signet records and, if necessary, further amended by the king before it was signed.[28]

Kings were continuously confronted by suitors, in person or through intermediaries, with petitions oral or written, that required his decision and his signature (sign manual). Lancastrian kings received and answered requests every day after dinner.[29]

The king was never free from suitors: in his private quarters, moving around his palace, at meals or in chapel, when hunting or travelling. Suitors were notoriously importunate in asking: Henry VI found this particularly hard to resist. We have no notion how many requests were refused: rejected petitions were not filed as warrants. Many, indeed, were always oral – for intercession or for favours that never went through the writing offices; very occasionally letters patent were warranted by the king by word of mouth. Strikings-out may indicate how bills were amended or curtailed before they were signed. Rarely can we know for this period about competition for offices, what other issues such as competence or loyalty were considered, still less whether the most meritorious candidate won. The need to promote royal princes or sisters-in-law was often paramount: to this end Earl Rivers, Edward IV's father-in-law, was able to commit his king to almost anything.[30] The king's need to reward and his clients' desire for a proviso often coincided: it was 'by order of the king' that some provisos were enrolled.[31]

Access was crucial. No access normally meant no patronage. The advantage rested with those known to the king, those able to put their case in person, or those supported by his attendants, in all cases his ministers and household. The king lived in their company. They served him in bed, at table and in chapel, in public and at leisure, on duty and off guard, shared his recreations and heard his conversations. Kings were never off duty. It is hardly surprising that attendants so often secured the further favours that they really needed to finance their careers as courtiers or that kings sometimes asked their opinions. Nor that they told him what he wanted to know. The literary stereotype of the courtier was of a flatterer, who pandered to his ruler to his own advantage.[32] Why anger him whom one needed to please? Moreover it was one of their functions to control access to the king, which was as much in their interests – to confine patronage to themselves and exclude competition – as it was to the king. Archbishop Scrope's rebels in 1405 and those of Jack Cade in 1450 alike found that the courtiers whom they wished to denounce refused them access to the king.[33] It was not difficult to be on the margins of the household, or even in the great hall, which did not guarantee even a sight of the king. It was harder to enter the semi-public great and presence chambers, where embassies were received and books presented to the king. To almost everyone, the king's bedchamber, closet and oratory were closed.

Access in person was not essential. It was inconvenient even for a king's mother, consort, brothers, children, ministers or ambassadors to sue in person. Most central officials, local elites and complainants had no access in person. Their route forward was via intermediaries – those able to intercede with the king – such as ministers, the great nobility and members of the upper household. John Paston III, for example, relied on his brother-in-law Sir George Browne, his friend Sir James Ratcliffe 'and others of my acquaintance which wait most upon the king and lie nightly in his chamber to put [in] their good wills'. Securing access and seeing the warrant through every stage beyond took St Alban's Abbey five weeks in 1461 and was too daunting for Sir William Plumpton's agent to contemplate.[34] Always some individuals were particularly well-placed to help, with readier access and the king's trust. They were more likely to succeed. Chancery staff turned to the chancellor, the lower household to their steward and even the chamber staff to their chamberlain to put their cases. Suitors paid for this service: some well-placed individuals, for example Lord Chamberlain Hastings, his contemporary Lord Herbert and the squire William Catesby, were fed by numerous monasteries, boroughs and noblemen, whose mouthpieces with the king they were. Their identity is no surprise. Hastings was Edward IV's childhood friend, intimate and ruler of the chamber throughout his reign, Herbert bore more provisos in 1465 from the king's chamber on more occasions than anyone but the chancellor,[35] and Catesby, notoriously, was the 'Cat ... that ruleth all England under a Hog'. They were the king's favourites.

Every king had favourites, who benefited unduly both from royal patronage and from those who used them as intermediaries. Royal favour conferred political power: because favourites influenced royal decisions, they had influence elsewhere. They were courted and rivals feared to cross them. Aspirants sought to enter their service and parents placed their children in their households. They became the chosen avenue to royal favour both of less favoured courtiers and backwoodsmen, who expected their leader to deliver. Securing access and favour for oneself and one's clients and denying it to others were their objectives. If successful they could control and manage the king. This kind of exclusivity was reputedly sought by the maternal kin of the young Edward V. Something approaching it may have been secured by successive favourites of Henry VI, especially Suffolk, first as steward of the household and latterly when powerful enough to dispense with formal office. Edward IV, in contrast, received many suitors and intermediaries in person. The favourite was one origin of political factions. Others were mutual political interest, shared political principles and common enemies. Henry IV, Richard III and Edward IV were made kings by factions. Political failures stimulated hostility towards Henry's Lancastrian clique, forcing him to seek counsel more widely, whereas Edward himself chose to move beyond the Nevilles. The key issue then proved to be foreign policy, which was also a distinguishing feature of the rival factions that alternated in power in Henry IV's last years according to whether the king or his heir had the upper hand. Common enemies brought York and the Nevilles together against Somerset in 1453 and Edward IV to power in 1461. Fear of Warwick reinforced the natural alliance between the Wydevilles and Herberts in the late 1460s. Evidence about the conduct of factions is scanty. Given that most posts were held for life and that many officials were clerics, it is likely that factions affected fewer administrators and penetrated less deeply than under Henry VIII. The court appears less organised and patronage less intense. Factional differences, however, ran just as high. The state trials of royal dukes in 1447 and 1478, the lasting resentment of the Wydevilles at Hastings' captaincy of Calais and the dirty tricks perpetrated by each on the other during Edward IV's last years compare with some of Henry VIII's bloody coups. Fifteenth-century factionalism generated rebellions and the elimination of rivals, as in 1455 and 1469. Strong kings kept divisions under control: peaceful co-existence must have been the norm. The events of 1483 reveal what could happen when such control was removed.

Favourites counselled the king on more than particular cases of patronage. Whilst obliged to seek advice, a king could take it wherever he chose. He may well have received more advice in the household than he wanted from those from whom he did not seek it and whom Fortescue, at least, thought unqualified.[36] Some men were seldom formally described as councillors, formally appointed, or amongst those paid salaries. Lander identified 124 men called councillors of Edward IV and 227 of Henry VII. Only a handful attended regularly, on average in single figures – the three ministers and other functionaries. We know this from the records of the council: acts that the councillors had signed. Lander ably demonstrated considerable activity on certain issues, notably Calais.[37] These technical and convoluted negotiations required the diplomatic, financial and logistical expertise of professionals. That they lacked any discernible political dimension, were time-consuming and boring explains why most councillors, most aristocrats and indeed most kings absented themselves. Leave it to the experts! Kings reserved the last word.

Council minutes do not explain why several meetings were held each week during the law-terms. We have records for only a minority of meetings and for relatively little in all. What did they find to discuss? We cannot know for how long they met, nor how much discussion preceded the signed acts. What we have are action minutes: minutes recording formal decisions. Rare enough in many modern committees, how much rarer formal decisions were when governments covered less ground, were wedded to routine and had no desire to change things. Apart from decision-making, there was co-ordination, monitoring and budgeting to be done: co-ordination of official actions above and between departments, the monitoring of and the balancing of royal receipts and payments, the managing of cash flow and the financing of major enterprises. Discussion by itself generated no results and no minutes. What are missing from surviving council records (and indeed the public records as a whole) are the subsidiary working papers that were surely once commonplace and on which the council based its work. One surviving example, relating to Edward V's minority, reveals financial discussions by administrators at a level above the exchequer on the basis of statistics that the exchequer archive no longer contains.[38] Just as Elizabethan councillors pored over monthly county muster returns, so their fifteenth-century counterparts immersed themselves in administrative detail. Embassies, parliaments, coronations, royal marriages and funerals, and foreign expeditions made enormous bureaucratic demands, many of them met by the council.

Signed minutes were seldom kept. Though identifying those responsible for particular acts, they protected them from personal accountability by association with others. There were times when minutes were formally signed, probably at the instance of the clerk: when councillors were held accountable to the Commons under Henry VI, shared responsibility in his minority and protectorates, and in times of high political crisis. When Edward IV decided to abandon his invasion of France and accept the French king's terms at Picquigny in 1475, his council of war was obliged to sign a council minute approving the highly unpopular decision. Was it to cover himself that Lord Howard commissioned a registered copy (exemplification)?[39] At such times, the council may have been afforced by members of the high nobility who were, however, just as capable of staying away when unpleasant decisions had to be faced. Those nominated to York's first protectorate council in 1454 furnished themselves with ample get-out clauses when appointed and took advantage of them to avoid (and prevent) the duke's formal trial of his rival Somerset.[40] On other occasions also historians have noted that those voting numbered less than those attending:[41] defeated minorities, it appears, did not yet accept majority rules.

Some councils were attended by the king in person. The distinctions between a full meeting of the council, the great council and the peers in parliament are indistinct. All were places where the king formally took counsel. All were attended by the lords temporal, ministers, judges, whoever else the king wished to consult and – in the case of parliament – the elected Commons. Great councils were not necessarily better attended than ordinary councils and there was often poor attendance at parliament by the Lords, especially the abbots and barons. Meetings of the council itself took place regularly, but might be convened anywhere, wherever the king was from whoever he chose. It was not impossible to have more than one meeting at once, one with the king and one at Westminster. Meetings of the great council were preceded by formal summonses under the privy seal (which therefore seldom survive), sometimes specifying the purpose of the meeting. Like the council, but unlike parliament, no permanent record was kept. Its minutes resemble those of the council and are not always distinguishable. The great council was not integrated with the royal administrative and warranting processes. The results of its deliberations do not always mention the great council. Only a handful of its acts are known. Lacking legislative powers, it could bind the peerage and whoever else attended. Sessions of the great council were common in the 1450s, 1460s and 1470s, when parliaments were infrequent. It was a more flexible body, that could be assembled more quickly, at less energy and cost, often met outside London and could fulfil much of parliament's consultative role. Great councils served as ceremonial occasions to receive embassies, opportunities to secure advances of money secured on future taxes, occasions for disciplining disobedient magnates, for reconciling differences between factions, between those disaffected and the king, and for setting up forthcoming parliaments.[42] They did matter politically and thus are often mentioned in the chronicles.

Fortescue deplores how Henry VI's councils were dominated by lords

> which had near hand as many matters of their own to be entreated in the council as had the king. ... They were so occupied with their own matters and with the matters of their

kin, their tenants and servants that they attended but a little and then nothing to the king's matters. And also there were but few matters of the king, but the matters touched the said councillors, their cousins and kindred or their tenants and servants or such other as they owed favour unto ... Then could no matter treated in the council be kept private, for the lords oftentimes told their own councillors and servants that they had served them and sued to them for those matters, how they had sped them and who was against them.[43]

Inadvertently Fortescue reminds us that council meetings pooled viewpoints and experience and served more than the king. They brought different parties together. Of course lords told their clients: like the earl of Northumberland about 1477, they wanted credit for their good lordship.[44] If any 'low man ... in that counsel ... durst [not] say against the opinion of any of the said great lords',[45] he was acknowledging the realities of power that great councils were meant to reflect.

Some of these observations apply also to parliament, which was much more than the king's greatest council. The Lords alone sat in the parliament chamber: outsiders were halted by a bar. The king frequently, perhaps generally, presided and participated in discussions. He did not work *with* parliament, he was part *of* parliament, worked *within* it, specifically *within* the Lords. It was *to* the Lords and sometimes to representatives of the Commons that kings made their speeches and made the formal commitments entered on the parliament roll by the clerk of parliament. Within the chamber the king often presided, participated in discussion and perhaps constrained debate, despite Henry's promise in 1407 not to do so again.[46] There was a direct interchange between the king and Lords and amongst the Lords as a group. On some issues peers responded individually to questions posed to them. Surviving fragments of their journals reveal them in detailed discussions and performing such essentially consultative and administrative tasks as approving the king's war strategy, negotiating with merchants and scrutinising draft treaties in which the Commons had no part.[47] The Lords had a role in advice both separate to and additional to the Commons. Not surprisingly, since they were consulted more fully and worked more closely with the king, the Lords represented the king's views to the Commons in 1461 and took a magisterial tone in inter-house transactions.[48] The impression from the parliament roll that what the Commons did took place off stage is a faithful record of what its compiler the clerk of parliament, sitting with the Lords, actually saw. It also reflects the government's view.

Parliament, great council, council and advisers counselled the king with whom power of decision really rested. The king really was the fundamental element in the whole system. Kings needed to assess the flood of advice that came to them, to balance their patronage, to resist importunate individuals and interest groups and to determine policy. Their task was obviously impossible. Much had to be delegated, whilst the king always retained the power of decision. Kings needed to know when to act and when inactivity sufficed. They needed discrimination, the capacity to judge between alternative options, the self-belief to override contrary and often expert views, and the strength of will to impose their decision and to hold it despite contrary pressures. Henry V, famously, could do all things, for the brief period that he ruled. He continued making decisions on domestic issues even whilst campaigning abroad. Other kings were not so capable. Several times Edward IV did too little and let things slide. Henry IV and Richard III were pushed off course by sheer pressure of circumstances. Delegation and reliance on favourites could identify a king with a particular faction, driving their foes into opposition, or even obscure the king himself. Henry IV relied unduly on his Lancastrian retainers. Henry VI's reign can be divided into the prevalent influences of Cardinal Beaufort, Suffolk, Somerset and Buckingham. Henry VII's experience suggests that absorption in administrative detail rather than politics was as dangerous as the reverse.

Government and the political system did not change fundamentally between 1399 and 1509. The relationship between the king and his magnates, the king and his subjects, the king and parliament, and the different houses of parliament fluctuated, but did not fundamentally shift. Regimes constantly reacted to circumstances demanding short-term remedial or corrective action. Disorder needed quelling, truces needed extending, debts needed paying, crises needed confronting. Even campaigns against lawlessness, as in 1414 and the 1470s, were provoked. It is hard to see in such reactions that governments formulated their own policies. Relatively few developments can be pinned down to deliberate government decisions, the most important – which coloured the whole century – being Henry V's invasion of France. His initial victory and subsequent defeats created an aggressive climate of opinion that subsequent kings pandered to and which constrained them. Most decisions on foreign policy and defence were short term, because of events elsewhere. Rarely, as in the mid-1460s, was there a choice to be made.

Changes within the system were nevertheless happening, constantly, and were being regulated, as can be perceived schematically from the results of administrative action and legislation. Edward IV's indentures of the marches and Henry VII's strict interpretation of the privileges of particular sanctuaries have both been seen, surely correctly, as precedents to the act of union and abolition of sanctuaries in the 1530s.[49] Progression from statute to statute has been charted in such diverse fields as the laws regulating treason, dress, labour, riot, livery and maintenance. Such developments are most easily interpreted as new or tougher remedies for new or worse offences, but that is not necessarily the case. New regulations on dress or sumptuary legislation may indeed mean existing laws were flouted, but the statutes of 1363, 1463 and 1483 reveal major changes in fashion, social stratification and re-assessments of status – royal kin, for instance, rising substantially in status.[50] The chronology of legislation needs careful handling – the preambles alone cannot suffice – but it can indicate social change, which seemed greater to those affected than from the vantage point of today. Crown and parliament were instruments for social stability and greater regulation.

Local government

Governments orchestrated networks of local officers everywhere. In every shire a sheriff accounted for the farm of the county, an escheator for the king's feudal revenues, an aulnager for the levy on cloth, in every port a customer and controller for customs and subsidies, at intervals collectors for parliamentary taxes and usually also receivers and lesser ministers for estate revenues. Everywhere coroners inquired into sudden death and treasure troves. The sheriff was the first port of call for the central courts, for the annual assizes and infrequent commissions, and for the standing commissions of the peace. A stream of commands were despatched from the central departments, the royal council and from the king himself: a host of writs were returned and actions taken in response. The government reached into every corner of the realm: more frequently, admittedly, in the midlands and the south than the north and west, indirectly in the palatine counties, but everywhere nevertheless.

Seen from the centre, the basic unit of local government was the county or shire and its principal sub-divisions the hundred, wapentake in Danelaw, lathe in Kent and rape in Sussex. The sheriff was still the king's principal agent. His financial duties brought him into constant and acrimonious contact with the exchequer. He was the county's chief police officer, leading the county posse, supervising the county gaol, servicing the courts and implementing their decisions. The sheriff was the recipient of all writs in civil suits from the central courts, responsible for proclaiming them in his county court and serving them, usually via the officers of hundreds and manors, for returning them with his responses, for distraining property, for outlawry, arrests and confinement. Both in civil and criminal cases, at the centre and locally, it was the sheriff who empanelled juries, produced defendants and sometimes conducted their hangings. As the elections to parliament of the county MPs (two knights of the shire) took place in his county court, he was the returning officer: on occasion, a role of the highest political importance. Since his appointment was annual, it is likely that continuity was normally provided by a county undersheriff who served from year to year, although the evidence is scanty – only the slightest archives remain anywhere – and even though the sheriffs' oaths *c.*1485 forbade the employment of a predecessor's undersheriff.[51]

Escheators, in contrast, had little to do, though the inquisitions *post mortem* that they held were, on occasion, politically sensitive. Far more important already were commissioners of the peace (JPs), the lowest criminal court. A quorum of designated justices was set. JPs met four times a year in quarter sessions, perhaps for a day at a time: they had not yet undertaken the mass of out-of-court work between sessions that so burdened their Elizabethan successors. They were supervised by the assize judges, who descended on their circuits each year and by the central court of king's bench, which frequently called in cases from the JPs by writ of *certiorari*. There were many occasional royal commissions, of oyer and terminer on serious criminal matters, *de valiis et fossatis* regarding protection against the seas and of array, for purposes of national defence. The exchequer also appointed its own customers, controllers and aulnagers, who regulated and taxed external and internal trade.

Market towns were subject to county government, but scores of towns managed their own affairs, as royal or seigneurial boroughs, subject merely to county oversight. Most charters prescribed one or more councils and courts, a hierarchy of officers chosen from those free of the borough, burgage tenure, the right to own property and raise revenue, and the obligation to pay an annual farm. Officers were chosen according to local rules that seldom allowed free election. Corporations were characteristically police authorities. They regulated their own economic affairs – trading standards, markets and fairs, apprenticeship – directly and frequently also through craft-gilds and other subordinate bodies. Courts normally handled specialised cases between parties – suits of debt, breach of covenant and trespass. Perceived from above, gilds were a means of controlling the workforce, who belonged to gilds, parishes and fraternities that harnessed their endeavours in structured and regulated ways. The largest towns were counties in themselves, with their own sheriffs, JPs and quarter sessions. Such county towns proliferated, from London and Bristol down to Southampton (1447) and even Scarborough in 1484. A few, such as Coventry and Bristol, were staple towns, with jurisdiction over recognisances for debt. Typically towns were governed by their principal citizens, whose richest members doubled as councillors and aldermen, intermarried and co-opted one another into office. Political, social and economic elites commonly coincided. Royal office bestowed legitimacy.

What all these positions had in common, bar exchequer officials and assize judges, was that officers were unpaid. They were chosen by the king from local men, sheriffs normally being leading county gentry, JPs a mixture of the principal aristocracy and those legally expert, and escheators and coroners hailing from the lesser gentry. County government was the preserve of the aristocracy, principally but not exclusively of residents. Selected from major figures in the shire, they lent their local standing to royal office, thus ensuring respect for the king's instructions and for their own administrative and judicial actions, and facilitating the implementation of royal commands and decisions. They served to gain the advantages of office. If some sheriffs sought exemption from such office, for most the substantial fee payable was compensation enough. Responsibility was delegated by the crown to local notables, who governed themselves – self-government at the king's command – subject to a string of instructions from various government agencies. In return, they exercised royal authority – a royal authority that legitimised their own otherwise dubious bullying. It was an alliance of mutual interest.

Disputes arose everywhere. Whilst resort to the central royal courts was an option, this involved settlement by outsiders, was costly and slow and infringed local autonomy. Many preferred cheaper and quicker alternatives, certainty and ease of enforcement, for which they were prepared to compromise. Whatever individuals may from time to time have intended, with an eye to tactics and personal advantage, their neighbours preferred settlement within the community, whether through its courts or by agreement. The common law did not 'provide the kind of mutual compact which people increasingly sought as the only workable means of bringing certain disagreements to an end'. Private settlement, though undocumented, was commonly the first step. Conciliation, mediation and arbitration was practised at all levels of society, within all types of community everywhere, 'whereby all parties could be pacified rather than one humiliated or punished'. They occurred both voluntarily and under pressure from superiors and peers. Some gilds automatically referred disagreements to arbitration. 'All English courts, from the manorial level upwards, made a practice of referring cases to arbitration.' Most took place within classes, the arbitration of cases between craftsmen by craftsmen, though exceptions are known, most frequently the selection of a social superior as umpire – the arbiter of last resort. Arbitration was adapted to the full range of possible quarrels. It was common, far more so than the relative handful of explicit records indicate. Since a mere fraction of cases in the royal courts reached a verdict, the presumption is that they were settled out of court.[52] Litigation and arbitration were complementary alternatives often used in concert.

Arbitration procedures were standardised across all social groups. First of all, agreement was needed to go to arbitration: at this stage the parties nominated the arbiters, undoubtedly maximising their advantage, and the timescale, a deadline for the award being set and, failing agreement, the final award. Most commonly each party selected one or more arbiters to join a balanced panel; sometimes an individual acceptable to both was chosen. At this point both parties sealed bonds to one another to abide by the award: the penalty, a large round sum, was forfeited if they failed to comply and could be pursued through the courts. These bonds, often enrolled in royal courts of record, are the most common evidence for arbitration. Next the panel met, received the submissions and evidences of either party, debated, conciliated, mediated and negotiated, usually without generating any intermediate evidence. Sometimes professional legal advice was invoked. An award was then devised, which was then implemented. Sometimes no agreement was reached and/or the umpire took over. Usually the award determined the principal issues, occasionally in great detail, offering something to each party in the interests of peace. All existing lawsuits should cease. Often ceremonial reconciliation was prescribed, a loveday sealed by worshipping or eating together. Thus the offending royal judge Sir Robert Tirwhit had to provide a banquet and humbly beg forgiveness.[53] Implementation ensued: transfers of land or money, collusive lawsuits – final concords or common recoveries – and deeds of implementation. Generally these do not refer to the now redundant award, which was discarded. Pressure from courts, lords, kin, friends and neighbours to submit to arbitration and abide the award and participants' efforts to outmanoeuvre, suborn or intimidate can be presumed, but are normally concealed.

Most arbitrations succeeded.[54] Some did not. Contestants refused to make concessions, declined to proceed to arbitration and failed to implement the award. Even some lovedays collapsed in violence. Individuals or their heirs resurrected disputes. Social pressures were exerted on the defaulters, who were shamed, coerced or suffered reprisals. Some cases were so technical that they were referred to the courts, yet others so intractable that they could not be solved by arbitration. It is these exceptional cases, *causes célèbres* such as the Ladbroke case, that are the best documented. Peaceful resolution of disputes within communities was common at all levels.

Arbitration operated hand in hand with the king's justice and local government. It was not an exception to the system. Exceptions there were, however. Past kings had granted away numerous franchises: the view of frankpledge exercised by many manorial court leets was an example; so too were the private hundreds in many parts of the country, the private liberties and even private shrievalties, such as Worcestershire. Though most franchises were obsolete, some in the north, such as Allertonshire and Howdenshire in Yorkshire, and the marcher lordships in Wales remained important. The counts palatine of Durham, Chester and Lancaster and the Welsh marcher lords exercised the full range of kingly powers – regalian rights. Or, that is, theoretically: in practice kings interfered directly. Rather more frequently they exerted pressure on the lords. Kings continued to create franchises. Edward IV granted a Norfolk liberty to the duke and elevated Raglan into a marcher lordship for his favourite Herbert.

Central authority was also devolved. The greatest franchise-holder was the king as lord of Cheshire and Lancashire and of a growing number of marcher lordships. Chester and Lancaster duplicated the institutions of central government and offered devolved systems on the spot to inhabitants. It was primarily for this reason – not merely because their archives survive – that the government of these counties appears so active and effective compared with that of their neighbours. Devolved government in the north and Wales also began during this period. The crown held the principality of Wales throughout, Lancaster lordships such as Kidwelly from 1399, those of the earldom of March from 1461, of the Despensers and Beauchamps from 1487, and others temporarily through forfeiture and wardship. When Edward IV established his son at Ludlow with a council for the government of the marches, he already controlled many lordships; other marcher lords were persuaded to co-operate in the management of their lordships. Henry VII was to re-establish the system under Prince Arthur. The dominance that Gloucester was permitted to build up in the north in

1471–83 was continued through a council at Sandal presided over first by his son and then a nephew. It is not altogether clear at what point thereafter it was revived. The councils of Wales and the north provided devolved government for their regions until the civil war.

7

ALTERNATIVE
PERCEPTIONS

Earlier chapters have touched on the vast range of ideas of which everyone in fifteenth-century England partook. They were not always or everywhere the same. They were affected and even altered according to rank and occupation, locality and the passage of time. Political values were not the same at court as in the provinces: fidelity, honour and justice had different meanings in different contexts.[1] So too had worship and service. Chapters 4 and 5 stressed how much (and inevitably) social orders diverged. How could a rural peasant share much with a great magnate? What common perspectives had a tenant and his landlord? What could commoners make of the elite codes of honour and chivalry? Were not their lifestyles and horizons inescapably alien to one another? One of Cade's manifestos denounced abuses of the statute of labourers – *the* classic piece of class legislation. Few aristocrats can have shared popular apprehensions of judicial descents. When, in fact, was the last harvest of heads? It was king's bench, the principal criminal court, that 'was grief-full to the shire of Kent'.[2] Were rebels harking back to folk memory when judicial eyres in the provinces were money-raising exercises akin to the great sessions in Wales?

Such variations did not add up to mutually exclusive aristocratic or plebeian sub-cultures. Co-operation and mutuality predominated over conflict. Such contrasts oversimplify. No two individuals, even in the fifteenth century, saw everything exactly the same. There were regional variations. Attitudes evolved over time. The principal constitutional ideas were neither rigid nor definitive. They were repeatedly reassessed, adapted to particular circumstances and re-formulated in their opening sermons to parliament by a succession of royal chancellors. Chancellors consciously selected the ideas most relevant to their needs and blended them to current requirements. Others did likewise, often unconsciously. Everybody had their own notion of the public interest and the commonweal. There was an unusual degree of national consensus in 1450, yet Cade, York, Warwick and others laid different stresses on the same ideas. There were alternative perceptions on many issues, certainly most political and constitutional matters, and these developed. Such alternative perceptions of class, place and a range of constitutional concepts are here explored. Political debates, the cut and thrust of politics, are deferred to later chapters.

Perceptions of social class

Fifteenth-century Englishmen were innocent of our sense of class, and especially of a middle class. The aristocracy were defined in part by what they were not or thought that they were not. They did not engage personally in trade, which was ignoble, nor did they labour with their hands in the fields. They were contemptuous of those of inferior class and birth: Robert Armburgh denounced his rivals and nieces by marriage as bastards born of 'churls and combsters'. An anonymous chronicler was offended when Cade strutted around in finery 'as if he had been a lord or a knight and yet he was but a knave and had his sword borne before him'. It was presumptuous for 'men of little substance or no wealth at all' to claim equal voices in elections to valiant knights.[3] Such snobbery can be multiplied.

The clergy, who are so revealing about their aristocratic patrons and, inadvertently, about themselves, were less sympathetic to the commons. Whatever their personal origins, they were outsiders, who aligned themselves with lords and landlords against presumptuous peasants. Thomas Walsingham's vitriolic denunciations of the rebels of 1381, who terrorised his abbey, set the tone. Adam of Usk feared the populace might acquire a taste for murdering their betters from the lynching of the Ricardian earls in 1400.[4] The Crowland continuator exhibited little sympathy, reporting that the Lincolnshire rebels of 1470, 'as though making a new alliance with the Kentishmen, took up arms against the laws and customs of the realm ... and paid the full penalty according to their deserts'. He attributed Fauconberg's rebellion to a desire for pillage.[5] The commons were typically depicted and characterised in the mass. We frequently learn what caused them to 'grudge'. One chronicler regularly records popular reactions to events in decidedly simple terms: the people were fearful, displeased, sad, angry and morally outraged in turn. Such emotions and sentiments conform to the contemporary stereotype that the commons were irrational, passionate and supposedly actuated by their feelings rather than by logic and reason. Commoners did not decide their political stance themselves, but were swayed by others. Generations of them, so kings declared, were 'blinded' by noble demagogues into insurrection. It was the leaders who mattered and who were slaughtered: the commons, 'because they were rough and simple', could safely be spared. 'As is always their habit', wrote the Crowland continuator in 1470, 'all the local people were sympathetic to the returned exiles'. 'The fickle nature of the Kentish folk', in 1471, justified for him Edward IV's vigorous repression. Edward himself was apprehensive in 1475 about 'the condition of his people and how easily they might be drawn into rebellions and strange schemes, if they were to find a leader'. Lacking the resources to be stable and 'therefore living by their casual labours', the people, to Bishop Russell's mind, 'be not without cause likened unto the unstable and wavering running water'. 'Let those who follow beware', warned the Crowland continuator in 1486, 'because they are set over a populace which is not only unsettled, but at the same time greedy for innovation'.[6] Already the people constituted the 'many-headed monster' of the literary elites of Tudor and Stuart England.[7]

Overt expressions of class hostility *from* inferiors *to* superiors are actually unusual.[8] The commons were seldom impelled to rebel, were generally restrained when they did and were respectful to their leaders, the aristocracy and crown alike. Far from exploiting civil war to assuage class antagonism, they seem often to have looked to their social superiors for remedy of grievances and for leadership in their insurrections, even expressing loyalty on occasion towards their lords and identifying themselves with them. Yet the comments above reveal a class hostility *from* the elite *towards* the people. The Peasants' Revolt and then Cade's Rebellion gave aristocrats good cause to fear the commons and to avoid offending them. 'In good faith', wrote Margaret Paston in 1462, 'men fear sore here of a common rising'.[9] The *Somnium Vigilantis* of 1459 and Russell's sermon in 1483 both presume contempt for the people's political capacity amongst the aristocratic and property-owning elites of parliament. Fifteenth-century parliaments did enact much legislation prejudicial to the commons. The aristocratic privilege of hunting and sumptuary legislation were both discriminatory. Control of wages did not cease with the Peasants' Revolt.[10]

Perceptions of place

The English *nation* and English *patriotism* are striking fifteenth-century phenomena. Many European monarchs appropriated chivalry for their foreign wars and to buttress their sovereignty at home. Olivier de la Marche and others stressed the approval of the prince and his role in bestowing and withdrawing honours. It was princes who promoted tournaments and ceremonial, princes who ennobled their subjects and princes also who founded and ruled such national curial orders of knighthood as the Garter and the Golden Fleece. The Hundred Years War had made Henry V into a chivalric and patriotic hero. His cause was a *just war* because the French denied him justice, so he claimed, and clergy, nobility, parliament and people agreed. Taxes were voted, the aristocracy enlisted and God gave his verdict at Agincourt and subsequent victories. Henry's victories were accepted as divine judgements, not least by the English church, which subscribed to the concept of the just war, prayed for success and celebrated it with the *Te Deum*. English pride burgeoned, was stimulated and repeatedly promoted by public ceremonies and by other skilful propaganda, for Henry VI's coronation expedition in 1429–31 and for the relief of Calais in 1436, when a minor success was celebrated in verse.[11] Henry VI promoted the national cults of St George and St John of Beverley. Even the burgesses of Shrewsbury must be aware, York presumed in 1452, 'what praise, dignity, honour and manhood were attributed by all nations to the people of this realm whilst the kingdom's sovereign lord stood possessed of his lordship in the realm of France and duchy of Normandy',[12] for which he, as a past lieutenant of France, claimed some credit. The treaty of Troyes (1420) justified the cause, legalised the dual monarchy and made traitors of non-subscribers and perjurers of those, like Philip the Good of Burgundy, who withdrew from the alliance at the Congress of Arras in 1435. 'The Scorn of the Duke of Burgundy' enlists chivalric shame in the cause of patriotism.[13] Dishonour and treason were alleged by humiliated patriots in parliament and amongst the commons against the 'duke of Somerset when he had the command of the same' and lost it. 'And what derogation, loss of merchandise and villainy is generally said and reported about the English nation for the loss of the same'.[14] It was not just a few nostalgic veterans who urged re-conquest. National pride moved parliament itself to vote taxes for further invasions in 1468, 1475, 1492 and 1513. Whatever his dynasty, Henry V was as untouchable a national hero for the Yorkists in 1460[15] as for the Tudors and for Shakespeare.

Such patriotism built on the sense of difference between the English and other nationalities, reflected for example in the separate English nations at early-fifteenth-century general councils of the Church. Fifteenth-century Englishmen, like all societies at all times, were suspicious of outsiders, of aliens, and discriminated against them accordingly. The early-sixteenth-century *Italian Relation* reported that the Englishmen valued only themselves.[16] They had good reason to fear the intentions of their enemies, the French and Scottish, but their hostility ran deeper than that. The fourteenth century had witnessed legislation against foreigners taking English jobs, exporting English bullion and trying English cases abroad, and against alien priories, supposed refuges of enemy nationals. The alien priories were dissolved in 1414. The Commons complained again of export of bullion in 1422 and of foreign clerks in 1436. Cardinal Beaufort, no less, was forced first to abandon his cardinalate and was later prosecuted for *praemunire*. All levels of Englishmen discriminated against all levels of foreigners, even including the foreign servants of foreign queens. Contacts could not be altogether cut, trade – in which their role was most resented – being especially important. Direct acquaintance made people neither more understanding nor better informed. It was in London, where 2 per cent of the population were aliens, that native Englishmen were most hostile, whether they were merchants who feared competition and envied alien privileges, or the mob. There was universal agreement that the activities of aliens needed to be controlled. A statute of 1404 forbade them to export gold and silver and required them to reside with English hosts: regulations that were commonly thought to be under-enforced. In 1422 the Commons believed that aliens were manipulating foreign exchange and in 1437 the stews of Southwark supposedly harboured enemy spies and criminals. Animosity towards aliens ran high in the 1430s, as fortunes in the Hundred Years War flagged and the *Libel of English Policy* preached English mercantilism and reached a peak in the anti-alien parliaments of 1439–42. Believing foreigners enriched themselves at English expense and aliens to be much wealthier than they actually were, parliament excluded them from the retail trade, regulated hosting more rigorously and introduced an annual alien poll tax, with disappointing results. At various times, in the 1430s, 1457 and in 1470–1, the commons attacked Flemish beerhouses at Southwark.[17]

Hostility towards foreigners extended also to the king's own continental subjects and the Celtic peoples of the British Isles, with whom there were obvious racial and linguistic differences. 'Racialism, in the sense that the late-medieval English believed themselves to be separate from and superior by birth to the celtic peoples of Ireland and Wales, was ingrained'.[18] Scotland, of course, was a foreign country, with which ancient animosities were constantly fuelled by occasional wars and frequent border infractions. A few Scots did live in England: many wisely secured denizenship when war broke out in 1449. Nominally the king's subjects, most Irish ignored royal authority. Frequently described as 'our enemies and rebels', they were expelled in 1422 and even subjected to the alien poll tax in 1440–3. In 1439 they were excluded from Bristol's corporation and the hoppers gild; they were re-admitted and discommoned in 1455.[19] The Welsh, a subject race, rose in Glyndŵr's rebellion against Henry IV, were defeated and subjected to punitive legislation, from which individuals however were exempted. They were excluded from the alien poll tax. Practice and reality often departed from theory or the law. Herberts and Tudors achieved high rank and office even in England. Such tolerance, however, should not be exaggerated: it was under Henry VII that Poynings' Law subjected all acts of the Irish parliament to that of England.

Many such people, especially the Celts, spoke outlandish languages. The Cornish were Celts. Although an extreme example, Cornishmen recall the distinctive dialects in so many parts of the realm. The striking contrasts between the languages of three late-fourteenth-century contemporaries, Langland the west midlander, the *Gawain* poet from the north-west, and the metropolitan Chaucer, were not wholly eradi-cated by the emergence of Chaucerian English as the national norm English was the language of Henry V and polite society from the four-teen-teens. Borderers and Kentishmen may not have understood one another. There were several different cultural provinces. The Kentishmen and the Lincolnshiremen found shire-consciousness a bond: membership of the same wapentake or riding could determine voting patterns.[20] Parliament restricted the vote and parliamentary seats to those actually resident within the relevant shires which the Pastons of Norfolk, at least, thought decisive against Sir John Howard of Stoke by Neyland in neighbouring Suffolk.[21] There was a strong sense of *country*, of counties and of the otherness of neighbouring units. What 'country' meant in the *Paston Letters* has been examined and deserves wider exploration.[22] Localism co-existed with and complemented nationalism and patriotism. Successive regimes saw advantage in stressing the north–south divide, especially the wildness of the northerners and their desire to destroy the southern parts of the realm, a view subscribed to by at least some southerners.[23] It really mattered where the line was drawn.

Perceptions of law, justice and crime

The *law* was also subject to different interpretations. Law is not an absolute rule, but relative: a dominant ideology, but not the only one. Our modern impartial set of rules is authoritative because consecrated by parliament and applies equally to all subjects and must be obeyed by all. We should not presume, Green warns, that their 'world [was] always juristically like ours'.[24] Fifteenth-century England possessed several systems of law – statute, common, canon (ecclesiastical), military (the law of arms) and customary – and several levels. Each had different areas of jurisdiction, generally complementary, sometimes overlapping or competitive. All these systems however were practical concrete expressions of the principles of *natural law* – divine law, that God had prescribed, or the law of reason – and all therefore corresponded with abstract notions of *justice*. They were all working to the same divine end. Supposedly, new laws were not made: old laws were discovered or new laws implemented pre-existing divine law. Confronted by earlier acts of parliament in 1460, York appealed to natural law, a higher authority, but only three years later the judges ruled that parliamentary statutes bound everyone. The dominant law was that of the king or the common law, which was administered through his courts by his justices: their writs prohibited certain actions in church courts and writs of *certiorari* frequently removed cases from local courts to those of the king. Albeit reluctantly, judges accepted in 1505 that statutes could change custom and override the common law itself.[25] The law they administered presumed the status quo and defended it: the social hierarchy, current property rights and order. Respect was demanded in the king's name through proclamations, by delegation, and in proceedings distinguished by robes, lore and ritual. The gibbet, quartering and public exhibition of severed limbs were deterrents to future offenders.

Law is not the same as *justice*. It is not absolute. It varies from country to country. Nor is it static. It varies from time to time. There were many new laws in fifteenth-century England. Kings, legislators and lawyers devised remedies for grievances, mainly remedies for new grievances, grievances that may have existed before but were not illegal. There were riots before the statute of riots (1410), but they were not illegal, or at least they were prosecuted as other offences. Law does not operate in a vacuum. It is moulded with society, changes with and reflects changing social attitudes. Many activities hitherto legal were outlawed in the late middle ages. *Crime* is the consequence of law: crimes are made when new laws are created and unmade when they are repealed. Those who continued to practise activities once forbidden henceforth committed crimes and were prosecuted, whilst the rest conformed to the new framework. Aspects of bastard feudalism that had been legal were proscribed. The very few prosecutions indicate both that some offended and that most potential offenders complied. Other laws, like specific sumptuary regulation,[26] became out of date and, ceasing to conform to current values, were updated or fell into disuse. The king's law was very much a lawyer's concept. It suited the *amour propre* of professional lawyers. It was a professional lawyer, Chief Baron Fray, who declared the law to be 'the highest inheritance that a king has'.[27] Lawyers' heightened sense of self-esteem was developed by a professional training, fostered by a common dress, the collegiality of the inns of court and corporate interests, and was justified by a distinctive code of ethics which they regulated themselves. Within the legal profession at Westminster, there was a hierarchy of ranks and career structure superior to the practices of provincial attorneys, which led through office-holding in the inns and through advocacy at the central courts to selection by the king as serjeants-at-law and justices, both of whom wore the distinctive coif. Serjeants had a monopoly of the lucrative pleading at common pleas: restrictive practices already existed. The common lawyers were well placed to proselytise and enforce their notion of the law as the king's legal advisers and as interpreters of the law in the central courts. Their discussions, as reported in the yearbooks, reveal the law changing. They also went beyond it. Chief Justice Husy's reading in 1485 of the oath against illegal livery of 1461 went well beyond the literal meaning of the words.[28]

Here Husy was acting as the king's officer. Judges were the king's men, royal employees, bound to the king by oath and obliged to give priority to the king's interests over those of others. 'You shall counsel our sovereign lord the king in his needs', begins the judge's oath of office,

> and that you shall not give any counsel or assent to any thing the which might turn to hurt or disinheriting of the king by any way or colour. And that you shall do & procure the profit of the king and of his crown in all things where you then reasonably may do.[29]

The king's justices were banned from counselling anybody else in a case involving the king. They were also forbidden to be retained or liveried by anyone else – a rule, not surprisingly, that Husy thought should apply to all. 'And in case that you be found on default hereafter', ominously ends their oath, 'you shall be at the king's will of body, lands and of behaviour to do thereof that that shall please the king'.[30] It was such principles that caused the incautious responses of the judges in 1387 to Richard II's questions. Fortescue assigned a high place to lawyers in government. Politically of course he was an extremist: the only judge to suffer attainder and exile during the Wars of the Roses. A man of little political sense, of power or palace politics, or why the lords mattered so much, he may not have been typical of the king's judges. His colleagues, in practice, were more discreet. They found both that York's claim to the crown and the attainder of Henry VII were above their learning.

The law was less absolute and definitive than professional lawyers wished. That the statute read thus – or, more commonly, was interpreted in a particular way – did not mean that everybody agreed. Experience of the law and legal consciousness was widespread. 'The legal mentality', writes Harriss, 'was already displacing the chivalric'.[31] So too was respect for the law, to which most landholders resorted in preference to violence. On the ground, the law was no absolute standard. There was no definitive code. It was uncertain, adversarial, costly, all or nothing. Some statutes passed unenforced, some of relatively recent date were discarded as out of date and yet others were considered counter-productive in particular localities. Conflicting laws and the various courts offered alternative ways of proceeding: it was not uncommon for the same suit to be pursued in different courts. Suitors and lawyers alike made the most of technicalities, overlapping jurisdictions and tactics to advantage their clients. Processes could be manipulated and subverted, although perhaps only so far. Many, perhaps most, parties preferred settlement out of court. Court actions could be suspended in favour of less formal mediation and arbitration. Litigation was a game. Both parties in a lawsuit almost invariably supposed themselves to be right. Lawyers were as likely to be seen as fomentors of quarrels and self-interested oppressors as peacemakers. On occasion the Commons themselves wished to exclude lawyers from their ranks.

Conceptions of the law varied with class, locality and occupation. It was the contention of king and lawyers that their activities benefited the poor and defenceless. The peasants of 1381 were hostile to both the law and lawyers, whom Tyler actually wanted dead, so that 'all things would then be regulated by the decrees of the common people'.[32] What he evidently meant was that peasant notions of law – their version of natural law, justice, fairness and equity – did not coincide with that of the law as practised by lawyers and that it should prevail. What he meant by the 'law of Winchester', which alone should remain, is ambiguous: one possible interpretation, that of the Domesday Book, the 'book of Winchester', was already frequently appealed to by rural communities across southern England who believed that it established their claims to ancient demesne and hence exemption from villeinage.[33] What was sought elsewhere, at St Albans, Bury, etc., was the righting of specific local wrongs. Green argues cogently for local preferences for their own law, for local resistance to intrusive royal law and hostility to its agents.[34] Such conceptions of the law, to those who asserted them, were just as legitimate and were hence enforced. The indictment of Henry VI's favourites by Cade's rebels in 1450 and the execution of Richard II's ministers in 1381 aped the procedures of the common law even if the law that the rebels applied did not conform to that of parliament or the royal courts.

Everywhere, of course, had its own law and customs, enshrined in collections of town ordinances and the practice of the manorial courts. The different inheritance customs and provisions for widows in adjoining manors illustrate the point. They were subordinate to royal justice and statute law and were slowly eroded by parliamentary legislation. Such intrusion was sometimes resisted. Jurors were reluctant to impose the death penalty, to indict their neighbours, or to answer all the articles tendered to them. Jurors who convicted neighbours of misdemeanours carrying fines balked at sending them to the gallows for felony. Their disapproval of informers is demonstrated by a 98 per cent acquittal rate.[35] They resisted new national conceptions of law that attacked their local interests. National laws protected the king's deer, but forest dwellers unashamedly took them, as a matter of course and necessity: 'Other shift have not we', declared Robin Hood.[36] Henry V found it impossible, in practice, to secure convictions for piracy from Devonshire jurors of sea captains, whose activities were acceptable and indeed praiseworthy locally. Instead westcountrymen petitioned parliament against the statute of truces (1414), which had made treason of their piracy, and secured its repeal in 1416.[37] The border clans of Redesdale and Tynedale lived by preying on the Scots, regardless of treaties or truces. Whatever the national law, border-reiving, poaching and highway robbery were not regarded as crimes on the northern borders, in the royal forests or in the pass of Alton. Robin Hood could be regarded as a hero. That certain types of crime (Professor Hanawalt's 'fur-collar crime')[38] were particularly associated with the aristocracy indicates that these did not destroy their reputations. This is what historians call *social crime*. Within a common framework of respect and preference for peaceful settlements, the law cannot be viewed purely through the eyes of the lawyers.

Crime varied from time to time and place to place. By our standards it appears endemic and blatant: 'Early Lancastrian England was not a well-ordered society', concludes Professor Allmand; 'violence was prevalent in late medieval society', declares Dr Kleineke.[39] This was not the perception of contemporaries who demanded, Lander wisely observes, 'that public order should not fall below some rather vague level which was generally regarded as tolerable'.[40] Their vociferous complaints in parliament may tell us that standards fell short at times, but not all the time. Most probably there was a steady improvement in law and order in the fourteenth and fifteenth centuries, but this is impossible to substantiate. The number of lawsuits and prosecutions appears to rise, but this perhaps was because offences increased with new legislation, because society itself repudiated activities hitherto anti-social rather than illegal. Repeated claims of lawlessness may indicate reduced tolerance rather than increased crime. Litigants constantly resorted to the courts instead of (or in addition to) violence. Yet not all of the new remedies enacted (and rightly hailed as innovative by Professor Bellamy[41]) were implemented much or indeed at all. More records need not mean more violence.[42] Much that we penalise today was not yet criminal and fell within the wider medieval definitions of acceptable behaviour. Disorder in particular areas fluctuated and some were worse than others: 'examples of awful violence abound among the south-western gentry'.[43] Yet there was no breakdown. Society and the courts continued to operate, peaceably for the most part. Perceptions varied.

Perceptions of government

Government can be perceived in many different ways. Supposedly it was ordained by God to impose order on the governed and hence for the common good. To kings it was both natural and their instrument of rule. To many others, it was the source of benefits, something they could manage and manipulate. For others again, the governed, it was arbitrary, exploitative and oppressive, something to exclude, resist, subvert or otherwise mitigate. Often it was considered corrupt.

Everybody subscribed to the commonweal. It is, and was, the most flexible of terms. The revolutionary Commonwealth government of the 1650s, for instance, differs markedly from the loose federation of Commonwealth countries or the Commonwealth of Australia that exists today. In the fifteenth century, the public interest was enshrined in the commonweal. That the commonweal was the objective of good government was agreed by everyone, from kings and ministers to commoners. However it was an ambiguous term capable of different interpretations. Governments typically identified the commonweal with

126

themselves, with the status quo that they represented and maintained. It justified their direction of affairs. It was used to urge everyone to pull together for the common purposes that governments had selected. In their hands, or when deployed in parliament or by academics, it was harmonious, unifying and essentially passive. The parliamentary Commons was concerned primarily with legislation that benefited all, what came under the Tudors to be the commonwealth business that was distinguished from matters of state. In 1485 there were two debates 'for the commonweal': one, over two days, sought remedies against counterfeit coin 'that reigns in the land deceiving the king's liege people'.[44] Next century the commonweal was to be the clarion call of those seeking to improve the Tudor economy and society in the interests of all.[45]

For fifteenth-century reformers and opponents, on the other hand, the commonweal was a touchstone, a measure against which the regime's deficiencies could be judged. They usually harked back as an inspiration to earlier precedents. Whatever was wrong with the commonweal, even in areas outside the normal purview of the state, could be held to the government's account in a thoroughly modern way. Governments were seen as responsible for everyone's prosperity and were blamed whenever times were economically adverse. Subjects often expected governments actively to pursue the common good, though not yet, unlike their Tudor counterparts, to engage in social and economic engineering. The commonweal already had revolutionary connotations. In the hands of reformers it could be a subversive and even explosive concept. York claimed in 1450 to interpret the commonweal and to act in its name and subsequently placed the commonweal above his allegiance: the *Somnium Vigilantis* refuted this ordering of priorities.[46] The term was open to interpretation and could mean different things to different men. The commonweal was invoked by both sides a decade later, first by Warwick and Clarence against Edward IV and in favour of reforms, and then by the king himself, for whom their objective was 'the final destruction of his most royal person and the subversion of this his realm and the commonweal of the same'.[47] The commonweal to which Richard III so confidently appealed in 1483–4 carried different connotations according to the audience – the corporations or mob of London, Lord Neville, parliament or county elites – and whether he was writing as duke, protector or king.[48] Was Richard numbered among 'these false persons which hath reigned many days amongst us' against whom the Commons railed in 1485?[49] The commonweal was alternatively interpreted in monarchical, aristocratic or even democratic terms. Just how democratic, however, was Cade's commonweal? One wonders whether already the 'poorer and meaner sort' were excluded from the commonwealth as they were by the seventeenth-century Levellers? Just how poor were the poor whom Gloucester cultivated? Surely his master of requests catered only for those with some property?

Acceptable and effective royal government demanded good and wholesome counsel for the king. Though free to seek it where he chose, we have already seen that he was hedged about by conventions and also by alternative expectations. Parliament and subjects agreed that counsellors should be *sufficient*. They should also be representative. Under Henry IV, during Henry VI's minority, and in his first protectorate, balanced councils representative of the first two estates – the lords spiritual and temporal and the Commons – were set up in preference to either a council of magnates or of administrators, though both were always present. There was a convention that it was the most senior of his subjects – 'the great nobility of the blood royal' – who were a king's most appropriate councillors, his 'natural councillors'.[50] Such men could afford to be independent and need not exploit the opportunity to enrich themselves. Lesser men were out for what they could get and were too easily overawed. Nobody was more appropriate during the 1450s than York, so he himself considered and so many others in many stations of life also supposed. York did not so much offer his services as councillor – chief councillor – in 1450 as force himself on the king. Two successive dukes of Gloucester in 1422 and 1483 considered themselves entitled to be protectors and chief councillors to their under-age royal nephews. It was therefore those of lower rank, such as the former Lancastrian retainers whom Henry IV elevated into councillors, who were most likely to be thought unworthy. Cade's rebels and York alike disparaged those councillors 'brought up of nought',[51] yet they were for the most part aristocratic, if not from the highest echelons, and included two bishops. Amongst them were men of knightly, baronial and even comital stock, some of whom had behind them long and indeed distinguished careers in royal service both in peace and war.

The king was ultimately entitled to his free will; as God's representative he was above direct criticism. If his rule was evil, therefore, the convention from the thirteenth century onwards was that it was not he himself who was at fault, but his evil councillors. The solution was to substitute good and sufficient councillors: in practical terms, men of substance and experience, his natural councillors. The old evil councillors should be punished as traitors. Fear of denunciation as an evil councillor, of being held to account by parliament or the people, or even of being murdered were uppermost among the councillors of York's first protectorate. They had no wish to be labelled evil councillors nor to suffer the possible consequences. When Lord Cromwell demanded safe access and egress as a councillor, he was voicing a more general concern;[52] many councillors, as Fortescue observed, 'the people have oftentimes slain for the miscounselling of their sovereign lord'. It was difficult if not impossible to combine the role of the king's councillor with public accountability. They could 'in no thing restrain his power, liberty or prerogative'. Although Henry IV's parliaments insisted on approving the king's council, they never actually nominated it. On occasion, it appears that councillors tried to act in the public interest – the interests of the crown rather than the actual incumbent king – when trying to restrict Henry IV's profligacy or Henry VI's patronage.

Fortescue wrestled with the problem of counsel. He argued that it was a breach of prerogative for the king to 'put from him and alienate the same [royal possessions] to his own hurt and harm'. What was needed was an independent council to restrain the king. Fortescue recommended this to the Readeption government. No king should be 'counselled by men of his chamber, of his household, nor other which can not counsel him', nor by private individuals who had got themselves appointed, nor by magnates:

> it is to be considered, how that the old council in England, which was most of great lords that more attended to their own matters than to the good universal profit. And therefore procured themselves to be of the council, which was near of as great charge to the king as this council shall be and no thing of such profit.

Instead he wanted 'a worshipful and a notable council established' numbering thirty-two, twelve churchmen, twelve laymen, to include only eight peers (four spiritual or temporal) or less, to be selected 'of the most wise and indifferent that can be chosen in all the land' and motivated by 'the prosperity and honour of the land [and] the surety and welfare of the king'.[53] He wanted a council of experts instead of the council of great men that he considered self-interested. The Readeption was too brief to allow for a fair trial. Obviously Fortescue's prescription conflicted with the perceptions of peers and others about their role. It was also anachronistic in its emphasis on the clergy and its neglect of the realities of power. It did not attract kings, who did not want independent councillors who limited their actions, but servants who did as they were told. Whatever the theory, kings regarded councillors as servants. They wanted advice on how to fulfil their objectives, not advice against them, their tasks performed and their commands obeyed. Household men gave the counsel that Fortescue deplored because kings invited, valued or tolerated it. This was as true of Henry IV, with his Lancastrian imports, as of Bray, Belknap, Empson and Dudley under Henry VII. Henry IV valued lesser men, more dependent on himself and committed to his partisan Lancastrian interests, whilst Henry VII favoured technocrats, more useful, more dependent and more willing agents of unscrupulous policies. Nobody wanted counsel purely from appointed professionals except the professionals themselves.

Similarly Fortescue thought that service to the king should be exclusive. Modern historians, who tend to be the king's men, have often agreed.[54] Fortescue was a centralist who saw rule in terms of Westminster and not the necessity for acquiescence, co-operation and assent in the provinces on which mixed monarchy relied. Exclusivity of service would indeed have removed from royal service certain conflicts of seigneurial with royal interest, if this were thought desirable. Such dual service however was a means whereby lords exerted influence on the king and the king on lords. Exclusivity could therefore have severed kings from opinion on the ground, very dangerously: Fortescue, notes Watts, was condemning 'the very essence of late medieval government'.[55] Moreover such exclusively royal retainers were nowhere more than an element than in the localities: they were favourites, whose special status was liable to disrupt local power structures temporarily without replacing them. Exclusive retention of duchy officers in the north midlands by Lord Hastings, who was not active locally, may have prevented the interpolation of any seigneurial hegemony,[56] but left politics to be transacted at a lower level. In proposing that royal institutions should serve solely the king's needs, Fortescue failed to appreciate the government's service role, the realities of power and the manner in which pursuit of the king's needs could infringe the interests of subjects. Henry VII's emphasis on the pursuit of royal rights and the mulcting of his subjects, often for technical offences or no offences at all, 'light matters only upon surmise', offended contemporary notions of justice, even those of his agent Edmund Dudley, who identified eighty-four cases of injustice.[57] Henry VIII wisely chose to reconcile himself with the political nation by renouncing and punishing his father's ministers, thus staving off any explosion – had, of course, one been looming. Historians cannot know the might-have-beens of history.

Fortescue's critique started from the financial difficulties of Henry VI and his consequent political impotence. To rebuild royal revenues meant reconstructing royal power, reasserting royal authority over even the greatest subjects and removing any need for taxation. What stood in the way, so he believed, was *patronage*: kings' insistence on giving away their wealth to those they favoured. Nor was he alone: the somewhat earlier poems *Mum and Sothsegger* and *Richard the Redeless* took the same line. We are inclined to agree. We live in an age of equal opportunities for all, which bans discrimination on grounds of race, sex, religion, disability or age, in which promotion and success on merit is preferred to privilege, often indeed objectively measured through competitive examinations, personality tests, referees and interviews, and in which nepotism is frowned upon. 'It is not what you know but who you know' has supposedly been consigned to the dustbin of history. Generally we consider patronage to be bad and therefore believe that it was bad also in the past. Fifteenth-century historians have used it to 'characterise the workings of the social, political and governmental institutions of an entire society'.[58] We have been too hasty. 'Is patronage inherently a corrupt thing?', asked Professor Hurstfield, before concluding that it is morally neutral.[59] Patronage is merely a mechanism, like any other, comparable to lordship, kinship and neighbourliness, which is capable of good use and abuse. 'Patronage worked for good and bad', writes Richmond, 'depending upon the particular circumstances of persons, place, time and matter involved.'[60] Patronage was 'the essential lubricant of government' that only became an issue when it was not working.[61] Inevitably patronage appeared differently to those who secured it than to those who were disappointed. So, too, today. The losers are always dissatisfied: with all our regulations, the wrong people still advance.

Such safeguards did not exist in the fifteenth century, when superiors seeking service and inferiors in need of employment or advancement generally relied on patronage. Not everyone could be rewarded: some had to be disappointed. If resentment were to be avoided, patronage had to be balanced. Because the Lancastrian retainers of Henry IV and the northerners of Richard III were cliques, they were resented and perhaps lost their patron as much loyalty as they brought. Jealousy contributed to demands that royal favourites be stripped of their rewards both in 1450 and 1469. With patronage came conflicts of interest. Kings insisted on their right to patronise whom they chose to whatever extent they chose. Their main criteria were often political. Their need to patronise particular individuals did not necessarily correlate with deserts, merits or with the best performance of the functions of an office, and might conflict with the criteria of suitability and the public interest applied by their critics. Offices were treated as sinecures, exercised through deputies and exploited for profit. When magnates interceded with the king for others, it was gratitude towards themselves from the recipient and the latter's service to themselves that they sought. Service to the king came second. Often the king rewarded clients of magnates because he wanted influence with them. Buying loyalty and service, through grants of land or annuities, reduced the king's income and made him dependent on taxation. Henry IV and VI wanted to increase or maintain their patronage, whereas the Commons wanted it curbed and revoked through acts of resumption. Edward IV, in contrast, used resumptions to review outdated patronage and to renew grantees' gratitude through provisos of exemption. What was excessive was a matter of personal perception. The emoluments of judges, for life only and one office alone, were enough for anyone to Fortescue's mind.[62] That courtiers should have their grants resumed was common ground between Cade's rebels and successive houses of Commons. They gave overwhelming priority to financial issues, born of a self-interested hostility to taxation, which they equated with the public interest, and Fortescue had a professional's preference for government by professionals. Neither took full account of the political role of patronage. Kings had to balance issues in a manner that Fortescue did not fully understand or care about.

Fortescue was right however in the importance he attached to taxation, which was a highly controversial subject in the fifteenth century. Foreign wars required taxation, which parliaments were persuaded to vote, but never indefinitely, even for Henry V. The doctrine of *necessity* obliged all subjects to offer supplies for their own defence. Actually, however, the Commons were reluctant to respond, especially for unsuccessful wars, and became less willing as the century progressed. Certain towns secured permanent reductions in their tax liabilities on grounds of poverty, sometimes dubious. In 1449–50 and on most subsequent occasions the taxes voted were inadequate. There were repeated experiments with new taxes designed to shrug off some of the burden on to others. In 1404, 1453 and 1472 the vote was conditional on the campaign taking place.[63] Kings even had to manage without. For ordinary expenses, it was argued, kings should rely on their own resources. For Henry IV, this was the duchy of Lancaster. Grants should be resumed. Whereas Henry VI resisted resumptions, Edward IV engaged in them voluntarily in 1461, 1465, 1467 and 1473. Hence the universal popularity of Edward IV's declaration of intent in 1467 'to live upon my own and not to charge my subjects but in great and urgent causes, concerning more the weal of themselves and the defence of this land, rather than mine own pleasure'.[64] Thus softened up, the Commons willingly voted taxation for the invasion of France next year, which never happened. Although they succumbed to Edward's persuasions for a further invasion of France in 1472–5, they experimented again with ineffective taxes and failed to vote enough or as much as they could afford, which was secured, instead, by a forced gift (benevolence). 'Such attitudes meant that from the 1470s until well into the reign of Henry VIII the kings of England could not afford an aggressive foreign policy which involved anything like prolonged campaigning'.[65] Edward had been three years at war with Scotland in 1483 when he obtained parliamentary support for a third time for war with France, but he could not obtain a lay subsidy; he did extract a tenth from the clergy. Richard III curried favour with the propertied by abolishing benevolences, but subsequently aroused hostility by reviving them. Henry VII, the beneficiary of recovery from the deep late-fifteenth-century slump, secured three votes of taxation in 1489, 1492 and 1497.[66]

Hostility to taxation, especially for unsuccessful war, was shared by the peasants of 1381, critics of Henry IV, Cade's rebels in 1450 and by a whole series of subsequent popular insurgents, who cannot easily be shown to have subscribed to the doctrine of necessity. It made them grouch.[67] They objected when Henry IV 'took their goods and did not pay for them'. Popular objections to taxation burgeoned even though the tax-burden was low and taxpayers suffered only relative deprivation. Edward IV's promise of 1467 coupled with his misappropriated tax became a charge against him in 1469.[68] It may have been more important than just one count among many, to judge from the king's apprehension of popular disturbances in 1475, when he remitted an uncollected instalment following his peace with France. In taxing themselves more easily, the Tudor Commons lost touch with the commons proper. The Yorkshire Rebellion of 1489, which recruited 20,000 northcountrymen, was a response to unprecedented taxation that ignored past exemptions: the Commons had again sought to redistribute the burden from themselves. Similarly the Cornish Rising of 1497, which aroused the whole west country and brought insurgents as far as Blackheath, was primarily a reaction against taxation. Although quite light, this subsidy was newfangled and universal, touched those who did not traditionally pay tax: it was these factors, combined with impressment of ships and men which reduced local capacity to pay, that prompted the explosion.[69] Whilst resistance to parliamentary taxation was perhaps predominantly a plebeian phenomenon, it is striking that aristocrats, townsmen and churchmen alike were unwilling taxpayers – necessity, it seems, was an obligation reluctantly acknowledged – and that one at least one leader in 1489 and many rebels in 1497 were gentry.[70] Resistance to taxation coincided with revolt in 1450 and was an element in insurgency under Edward IV, but thereafter the two separated. If still unhappy about taxes, the elite continued to vote them, though less than kings wanted and less than they could afford: hence the Amicable Grant (1523), the Forced Gift (1614) and the Forced Loan (1626), and the gradual but continuous erosion of assessments. The populace, however, still rebelled on occasion: indeed the tax revolt was a distinctively popular style of uprising well beyond the Wars of the Roses, which is, indeed, almost at the beginning of this story.[71]

Perceptions of treason and corruption

Treason existed to protect the king. To at least some commons, it protected the commonweal. The definition of the lawyers differs markedly from the conceptions of kings, aristocrats and commons. The statute of 1352 had been too narrow for Richard II, who had expanded it to include exciting the Commons to remedy or reform matters touching the king's person, government or regality. Such lengths were found tyrannical in 1399, when complaints against new and unsuspected treasons that one could not guard against secured reversion to the 1352 statute. Appeals of treason and treason trials in domestic cases by the court of chivalry were abolished.[72] The definition of treason was extended by the king's justices to embrace seditious words and imagining the king's death by necromancy. Men were executed for both offences, but these were resisted by jurors and famously, in the Burdet case, by the king's own brother Clarence. In 1414 breaking a truce was made treasonable and in 1423–4 breaking out of prison was made treason to destroy Sir John Mortimer. In both cases there was resistance to the new counts, neither of which endured, both by jurors and in parliament: the king's legal teams and their subjects evidently saw issues differently.[73] In 1404 the Lords decided that although Northumberland was in concert with his rebel son Hotspur, he had not actually committed treason, but merely trespass. Much later, even Henry VIII failed to have Thomas Lord Dacre convicted by his peers. Cade's rebels in 1450 and York thereafter considered their actions not to be treasonable, but legitimate protest and petitioning.[74] Opinions in particular cases differed. Whatever might have been had he come to trial in 1447, many doubted that

Duke Humphrey was a traitor. So too with Clarence in 1478. 'Were he faulty were he faultless', wrote Thomas More.[75]

Kings were dissatisfied with such narrow definitions, which were progressively extended by judicial interpretations of what contributed to the eventual death of a king. Henry IV, Edward IV and Henry VII found it convenient to 'ordain' the penalties of treason against enemies in the field without recourse to trial by peers in parliament, where defendants might be acquitted. Henry VI's courtiers overreached themselves in 1450 if they really said that traitors were whoever the king wills or laid treason charges against those whose forfeited possessions they coveted.[76] Doubts about York's fidelity, given the 'strange language' of the commons and his own uninvited return in force from Ireland, were more excusable: Henry VI excused them. Edward IV in 1461 and Henry VII in 1485 had enemies attainted for actions prior to their usurpations. Doubters were vindicated in 1495 when the *de facto* act confirmed that loyalty to a *de facto* king was not treasonable.

Different kings viewed traitors differently. If the Despensers had dared to execute a prince of the blood royal in 1322, Richard II in 1397 and Henry VI in 1447 apparently balked at show trials of successive dukes of Gloucester. Edward IV's execution of Clarence was shocking even in the context of the routine bloodletting that followed the battles of the Wars of the Roses. Royal blood several times saved Edmund Earl of March (d. 1425), Edward (d. 1415) and Richard Duke of York (d. 1460): the latter indeed thought it rendered him incapable of treason.[77] If some treasons were beyond reconciliation, Henry IV and V, Edward IV and even Henry VII restored repentant traitors and their heirs. Henry V and Henry VII, however, were merciless to their own traitors, each having executed in Henry Lord FitzHugh and Sir William Stanley intimates apparently guilty only of misprision of treason – mere knowledge and concealment. Perceptions of treason and loyalty amongst lesser men also depended upon one's political stance. It was necessary to reconcile to their successors those of honour and tender conscience who had sworn allegiance that Richard II had abdicated, that Henry VI had broken the 1460 *Accord* and that Edward V was illegitimate. Sir Thomas Erpingham's support for Bolingbroke's invasion was justified by the accession of Henry IV and his role in repressing the Ricardian earls in 1400 earned him the praise of parliament. To unreconciled Ricardians he was 'the traitor Erpingham'.[78]

The statute of 1352 and the revolution of 1399 did not define accroaching the king's power as treason. This weapon was used by critics of royal favourites before 1399 and was still apparently required thereafter. Something closely akin to it was current in 1450. Most of the charges against the king's favourite Suffolk fell short of the statutory definition, yet it was treason with which he was charged by the Commons of one parliament and for which corruption of his blood was sought in the next, treason for which the shipmen executed him, and notorious treason that Cade presumed. Cade's rebels judged the king's advisers by results: by the loss of France, the commons' misery and the misappropriation of public funds. They adjudged them traitors for denouncing 'Good Duke Humphrey' as a traitor, for attributing designs on the throne to York and for regarding the rebels themselves as traitors. It was treason in their eyes to deny them access to the king. They meant business: not only did they eliminate several ministers, but they formally indicted other courtiers as traitors in the areas under their control. Cade's men wanted them tried and punished, as indeed did York, who accepted the validity of the indictments. 'Away, traitors, away', cried Cade.[79]

Professor Green has demonstrated antecedents to such attitudes. Treason already had a meaning – was, indeed, a keyword – before it was appropriated by statute in 1352 to protect the king and remained current thereafter. Petty treason, the betrayal of one's master, was not a variant of high treason, but incorporated the original meaning. The essence was betrayal of trust – even within the family, even by a superior of an inferior, even by a king. Richard II, who reneged on a pardon, was both a perjurer and a traitor. Chaucer's parson identifies a giver of 'wicked counsel ... as a traitor, for he deceiveth him that trusts in him'. The rebels of 1381 executed the king's chief justice, chancellor and councillors as traitors. They were loyal and acting legitimately. They saw themselves as 'true commons', just as the Lollards dubbed themselves 'true preachers', 'true priests' and 'true Christian men'. Cade's rebels, also 'true commons', associated themselves with 'true lords' and 'true blood'.[80] These were ominous precedents for York's 'true lords' and 'true councillors' the following autumn.[81]

The original local grievances of the Kentish insurgents were progressively refined through Cade's manifestos into issues of more general appeal. Three such charges were then elevated by Cade and York into more general principles, which in practice revived the notion of accroachment of the crown and equated it with treason. Evil counsel, first of all, was treasonable. To tell the king that he was above the law, in breach of his coronation oath, was the 'highest point of treason that any subject may commit against his prince, to make him live in perjury'. Secondly, Cade's condemnation of those soliciting grants from the king to his loss was elevated by York into subversion of the law, 'the most treason on earth that can be thought', since offenders thereby impoverished and disinherited the king. And, thirdly, the deprivation of his French realm 'caused our sovereign lord to live contrarily, the which is the most treason that may be done to any prince'.[82] None of these strained definitions can be accommodated with statute law. They represent instead an alternative, public, notion of betrayal. Treason in their eyes was not merely an offence against the king, but was also – or rather – against the commonweal and the common profit of the realm. It was treacherous to act against the public interest.

Some popular charges of treason relate to offences that today we would call corrupt. Every era witnesses charges of *corruption*, which entail the subversion of public decision-making and justice to private advantage, typically private profit from public office. Hurstfield devised a threefold test of corruption: was money given; did it thereby damage the state; how and why?[83] Corruption is not an absolute concept and has changed enormously over five centuries. Today government central and local must operate in the public interest, not to the private advantage or profit of politicians or civil servants. Justice must not be bought. Many rules prohibit bribery, prevent payments to MPs for asking parliamentary questions, register their external income and ensure that personal interests are excluded from public decisions. Even today, despite the Neil committee on public life, lines (Hurstfield's 'frontiers') are drawn between what is permissible and what is not, so – for example – some public bodies are omitted and MPs are allowed external income from other employment. When fifteenth-century people wrote of corruption, though they did not use the term, they drew their lines in different places. Maintaining someone else's lawsuit, which we forbid, was legal, but certain associated practices were outlawed. Fees were charged for all documents issued by central government, a tariff being imposed in 1433; fines were charged in some cases and suitors commonly paid extra to clerks (whose salaries were inadequate) for speed, enrolments or decoration of documents and for extra services such as searches and copies undertaken on a free-lance basis. At the decision-making level, royal favourites, ministers and councillors received annuities, gifts and free breakfasts for their advice, patronage and intercession. The term 'corruption', in Hurstfield's words, is 'subjective', or rather relative and subject to conventions that change over time. Far from subverting the public interest, a gift may be merely 'a payment to an official ... that is the accepted convention'.[84] It was a necessary supplement to an inadequate salary.

The most fundamental difference is that judges and officers were royal servants not public servants, and were expected to act in the interests of the king, not some abstract public interest. What if the king's officer served the public interest to the king's loss?

Fifteenth-century kings accepted that service and office had to be worthwhile if it were to be undertaken. If the pay alone was insufficient, as it always was for the men of substance who were preferred, there needed to be other compensations, such as authority and perquisites, inevitably either at the king's unacknowledged expense or rendered by his subjects. Accountants delayed liveries of receipts and used them for other purposes. Captains claimed pay for deserters and were less than assiduous in filling gaps in the ranks. Menials claimed used items as perquisites and sold off leftovers, sometimes being tempted to include what was not yet waste; officers of the ordnance and navy suffered similar temptations. Royal parks and other facilities were exploited by the officers. Hence the expenses of government, especially the household, tended to rise independently of the service rendered. From time to time therefore, and indeed repeatedly, kings tried to draw lines between what was acceptable to them and what was not. Edward IV, it appears, found the level of profit of Lord Treasurer Essex was acceptable, but that of Lord Treasurer Kent was not.[85] Household ordnances of 1445, the mid-1470s and 1478 sought to regulate the royal household, defining duties and acceptable perquisites at great length and reinforcing daily and weekly the most meticulous accounting systems. Honest declarations of receipts and expenses by the king's caterers could be taken for granted. It was to restrict payments of wages to real men in real garrisons that Henry V devised his quarterly system of muster and review. Plenty of captains, it appears, saw no harm in abuses, favoured some men over others as York was accused about 1446, or spent the receipts on other non-military purposes.[86] A remarkable range of officers were sworn not to assent to anything against the king's interests, to try and stop such occurrences and, failing that, to report them to the royal council.

The late medieval judicial system differed in many particulars from our own. A fair trial and justice could not be presumed. Payments were commonly made by suitors to jurors and judges, to sheriffs and court officials, with predictable effects on the verdict. Such payments could not be stopped, kings realised, but they could be restricted.

> You shall not take by you or by any other person privily nor openly any gift or reward of gold or of silver nor of any other thing which might turn you to profit, but if it be meat or

drink or of little value, of any man that shall have any plea or process before you so long as before yourself those pleas and processes shall [be] so hanging nor after for that [particular] cause. And that you shall take no fee nor robe of any person great or small in any case but of the king himself.

Bias and perversion of justice should be prevented.

You shall not maintain by yourself nor by none other privily nor openly any plea or quarrel hanging in the king's court or elsewhere in the country. And you shall not delay any person common right for the letters of the king or of any other person or for common cause.

In such cases, indeed, the judge should ignore the letter and apply the law.[87] Such rules seem strikingly modern, but diverge nevertheless from modern practice. A free meal was acceptable, restrictions applied only to the particular case, and it was the crown as well as the parties that the judge needed to resist. That such rules were required tells its own story. Moreover the oath of office was impossibly idealistic: all kings intervened in such cases.[88] However much judges such as Fortescue and Husy might assert their probity, some continued to be retained,[89] to act as feoffees and to take sides in land disputes, without punishment.

Unjust judgements obviously had victims. So too had the extension of royal patronage to the private advantage of favourites by procuring the condemnation to forfeiture of the innocent, as was alleged in 1450 and 1469, the levying of inflated charges for royal service, the uneven application of purveyance and the delay of payments to suppliers. Apart from being bad in themselves, they brought the king into disrepute with his subjects. 'Nothing you shall take of my person', swore exchequer barons, 'to do wrong or right to delay or for to deliver or delay the people the which have to do before you.' Nor might the law be biased in its application or due payments to suppliers delayed.[90] It was because such conduct occurred that attempts were made to stop or limit it. Yet popular perceptions of corruption commonly went further. There was nothing illegal about paying MPs, appointing tax collectors or indeed paying councillors to impede justice, yet all were regarded by Cade (and no doubt ourselves) as bribes. To impose the death penalty for taking 'any bribe for any bill of supplication or repetition or for speeding or letting (delaying) a case' was extremely harsh, still more so for the process of the green wax or purveyance, which were normal if unpopular facets of contemporary government.[91] Perhaps there ought to be have been a law against such practices, but there was not. If government and parliament did not share Cade's perception, the general public apparently did.

Historians have started from the presumption that the 1352 statute corresponded to contemporary understanding. A century later it still did not. A shared language conceals alternative perceptions. Alternative notions of treason were current and the eventual victory of the royal version lies beyond the scope of this book. The topics examined here are representative of many others where perceptions differed that are not explicitly discussed.

8

BASTARD FEUDALISM

An aristocrat was a monarch in miniature. Like the king, it was his will that governed his establishment, his initiative that mattered, and his decision how his resources were exploited and exercised. He had physical, emotional and other needs, the means to satisfy them, enough leisure and money to indulge his whims, sufficient staff and dependants to fulfil his commands. He too possessed authority – the power to command – and a mass of varied patronage with which to purchase service.[1] Aristocrats had kinsmen and favourites too: it was to Sir William and Sir Robert Plumpton's advantage that successive earls of Northumberland regarded them as cousins, however distant, and addressed them as such, though the former was obviously disadvantaged in disputes with the earl's brother [in-law] William Gascoigne. An aristocrat was also constrained by standards and conventions and beset with duties, obligations and responsibilities which he could, in the last resort, refuse. No more than the king could he know about or indeed be interested in everything. His court was his household. He had his own council and councillors. He recruited, retained and rewarded the manpower he required through a series of mechanisms to which modern historians have given the name *bastard feudalism.*

Peers counted individually for more than gentlemen and commanded far more men per head. Yet the distinctions between the lesser nobility – the barons and viscounts – and the richer knights and esquires were titular rather than substantial, mattered most in parliament and at court, and conferred merely precedence in their particular locality. The gentry were more numerous, held altogether more land than the nobility, and collectively commanded more manpower – including more aristocrats – than the peerage. Even the most marginal were *lords, masters,* and *employers.* They were served by as well as serving as the retainers, officers, employees and servants of greater men. It was not possible for gentry, even for John Hopton,[2] to stand aside from bastard feudalism. Most aristocrats were merely gentlemen, often scarcely discernible in our records, possessed of a single house in a single locality and barely the £10 a year qualifying income of their rank. Such small establishments may have dispensed with officers and accounts: certainly no accounts survive. So-called small landowners such as John Brome of Baddesley Clinton (War.) and Richard Clervaux of Croft (Yorks.), with £50 a year in income, were not actually small at all. They tower above those with £10. They qualified for knighthood, to be JPs and sheriffs, electors and knights of the shire, and often officiated. They had several properties, perhaps several residences: they needed and could afford to delegate.

It is from the far fewer big establishments that historians generalise. We must multiply small households five, ten or fifty times to arrive at that of a peer and substitute for each multifunctional menial a whole department, each with a head: the master cook, master butler and master pantler. For a manor or two in one vicinity, substitute half a dozen across a county, fifty or several hundred across England and Wales, organised regionally into receiverships. Elevate genteel attendants into heads of county families and upgrade household officers from clerks to knights. Greater worship arose from the service of men of honour. Magnates had enormous interests, geographically scattered, which they could not possibly manage or even visit themselves. They headed elaborate administrations generating extensive records. It was the scale, not the underlying relationships, that differed.

Aristocrats were adversely affected by the youth and inexperience, incompetence, ill-health and senility of any hereditary system. Fortunately their bureaucrats could run their estates without seigneurial intervention, although they were reluctant to take real decisions. Even though physically absent, the landholder remained the authority and initiative that moved his administration. Unfortunately we know little about this. Though everyone had a seal and the great had several, we possess no registers of out-letters or files of warrants like those of monasteries or the crown. We can observe John Lord Howard reckoning regularly with his officials and the 3rd duke of Buckingham checking estate records: as the only examples, we believe them untypical. It was the 1st duke who made the costly decision to erect a new garderobe to the chapel tower (£86 17s. 3½d) and to raise a wall (£20 9s. 3d) at Newport Castle in 1447–8. He received liveries at London and Stafford and charged to the same account his purchases of harness bought from a London saddler.[3] Aristocratic administrations were as awkward about every penny as those of crown. Every entry of decayed rent in a minister's account has a story about it. The rent was part of the charge for which the accountant was liable. We can be confident of the assiduity with which a tenant was sought, how reluctantly a lower rent was conceded or a failure to re-let was acknowledged. Such problems were not allowed at once, but were included in the arrears, then deferred or respited and only eventually conceded, on the lord's authority.

Structures and categories of service

At the heart of the aristocratic connection, as at the heart of government, was the aristocrat, his family and his household.[4] The household was a mini-court. It was there that the aristocrat lived, ate, slept and played. There also were his spouse and offspring, his unmarried siblings and less frequently, perhaps by the meal, his guests. Even the smallest household contained personal attendants – by definition genteel – and the menials, who cooked, brewed, baked, cleaned, groomed or combined several functions. All were male, all lived in except for the ubiquitous laundress, and all wore livery – gowns of a standard quality and hue. Committed manpower for any occasion, they made the necessary show at feasts and rites of passage, on journeys, for defence against burglars and attackers, and potentially also for offence. That Lord Strange 'keeps as great a Christmas as was ever in this country' at Lathom (Lancs.) reinforced the confidence in his 'especial good lord' both of his secretary and those resident thereabout.[5]

The household was the main charge upon a householder's estates. It was 'an investment in social standing'.[6] Aristocrats were rentiers, with little interest in what happened on the ground, whose estates were run for them by subordinate ministers overseen by superior officers of aristocratic rank: stewards, supervisors, receivers, receivers-general and auditors. *Legisperiti*, men learned in the law, were retained to advise and to represent. Attorneys and the more senior estate officials commonly sat on his council, which inspected, discussed, reviewed and decreed, often in their lord's absence, but always ultimately at his behest. All such officers were salaried, normally 2d a day (£3 0s. 8d per annum) at the lower levels, £5–£20 per annum in the higher echelons: sums that attracted gentry of different means and often permitted exercise by deputy. Many deputies and farmers of the demesnes were gentry also. Estate management was not the limit of their functions. All the lord's servants were available for any service.

Manorial courts were proof of lordship – of authority. Almost all aristocrats were lords – of manors, hundreds, liberties, marcher lordships, even counties palatine – with authority and jurisdiction over others. Lordship, however limited and geographically circumscribed, reinforced pre-eminence of rank. It demanded respect and conferred authority. A lord was ruler of his manor, unquestionable and unchallengeable. Manors, lands and estates were sources not just of revenue, but of authority and even power – the command of men or *manrede*, at a time when power was to be measured in terms of manpower. Throughout the fifteenth century it was illegal for anyone to retain people below the rank of gentleman by fee or livery, whether they be their own tenants or anyone else's. Tenants, rustic peasants rather than feudal vassals, were attendant exclusively on their lords, mustered by their estate officers and deployed by their lords as escorts, for forcible entries and ambushes and in the battles of the civil wars, for which they were paid. Humphrey Duke of Buckingham was acting entirely legally in mustering his tenants at pay in the 1450s, albeit only sometimes for legal purposes.[7]

Household, tenants and officers were the maximum to which anybody not a peer could *legally* extend their connection. They also constituted the irreducible core of the smallest aristocratic connection. This was how a William Floyer or James Hyde raised companies of three and five archers for the invasion of France in 1475.[8] For great men, the household was the centre of a much wider connection. At the heart was the lord, surrounded by aristocrats, who accompanied and attended him at all times, entertained and advised him. They were the most committed and most numerous aristocratic retainers of any lords. Magnates had their chief officers, councillors and favourites: evidently Sir William Brandon was favourite (and *alter ego*) of the last Mowbray duke of Norfolk, whilst for Lady Joan Hungerford it was her household chaplain John Pratt who counted for most. Magnates like kings retired into their private quarters, themselves semi-public, rather than dining in hall and access was restricted. Guests visited every day, often with their own trains. Liveried servants, costly furnishings and plate, lavish helpings and elaborate ceremonial made for a magnificent display. Great households required greater houses: a handful of castles or houses were upgraded to fifteenth-century standards or constructed from scratch at great expense and many others were allowed to decay. If great households were more sedentary and moved less often than of yore, it was partly because there was nowhere for them to go.

There were two other ways in which a lord could extend his authority by adding to those committed to him others who were not his natural dependants. These were extraordinary retainers and those merely liveried. Insofar as they can be studied, distributions of livery were designed as short-term measures to extend retinues cheaply amongst those who were outside the connections listed above, such as the tenants of others and townsmen; one's own tenants were included. George Lord Bergavenny, uniquely, was twice indicted for liverying hundreds of Kentish rustics. In crises, such as the king's madness in 1454 when Buckingham had 2,000 Stafford knots made as livery badges,[9] nobody could afford to regard such rules. It was presumably not dukes themselves but their officers who actually distributed the robes and badges.

Extraordinary retainers, whether bound by contract (indentured retainers) or mere annuitants, were always peripheral to any connection. Their individual accretions of manpower could hardly match their lord's and originated anyway beyond his natural geographical sway. Some may indeed have been secondary connections, compatible with other ties or deliberately contracted those of influence with other lords. We can seldom tell. It is usually up to the personal judgement of historians which tie took priority, if any did: fees from both Warwick and Ferrers of Chartley need not imply a transfer from one lord to another. Fees imposed a duty at least to safeguard one's lord and save his life: hence the shocked laments both of John Skelton and William Peeris at Northumberland's murder in 1489.[10] Retainer did not supersede or supplant any previous ties. It was contracted in the light of existing ties and because the associated obligations were compatible with them.

Extraordinary retainers were valued because of their independent standing, the personal followings they brought with them – 290 famously in Walter Strickland's case in 1448 – and because they extended the area subject to their lord's authority. Their own connections and spheres of influence, though subsumed, remained intact. It was by formal contracts, for example, that Lord Audley was retained by the earl of Wiltshire in 1457, Lord Grey of Codnor (1464) by Lord Hastings, and the earl of Northumberland (1474) by the duke of Gloucester. Clusters of indentures sometimes survive for special reasons, such as York's bid for the English throne in 1460 and Warwick's campaigns against the northern Lancastrians in 1461–2.[11] Annuities are much more common.

Highly expensive to recruit and maintain, extraordinary retainers were never numerous. They declined in importance. Indentured retaining had virtually ceased before it was further restricted in 1468 and had disappeared before it was banned in 1504. Yet historians have preoccupied themselves with these secondary groups. Admittedly it was these also that concerned contemporary legislators. Service in households and tenancies of land were universal, natural, stable and inescapable features of contemporary society. To suppress them was to destroy society. Extraordinary retaining, however, need not be so disciplined. Short-term contracts were already forbidden, only retaining for life being allowed. Since 1390 retaining had been a privilege of the peerage, who had been allowed only to retain aristocrats: the Scottish marches, where gunners and other professionals were required, and royal campaigns abroad were exceptions. Surviving cases of illegal livery were infrequent, involved few individuals and probably faithfully represent activities that raised more objections than the actual numbers warrant. Whether or not it was in response to legislation, those peers who ceased to recruit non-resident gentry or to distribute livery were denying themselves nothing substantial.

Not altogether dissimilar were offices on large estates, which were increasingly filled by gentry and which multiplied over time, perhaps as a legitimate way of recruiting extraordinary retainers. Their political importance has generally been neglected. Such offices were normally granted to local men, whose standing reinforced that of the lord. In some places, distanced from the lord's principal estates and residence and where the lord was otherwise absent, such office-holders may have been essential for the lord's will to be executed. To recipients, such posts had four obvious attractions. They were a source of profit – often a significant accretion: £3 was not trivial to a gentleman or £10 to a knight, and there may have been other ancillary spin-offs, such as leases and *douceurs*. Some were sinecures, incomes without duties, or exercisable by deputy, leaving both a net gain and patronage: Sir William Plumpton readily deputised as steward of Knaresborough (Yorks.). They also brought authority and prestige. Subject to the lord's will, his tenants were attendant on the officer, at his command for his own purposes, and reflected on him the standing and prestige of his lord. In many stand-offs that may have sufficed. Both Warwick and Clarence expected Henry Vernon to mobilise their tenants in 1471. Like their sixteenth-century counterparts, aristocratic officers may already have counted as their own the tenants of the ecclesiastical institutions to which they were stewards. Finally, such officers had access to the lord's patronage, intercession with other lords and the king, and his good lordship.

To be served by the gentry was important to all lords. Contemporaries were impressed by the quality of servants – their relatively high rank – which enhanced a lord's status. Individually they were more genteel and doubtless militarily more effective. Their connections and their own resources were added to those of their lord. What is generally forgotten, however, is that their resources were *addi-*

tional to the lord's own. Lords had their own manpower. Their house-holds, tenants and officers were always the largest element in a connection, several or many times that of an indentured retainer or annuitant and committed solely to them. If lords sometimes formally contracted with retainers, they paid them significant proportions of their revenues only rarely – the exceptions being the uniquely wealthy and ambitious John of Gaunt and the heavily subsidised wardens of the Scottish marches.[12]

A final category were the professionals: the common, civil and canon lawyers, especially the former. Commonly feed with small annu-ities, heavily supplemented by pay and expenses whenever work was undertaken, these ranged from the local men of affairs, innocent of qualifications and much if any formal training, and attornies in the central courts, to the career common lawyers who had attended the inns of courts, had London practices and were eligible for or destined to become serjeants-at-law and judges. Whatever the statutes might say, Chief Justice Fairfax and Chief Baron Andrew were not alone in serving the Percies and the Hungerfords and noble arbitrators commonly called on the expertise of the king's justices.[13] Both at the bottom level, where Thomas Troponell financed his modest estate, and higher up, where Justice Townshend and Serjeant Kebell made their pile, the profits of law far exceeded those from farming. Lawyers were well placed to learn first of potential land-sales and exploit them before other people. They had the necessary resources because like modern consultants they served not one but many clients. They were not tied agents: exclusive loyalty and perhaps confidentiality was not to be expected. Similarly, though perhaps to a lesser extent, professional estate officers acted as auditors, receivers or supervisors on half a dozen estates. Some men amassed stewardships and fees. Invariably influen-tial, it was not their loyalty that was being bought, but their influence with their masters, frequently the king. It was this reason that Dartford Priory always appointed a royal councillor as steward and in 1534 insisted on the king's principal minister Thomas Cromwell rather than his nominee.[14] Such men would never imperil their own master's interest – or, by inference, their own – by acting against his wishes. How many of the other annuities that we know about were designed not to secure the service of the individual but sympathetic access through him to his lord? A second fee need not indicate a *transfer* of service and probably seldom did.

Bastard feudalism also operated in towns. Richard Clitherow esquire at Newcastle, William Gosse esquire of Bridgewater and even Alderman Thomas Wetherby at Norwich were clients respectively of the earl of Westmorland, duchess of York and duke of Norfolk.[15] Many lords had towns of their own: two-thirds of English boroughs were seigneurial rather than royal.[16] In the Cotswolds alone the wool towns of Castle Combe (Wilts.) were subject to Fastolf, Stroud (Glos.) to York, and Fairford (Glos.) and Burford (Oxon.) to Warwick. County towns like Warwick, Salisbury (Wilts.), St Albans (Herts.) and Bury St Edmunds (Suff.) were subject respectively to the earl of Warwick, bishop of Salisbury and the abbots of St Albans and Bury. Towns served their surrounding hinterlands. Most were under the authority of the county officers and the influence of the county magnates. Noble rule extended into Derby.[17] Urban contingents, small in number, featured in campaigns against foreign and domestic enemies, always under overall aristocratic command. Towns deferred to local magnates, frequently sending gifts to them at home or when in the town, at quarter sessions for example, and sought their advice and directions when faced with royal commands or political decisions. Boroughs that elected gentry as MPs were admitting aristocratic superiority. That many gentry were also employed by boroughs or resident in them recognised that aristocrats were more likely to carry weight with other aristocrats.[18] Lords presumed they could secure elections for boroughs for their clients, wrote letters requesting seats and sometimes prevailed. Many landowners had properties in towns, resided there with household servants, employed rent collectors and other officials, and liveried local men. Lord Grey of Codnor was indicted repeatedly for illegal livery in Nottingham – an activity he evidently considered normal:[19] perhaps it was, other aristocrats being more successful in escaping prosecution. Kings frequently ordered towns not to permit such retaining. They equated royal boroughs with the crown lands and duchy of Lancaster, which were distinctively their own. Retaining in towns constantly recurred and was ineradicable.

The spirit of service

Only indentures of retainer spell out the nature of the contract between a lord and a retainer. Typically a lord retained his man in peace and war against all comers except the king, for which he paid an annual fee, expenses and promised his good lordship in the retainer's just cause. Household and wartime service was no longer specified. After 1430 allegiance was explicitly reserved. Each contract enshrined a balance of advantage, perhaps hard negotiation, that is normally concealed from us. The standard templates used by the two Richard Nevilles, earls of Salisbury and Warwick, and by Humphrey Duke of

Buckingham suggest that they made more contracts than currently survive. Comparison reveals where terms differed. When Robert Eure indented with Salisbury, he sought 'not [to] be constrained to be of counsel ... against the said Thomas [Lumley]', but had to drop the clause.[20] The fees paid varied according to the lord's estimation of the worth of the retainer and the extent of the latter's desire to serve. Salisbury's list of fees from Middleham (Yorks.) about 1457 extend from a mere £1 6s. 8d paid to Ralph Pollard up to £20 to Lord Fauconberg.[21] For none of them was this more than a supplement to their income – though no less attractive as an extra. Retainers hoped for further rewards, for access to royal patronage as Sir William Plumpton undoubtedly did and for the good lordship that is discussed below.

Indentures of retainer were voluntary contracts – free will agreements carrying particular weight. A lord had to choose whom to retain – he could not afford very many. Peers were sparing in their fees. Costs and obligations were incurred in return for services undefined, perhaps different in every instance, which the lord thought worthwhile and expected to be delivered. The retainer knew what was involved: service in the lord's household, escort duty, attendance at a day's notice, with his connection, and so on. It was in the light of pre-existing commitments, not all bastard feudal, that he engaged himself. Retainer by several lords was no problem if the services demanded were compatible. When they were not, retainers sometimes inserted exclusion clauses; by acceptance, the lord testified that the residual services were still worth the price. In 1433 John Wensley reasonably declined to counsel Lord FitzHugh against 'those persons that are or shall be of kin or alliance to the same John' and Sir James Strangways in 1446 excluded his 'kin and allies within the third degree of marriage'. Here they were stating what was surely the norm. Action against nuclear families or kinsfolk with identical interests was always unattainable. Eure was explicitly permitted to act for his brother and his children *against* his new lord 'if any matters of difference in law happen to fall betwixt them, which God forbid'. Thomas Wombwell reserved his loyalty to York, Strangways to the bishop of Durham and duchess of Norfolk, Richard Musgrave to Lords Clifford and Dacre in 1456 and Sir Thomas Stathum in 1464 to Lord Grey of Codnor for life. Stathum promised exclusive loyalty to Lord Hastings on Grey's death,[22] which was all that Hastings sought.

Mutual self-interest necessarily underpinned each agreement and might change, resulting in its termination. These were formal legal contracts – the most formal type of retainer – which were typically

completed in duplicate, each party having a copy, were sealed inter-
changeably and were enforceable at law. An annuity could be
discontinued for non-performance. Theoretically payment could be
enforced through the law courts. More important may have been the
moral component – the pledge of honour. An oath of fealty was
commonplace for the livery of inheritance. Although seldom
mentioned in the indenture itself, the oath was more probably an original feature and a normal accompaniment than a later development.
Reference to the oath appears late in the indentures. Apparently it was
the repeatedly perjured York himself who first required his retainers to
bind themselves in writing 'by the faith of his body ... for to do true
(sometimes diligent) and faithful service', George Darell first in 1453,
John Allington in 1456 and three others in 1460; the earl of Wiltshire
and Lord Hastings, who made such contracts in 1457 and from 1461,
had been York's own retainers. Sir Simon Mountford in 1469 bound
himself on his 'faith and honour of knighthood'. Abraham Metcalf
alone promised to be the 'sworn man' of Lord FitzHugh.[23] That Sir
John Paston prided himself on never being the sworn man of any
lord[24] implies that many others were and that swearing an oath was a
more binding commitment. They pledged their *faith* – sometimes,
specifically, their *honour* as *true* knights – whilst the lord promised his
good lordship in his retainer's *just* cause. Faith, good lordship and
justice were not empty phrases, but contemporary values laden with
meaning that nobody would commit with perjury (so akin to treason)
in mind. It is difficult not to believe that such indentures meant exactly
what they said.

Actually such contracts were severed, by mutual consent; outdated,
for example by the death of either party; and broken under intolerable
strains. What contract cannot be? Under pain of death or changed
circumstances, any contract can pass the point where it is tenable, especially when dependent on honour or obligation rather than legally
enforceable. The same applies to all other ties. The intention at the
time of the contract was to keep its terms.[25] Arguing from silence,
most were observed. The difficulty of historians is to detect and
comprehend where mutual interest dissolves. We cannot tell how
formal the release of obligations and the severing of contractual ties
had to be.

McFarlane assumed that indentures typified the other varieties of
retainer that were not so explicit. Often, no doubt, he was correct.
Many baronial letters patent or warrants merely implement indentures.
So perhaps do many of the fees listed in receivers' accounts, 'for his
retainer', without further detail. Yet indentures of retainer were untyp-

ical of many bastard feudal relationships. Fifteenth-century indentures no longer specify household service, which involved obligations of a special kind. Tenants, lawyers, estate officers and the merely liveried differed again. Indentured retainers and annuitants were extraordinary, expensive and always few: a mere handful were declared against tax by peers in 1436.[26] They appear surprisingly few until one appreciates that no lord could afford many: a hundred could have bankrupted even York or the Kingmaker. It is inherently unlikely that all gentry could have been retained. Only 456 out of 3,173 MPs in 1386–1421, a mere 14 per cent, 'had known links with magnates ... close enough to cast doubt upon their political independence'.[27] Shortage of evidence means that little account can be taken of household service, where most aristocrats served the great, or of service by gentry to gentry, churchmen, monasteries and towns. When allowance is made for these, the statistics appear less convincing. We can list the personnel of only one fifteenth-century aristocratic household – that of Howard – and then only briefly. York and Warwick raised hundreds of men from their households, their estates and the connections of aristocratic retainers, only a fraction of whom were indentured or feed.

Family and household, in contemporary parlance, were coterminous. Servants were members of the householder's family, in the same relationship as children, bound by loyalty as strong as that to their own blood kin. Murdering your master was equated with treason – more shocking than normal murder – and carried the same penalties. Service excused Sir Thomas Tresham's allegiance to Henry VI even to Edward IV; it was a wrench for that former household servant John Paston III to withdraw from the service of the Mowbrays. 'To associate oneself with the head of a great lineage – whether as an equal or a subordinate – was to enter a relationship which had something in common with the blood tie itself.'[28] Many families were hereditarily predisposed to serve particular families. Tenants, too, were bound by more than economic and contractual ties and frequently identified themselves with the estate, with the ancient lords, even long after forfeitures.[29] Newcomers, purchasers, had to wait to make their mark.

Command and authority over men was an essential attribute of the aristocrat. It was a source of authority and prestige. He needed it to make a show – the conspicuous display appropriate to his rank. No aristocrat ever went unescorted: to church, to hunt, to quarter sessions and the county court, to dine or to visit his lord. John Duke of Bedford brought twenty men with him to dine with Warwick at Rouen in 1431. Attendance by five menservants by itself should have secured an audience with Lord and Lady Scrope, so Katherine Chaderton indignantly observed.[30] Staff accompanied their lords on their progresses, to court, great councils, parliaments and state ceremonies, where they added to the display and – much more rarely – on military service against invaders and rebels. From them were drawn many of their lord's retinue of war for overseas service. A magnate like Buckingham could call out men from all parts of his estate – from the midlands or south-east – either separately or together, and direct them to local targets – arresting Sir Thomas Malory, for instance – or to a full-scale battle at St Albans.[31] That was what lords wanted from their connections.

The aristocratic household was the hub of polite society, aristocratic society and power relationships of a whole area, in every area, not merely the estates that the lord held nearby. Magnates had to live like magnates if they were to be respected as such. Respect inclined men to defer, to oblige and to follow the great man's lead. There was a natural disposition to serve the great man and to seek his service: witness the Pastons' ambiguous relationships with the dukes of Norfolk, the ties of many Northumbrians and Yorkshiremen with the Percies and, at a lower level, Edmund Capes' desire to follow his father in estate office. Magnates had many well-willers whom they had not formally retained and did not pay. The household performed this function for the earls of Arundel in fifteenth-century Sussex and the earl of Worcester in early-sixteenth-century south Wales. It helped convert a magnate like Warwick in the west midlands, where he held only a fraction of the total land interspersed with many other properties, into a ruler whose authority transcended his estates and embraced the whole region. It was not the only factor. A long history created a presumption in a lord's favour that endured from generation to generation. Inheritances were a better foundation than forfeitures. The dispossessed were liable to be restored: hence recipients often compounded with them.

Long-standing connections existed and endured without personal contributions from the lord. Personal relationships may have mattered in forging new links and lords could certainly drive retainers away: a lord of poor judgement, whose service harmed rather than advanced his men and denied them royal approval or whose own interests took priority, could alienate his followers. York's rebellions against Henry VI perhaps explain the particularly explicit allegiance clause in George Darell's 1453 indenture.[32] Warwick found his retainers unwilling to serve against the king in 1470.[33] It was apparently Northumberland's desertion of Richard III and the tough line that he had to take against Yorkshire tax-rebels in 1489, with whom he may have sympathised just as much as his retainers, that caused his feed men to desert him and shamefully leave him to his fate.[34] So, too, ought Pastons to have done, whose bonds to Norfolk, which included household service, appear irrevocably shattered by his siege of Caister, the killing of their servant and their own subsequent indictment. Sir John nevertheless declared his willingness to serve the duke if the issue was settled in his favour and in 1476, when John III formally withdrew from ducal service – rather late in the day! – he promised to notify the duchess if he joined any other lord.[35] He was offering her first refusal. Their bonds of service, once contracted, were not easily or willingly broken. Personalities counted for less than is generally supposed: particularly to tenants.[36]

Good lordship

Bastard feudalism was a command relationship. Lords were rulers of their connections and localities. Robert Armburgh wrote hectoring and threatening letters to his ministers and lessees. Fearful of poaching, the 5th earl of Northumberland ordered a review of woods, parks and game at Topcliffe, of horses and cattle removed from his park of Spofford, and required poachers to appear before him. His father did not ask, but ordered his brother [in-law] William Gascoigne to take a surety to keep the peace. The earls ordered the Plumptons to arrest traitors, to incarcerate them pending another command, to drive horses and cattle from Spofford Park, to supply a buck to the city of York and to attend them immediately on the Scottish borders or at their Yorkshire residence. Often on behalf also of the king, such commands commonly end with an abrupt reminder: 'See that you fail not, as you love me and as ever you think to have me your good lord and as ever I may trust you'.[37] Even, perhaps especially, in the household, where servants were directly under their employer's eye and where the relationship was especially authoritarian, there were rules to be obeyed. Household ordinances and courtesy books stipulate hours of work, duties, dress, thrift and economy, personal conduct and lifestyle. All had to attend religious services in the chapel. Discipline extended to moral regulation. Henry Duke of Warwick and his sister put their servants on short commons for swearing and dismissed them for oppression. Servants who were unable or unwilling to do their duties, wasteful or unprofitable to their lord, were sacked. Many ex-household servants prosecuted for wearing livery and executed for crime early in the sixteenth century demonstrate dismissals to be commonplace.[38] We can regulate our own servants, declared John of Gaunt in 1384. Lords had an interest in doing so. It was 'disworship to my lord [of Norfolk] that two of his men should debate so near him'. 'There was', writes Rawcliffe, 'an implicit assumption that the "good lord" should be able to keep order among his retainers and tenants'. Dismissal from one household, ordered Edward IV, should not be followed by re-employment in another. It was the dismissed servants who resorted to crime, opined Thomas More, not those still within seigneurial households.[39]

Servants outside the household were overseen less closely. In return for their fees lords expected functions fulfilled, offices performed, *ad hoc* tasks executed and extraordinary duties fulfilled. Armburgh frequently stressed responsibilities to his ministers and lessees. Before feeing Sir William Stonor in 1478, John Lord Strange expected more than good intentions; 'if you deal as you ought I will be your good lord', he promised, but if not 'I am friended so to help my self' without Stonor's assistance.[40] Officers were liable for the conduct of their deputies. Perks had limits. The authority or rule delegated to them was subject to intervention, review and overrule. Some officers took oaths of office; many accountants and lessees took out bonds and sureties to the lord. Once in post, they were supervised, held accountable for revenues received, their expenses were disallowed and any liabilities were held against their moveable estates after death. Many lords sued erstwhile accountants in the royal courts, more commonly perhaps for their bonds than for the actual sum due; erring parkers and foresters were sued for trespass. Edward Duke of Buckingham was exceptional only in that his bonds submitted his accountants to his council.[41] Fees went on occasion unpaid, were formally suspended or even revoked.

Servants at all levels expected benefits from their lords, invoking their good lordship or good ladyship, good mastership or good fatherhood. This commonly involved annual fees or offices, perhaps a grant of land for life, or wages, the reimbursement of any costs and a share of the windfalls that fell in. Lords extended their patronage by borrowing that of others: hence retainers were appointed as deputies to their own offices, as stewards of the king or bishop, and by other lords. Ministers exercised royal patronage to their own advantage. It was because Thomas Beckwith was 'his aunt's son' that Lord Treasurer Essex proposed appointing him escheator of Yorkshire.[42] Durham Priory was besieged by aristocrats seeking parkerships, leases, livings and university studentships for their protégés. Though major Yorkshire landholders worth £290 a year, the Plumptons valued highly the estate offices at Knaresborough, Spofforth and Arkenden (Yorks.) granted by king, earl and abbey. Each conferred authority that enabled them to favour all kinds of people. Such benefits were worth the service involved and any earlier service needed to earn them. The recipient must be grateful to the right patron.

> As long as my lord of Northumberland's patent thereof stands good, so long will he have no deputy but such as shall please him and can him thank for the gift thereof and no man else and also do him service next the king.

When requesting payment of an annuity to a client, Lord Treasurer Scrope asked that it be done 'in such wise as he may know this my writing may turn into avail'. Do 'as the law will; for that offence', wrote Gloucester, 'the rather at the instance of this our letters'. Not to perform, in the last analysis, spelt dismissal: too dire a result to contemplate.

Yet Plumpton was not merely a suitor: he was courted. He was a lord himself, a royal officer, JP and officer on many estates. His tenants of Idle (Yorks.) formally petitioned him for action against vagabonds, suspect of robbery, who flouted morality by their idleness, extravagance, thriftlessness and illicit games. His courts performed a service: they could be convened to oblige a canon of Newburgh. He had patronage, perhaps no use to him, but of value to others, such as church livings. Lesser men feared to offend him: Edward Plumpton begged him 'to take no displeasure with me that I sent not to you afore, as my duty was'. Alarmed that they had offended him and anxious not to anger him, Prior Lister of Newburgh and Richard Ampleforth apologised, agreed to abide his judgement or to revise their conduct 'to your satisfaction' or 'at your pleasure'. Thomas Hawksworth hastily expressed pleasure that Plumpton had the rule of his client's mother. The Plumptons received many requests in various capacities from their equals and social inferiors, some for themselves, others for others. Master Anthony, a doctor sued by his patients, asked for protection against arrest until he could pay. A son asked for intercession for his mother, a landholder for bastard children without subsistence, the prior of St John for the commander of Ribston 'as to his servants & tenants in those parts, as well in his absence as his presence', a parson for a poor kinsman, another for a farmhold of a relative of his own tenant, the esquire Robert Eure for renewal of the tenancy of a widow of an officer who had left seven small children, and the gentleman Richard Bank for him to be 'tender and especial master' to the (?troublesome) sons of his son-in-law's tenant. The latter implies several levels of intercession, favours done and gratitude earned, before the matter reached Plumpton himself. Intercessors were themselves good lords who expected thanks from those they had helped: there was scope for many lesser good lords below the knightly Plumptons. Very few such matters can have been of direct interest to the Plumptons and some, such as renewals of leases, may have cost them something. All, however, bore fruit, generally thanks and offers of service, often 'after my power' – the limited capacity of the petitioner. 'As I and my said son may have cause to do you service', wrote Bank, presuming on past service, '& the rather for my prayer'. But not all those suing to the Plumptons were inferiors. The 4th earl of Northumberland requested the bailiwick of Sessay, of which Plumpton was guardian, for Edmund Capes in succession to his father and the return of stolen kine to their proper owner. His son asked for loan of a tame hart and a couple of running dogs. Do it, 'as you love me, to my very great pleasure', he promised, and 'I will be as well-willed to do things at your pleasure'.[43]

Where there were disputes, the gentry often sought peaceful solutions, through mediation, compromise or arbitration. Sometimes they were arbiters imposing their own remedies. Henry Doget remitted a tithe dispute to Sir William Stonor, accepting whatever 'rule as you like to set between us', even if it were to his loss.[44] Parties often turned for help to greater lords, whose standard response was to offer or impose arbitration, by themselves or others. Their councils contained all the expertise required. Their rank guaranteed respect for their awards: often decisions reverted to them alone, as umpires, when panels of arbiters picked by the parties failed to agree. King, parliament and the courts often delegated disputes to them. Desirous of peace between Sir William Plumpton and his own cousin Thomas Beckwith, Lord Treasurer Essex wanted 'the rule' taken on by Chief Baron Rouclif, who was both his deputy at the exchequer and newly connected to Plumpton by marriage. It was out of 'respect for Humphrey Earl of Stafford, who greatly desired to make peace', and presumably also at his request, that Simon Kinsman agreed to arbitration of his dispute with the widowed Joan Mulso in 1426. Following alleged threats from Sir John Malliverer's men against Sir William Plumpton's, the latter sued to Malliverer's lord Earl John Neville, who asked Malliverer to restrain his servants; if they have a case, 'let them complain unto me hereof and I shall see that they shall have such a remedy as shall accord with reason'.[45] It is a typical example: first of all a cessation of the trouble and then removal of the cause. The earl did not override their rights, offered them a hearing – doubtless terrifying enough and particularly if they were in the wrong! – and a remedy that was just, not necessarily in their favour. Who could reject *reason*?

Lords sometimes intervened anyway. Regarding 'a variance' with Richard Birnand, the next earl ordered an armistice until he returned to sort it out. Stop your debate with Gascoigne's affinity, he ordered, 'unto time he might come to the country and see a direction betwixt you ... as shall be to your heart's ease and worship': not the victory of one party, but the demarcation of the power and responsibilities of each. Intervening yet again in 'a grudge' between his retainers Sir William Plumpton and Sir William Beckwith, probably at the latter's request,

> I, intending the pacifying thereof, desire & pray you to forbear ... to do anything in that behalf against the said Sir William unto my next coming into Yorkshire. And then I shall show me in such wise for the reformation thereof, as I trust shall agree with right law and conscience.

Who could reject *conscience*? Plumpton had little choice, as 'you shall understand that the said Sir William Beckwith will commit himself unto my rule in all particulars'.[46] Retainers were often given no choice but to settle.

It was as feoffee of a close that the Kingmaker intervened on behalf of Thomas Scarborough, but he did not prejudge the issue. Plumpton must leave him in peaceful occupation 'unto time that, by such persons as thereupon by your both assents being elect and chosen, the matter be thoroughly determined which of you ought to have the same of right'. The earl was not arbiter himself, but deputed arbitration to a panel chosen by each side. Another dispute had four arbiters, with Sir Robert Plumpton as umpire if they could not agree, which, given that each side picked two allies, was not an infrequent occurrence. Mediation having failed, yet another was referred to the arbitration of Thomas Middleton and Sir Robert Plumpton, the latter being the lord of the lord of one of the principals. Armburgh submitted to the rule of the abbot of Merivale and two others. Lords were well able to enforce their decisions, especially those involving two of their clients: hence, perhaps, the one-sidedness of some such awards. Earl Richard Beauchamp prescribed for the unfortunate Burdets of Arrow (Warw.) a humiliating climbdown to the prior of Worcester. Harsh his verdict may have been, but not conspicuously unjust, any more than were those of the dukes of Buckingham criticised by modern historians. Equity, reason, meticulous care and provision for all eventualities are normal. They were conspicuous in the awards of Ralph Lord Cromwell.[47]

Many arbitrations succeeded. Some did not. Suing at common pleas for the penalty in the defaulter's bond took both parties back to the courts, which they had sought to prevent, and verdicts were hard to enforce. Some celebrated cases of long-standing disputes several times unsuccessfully arbitrated are known. Lords often exerted pressure to comply. It is unlikely in 1437, when Richard Hotoft defaulted, that an angry rebuke from his master Stafford was the sum of his displeasure. Following another such failure, 'I willing the pacifying and reformation hereof, by the advice of you and other of my counsel', Northumberland ordered Plumpton to produce the parties next time he was at York. A settlement was to be imposed. So too in the case of Lawrence Lowe, to whom Clarence's household treasurer was 'to declare unto you in that behalf our intent furthermore' because 'contrary to your promise [you] sue, vex and trouble continually our tenants of our lordship of Ashbourne' (Derby.). Arbitration even provided acceptable remedies in crimes of violence. Compensation for death or injury much like the Anglo-Saxon wergild in modern personal injuries cases was precribed by lords as diverse as Buckingham (1455), York (1459), Lord Stanley in the north-west and even Henry VI in the 1458 Loveday at St Paul's. The sum of £40 covered the future Lord Hastings' murder of Robert Pierpoint.[48]

Recipients of such requests often had no personal interest other than the desire to keep order or to be good lords. Northumberland was obliging others over Sessay and cattle-rustling. Sometimes only intercession with those too exalted or unknown to the petitioner was required. Sir William Plumpton was asked to intercede with Sir Richard Aldborough for the return of beasts to Dame Isabel Ilderton pending an arbitration, his son to ask Sir Robert Ughtred to propose to the tenants of Coxwold to appoint as their clerk the brother of a Newburgh canon, and Sir Richard Empson asked Sir William Gascoigne to intercede with his kinsman Plumpton to stop his servants molesting Richard Fulbarn. Robert Armburgh twice solicited Lady Ferrers of Chartley 'that you vouchsafe so to stir my gracious lord your husband that he show such gracious lordship and help in this case that my right may be saved at the reverence of God'. To Clement Spicer he wrote:

> I pray you to speak to my lord of Buckingham, which is your good lord, and prayeth him to speak with my lord of Exeter and pray him that he would charge both Chaunceys, which be his men, that they let off their hands and suffer our farmers and tenants [to] sit in peace and that they make none such wrong

entries, and that he vouchsafe to charge them also to bring
their evidences when my lord and yours and my lord of Exeter
come next to Westminster before them and their council ...
that who can show best evidence rejoice the livelihood.

John Chauncey had selected as feoffees 'two mighty princes', whose
involvement caused Armburgh to lament 'I am never like to rejoice
that'. Armburgh nevertheless hoped to bring them to compromise
through their lords who, actually, had no direct interest in the result
and might well consider a just solution fulfilled their obligations.[49]
There were many trivial matters (from a magnate's angle) that were
better delegated. Regarding 'the variance and discord [which] is
depending betwixt my servant Thomas Saxston and Richard
Ampleforth' at Spofford, Northumberland delegated to Plumpton as
steward the investigation, maintenance of order and amicable solution.
'And for so much as you have the rule there under me', he went on,

> I pray you to show you of similar disposition if any matter of
> variance hereafter happen within your said rule, so that the
> parties sue not to me, if by your discreet wisdom you can
> reform it, as my very trust is in you ... Cousin, I pray you to
> see this matter pacified, that there be no more calling upon
> me therefore, as my very trust is in you.

Plumpton was assured on Ampleford's behalf of his willingness to do
whatever was needed to end the dispute.[50] A magnate's desire to keep
order, which he regarded as good lordship, did not mean that he
wanted to handle every case himself. What were his staff for?
Most of these suitors and beneficiaries, we may deduce, were not
actually retained, but might nevertheless be satisfied. Good lordship
itself was promised by lords to their retainers in their just cause: an
ambiguous phrase which, as we have seen, need not mean support in
an unjust case. The Chaunceys had hoped to deter Armburgh by
selecting magnates as feoffees – a capacity in which two dukes felt
obliged to defend their feoffor. Both might however prefer a just solution to backing their men to the hilt against right and justice. The
danger was that lesser men invoking good lordship would drag greater
men into conflict, thus converting a minor dispute into something
major. Supposedly this was what threatened in 1468, when Clarence,
Shrewsbury and Mountjoy were embroiled in a Derbyshire quarrel.[51]
Lords were anxious to avoid this. Lamenting a trespass by a poor man
'sometime belonging to me' against your servant, Robert Warcop

refused to involve himself and referred the matter to Sir Robert Plumpton to 'rule him as it shall please you & ... bring him to a reasonable end'. When Plumpton as estates steward of Lilleshall Abbey took the side of Robert Walkingham against Dame Joyce Percy, she appealed to George Earl of Shrewsbury, who interceded with the abbey, which told Plumpton to do her right. As Shrewsbury was 'our very good and tender lord in all our rightful causes, ... we may in no wise abide the displeasure of our said lord'. If you will not, we 'must set some other person in your room that will not wrong her'. Undeterred, perhaps calling the abbey's bluff, Plumpton heard next from Shrewsbury direct. Do her right. If there is justice on Walkingham's side, he will be compensated.[52] Nobody in Derbyshire could negate the earl's influence. When Robert Catesby appealed to the queen in his dispute with John Hugford, a Warwick retainer, the queen's councillors refused assistance for fear of arousing 'a grudge' between her and Hugford's master the earl. Likewise Sir William Plumpton's attempts to become JP, master forester and steward of Knaresborough, where Northumberland had 'the chief rule under the king' without being beholden to him, failed because neither king, dukes, courtiers nor council wished to make an enemy of the earl for a mere knight.[53] The earl did indeed advance Plumpton in all these ways and kept his service as well as those other retainers with whom he quarrelled. Plumpton was never allowed, in Strange's words, to over-master him. He had to know and keep his place.

The king's men

Kings had their own manpower: the tenants of the crown lands, queens' lands, principality of Wales, duchies of Cornwall and Lancaster, and the county of Chester. 'Forsooth', quoth Fortescue, 'the greatest lord's livelihood in England may not suffice to reward so many men', even if he divided it among his servants.[54] However the king's officers exercised their authority on behalf of themselves and their lords and added the king's tenants to their own. This was not new. What may have been new was successive kings' anxiety intermittently to share the benefits. Richard II extended his affinity into the provinces by systematically appointing his household knights to county office. In the west midlands this competed with, rivalled and sought to supplant existing connections, secure in Richard's backing and perhaps his self-conscious direction.[55] Henry IV inherited ready-made Lancastrian connections in many areas. Sir Thomas Erpingham, linchpin of the duchy of Lancaster in Norfolk, continued to represent his interests as king. As the original Lancastrian connection declined after 1399, private connections were constructed by local duchy officers in East Anglia and (less successfully) in the north midlands (and, by implication, elsewhere) that eventually escaped crown control.

Twelve of Edward IV's household knights should hale out 'of every country' and a further forty esquires 'of sundry shires', explicitly so 'it may be known the disposition of the countries'. The king could thereby greatly extend his information and authority and be able to confront any offender with his offence to his face.[56] Whether all courtiers perceived their role this way or performed is not recorded. A later act requiring annuitants to obey the king's summons to arms reveals this was not happening automatically. Royal service offered a better means to pursue private ends. It carried a cachet.[57] A display of 'your true mind and faithful [al]legiance towards us' could secure the most flattering and potentially profitable of royal letters: 'assuring you, that by this your demeaning you have ministered unto us cause, as [we are en]gaged to remember you in time to come in anything that may be to your preferment and advancement, as ever did any our progenitors to our nobles in those parties'. It was as the king's servant, his representative at Pontefract, that Sir Richard Tunstall intervened in the quarrel of an officer with William Scargill, first advising Scargill to submit to his authority, then advising him again on pain of arrest and reference to the king and council. To be reported to Henry VII, on another occasion, was what Sir Robert Plumpton definitely did not want.[58]

Hence perhaps Edward IV's experiment in controlling the north midlands, lately riven by feuds and then subject to a magnate whom he had expelled, where his chamberlain Hastings was steward. Hastings' indentures of 1474–83, contracted at the king's command and for which no fees were paid, gave the king through Hastings first claim on the service from the duchy's local officers, feudal tenants and local gentry and prevented them from prioritising any other lord, at no cost to king or Hastings but, most probably, to their retainers' financial loss. It was at the king's own insistence at Burton-on-Trent (Derby.) in 1474 that the first dozen indentures were contracted.[59] Richard III made this objective yet more explicit in 1484, when Sir Marmaduke Constable was 'deputed and ordained to make his abode amongst you and to have the rule' of our honour of Tonbridge, and the inhabitants were forbidden to be 'retained with any person or persons whatsoever he or they be but that you be ready to attend wholly upon our said knight at all times that you by him shall be commanded to do us service'.[60] Outsiders were shut out: the manpower was the king's alone.

Kings normally relied on the nobility to rule the provinces and worked with and through them. Many were royal kin, some the closest – the king's uncles, brothers or sons – whose local power was fortified by their royal status and access to royal favour. Even lesser courtiers could condescend to provincial notables: two grooms of the royal chamber and ewery begged Sir William Plumpton for his good lordship to their 'trusty friend' Thomas Lodge, 'wherein you shall deserve thanks of God & your good lords at your coming to the king's house, with our daily service at all times'.[61] Every king had particular favourites. Powerful at the centre rather than in provincial landholding, they tapped royal resources, transmitted them to their dependants or bent the law in their favour. Such men could accrue wealth very rapidly, construct great estates by royal grant and enlist large followings (here called affinities) for which they had no initial need to pay. So, too, custodians and officers on estates of the king or his wards may have commanded the tenantry, added them temporarily to their own resources, and perhaps withheld them from anyone else. It was as the king's principal officers in the north-west that the Stanleys came to dominate two royal counties palatine. Similarly it was as officer and custodian of various estates that Sir Thomas Lovell commanded 1,325 men in 1508.[62] Such officers filled a void. Royal permission was not needed, but was useful, not least in assuring tenants and officers of access to royal favour in return for their service. Whilst important factors politically at the time and perhaps even momentarily irresistible, such affinities lacked deep roots and seldom outlived their creators. In 1483 Hastings' men supposedly passed to Buckingham, favourite of the month, and thence into oblivion. In contrast, long-established connections – like those of the Percies, Courtenays and Nevilles – survived interruptions of a decade, generation, or even more. Affinities were more successful, perhaps, in excluding any overriding aristocratic hegemony than in forestalling and settling local disputes.

Edward IV allowed regional rule to be exercised by his favourites: during the 1460s, the Nevilles in the north and west midlands, Herbert in Wales and Stafford of Southwick in the west country; from the mid 1470s, Gloucester in the north, the Stanleys in the north-west, Hastings in the north midlands and the queen's family in Wales. It was royal backing that made Abbot (later Bishop) Senhouse and Sir Richard Tunstall so powerful. Senhouse bullied Sir Thomas Malliverer, on the pain of Henry VII's displeasure. Tunstall rejected Sir Robert Plumpton's claim to a bondman: if he could show convincing evidence, 'you shall have such answer as of reason you shall be content with'.[63] Addressing his equal in rank and office, Tunstall as the king's chosen representative could write like a lord to an inferior. Both, like Archbishop Savage, had established roles in local society, though another, Surrey, admittedly had not. Kings in practice needed to rely on men of local standing. 'And as any office of our gift there falls void', wrote the king in 1489, 'we shall reserve them' for 'such men as in the said parties shall be meet and able for the same'.[64] James has demonstrated that Henry VIII really had no choice, but to rule Northumberland through the local magnate. Interpolated outsiders were liable to be disruptive and ineffective. The king's patronage, affinity and household was spread thinly across the realm and, as Horrox points out, 'could never be more than an element. Cost precluded the taking of all the gentry into the king's service'.[65] The royal affinity was an element in provincial societies, significant, but rarely dominant. It could not stand outside or ignore local associations, government and power structures. King's men needed access to those powerful locally, to intercede with them and to be respected and to add the other offices, associations and dependants through which aristocrats conventionally exercised and extended their influence. They were not always backed up by their master, who could not allow his whole relationship with magnates to be pre-empted by local actions. The king could not enforce his will, their wills, if local potentates were alienated and uncooperative.

9

PROVINCIAL
COMMUNITIES

Models of provincial society

Historians disagree about fifteenth-century provincial society. The sources are particularly inadequate and interpretations are strongly influenced by the preconceptions that each historian brings to them. The significance of witnessing a deed, for instance, depends on the stance of the particular historian.[1] New techniques in applying old evidence and in discerning patterns rest ultimately on acts of faith to which non-believers may not subscribe. Historians have created a score of generalisations about aristocratic society in the English provinces that may well be wrong. Current historians agree that magnates had essential interests to be protected at all costs and that these included their lands and local spheres of influence, which stemmed ultimately from manpower derived from that land.[2] However reasonable and unexceptional those starting points, subsequent chains of reasoning diverge.

Some historians have further deduced that land was not simply held, but had to be constantly protected against challenge, wherever it lay. Magnates had to be politically active wherever they had property.

> No magnate ... could afford to ignore the politics of each of the counties where his lands lay ... [Each] had to acquire enough followers in each of the counties where he had a concentration of estates to give him significant authority over the local officers and a large body of military support if litigation developed into violence.

Victory lay in control of local government, to be achieved via competitive recruitment of gentry outside the household and the creation and maintenance of a sphere of influence that was exclusive.

> The aim of every local magnate ... was to defeat or neutralise by accommodation the regional pretensions of his rivals in

order to achieve and maintain control of his 'country' ... The
dream of every nobleman was surely the unchallenged rule of
the locality, because everybody would look to him for justice
... The distinction between the affinity and the local *commu-
nitas* would all but disappear.[3]

An area of dominance was closely related to where a lord and his
retainers held estates, which changed constantly with the generations
and the transmission of estates, so magnates were constantly propelled
into collisions whence essential interests, pride and honour made
compromise impossible. The provinces were in conflict. Hence the
political transformations detected in certain counties over periods as
short as twenty years even though the political system and social structure remained essentially the same for centuries.

Several connections supposedly collapsed. It is natural to suppose
that minorities, long-lived dowagers and forfeitures interrupted
connections, caused interregnums or vacuums and required complete
rebuilding by the next heir. The de la Pole interest in East Anglia
lapsed for twenty years after 1415. In the west midlands the
Beauchamp connection experienced an interregnum between 1439
and 1449 and thereafter could not be reconstructed by the next two
lords, the Kingmaker and Clarence. The Courtenay earls of Devon
alienated their aristocratic retainers in the 1450s. These gaps were
filled by others. Hard facts underpin these interpretations, some of
them quite telling: the aristocratic component diminished from 19 per
cent to 9 per cent of the Courtenays' private armies between 1451 and
1455.[4] Such analyses however misunderstand bastard feudalism and
over-value individual contracts between peers and gentry. They
presume an improbably comprehensive knowledge of the personnel of
each retinue, the households being particularly obscure, and can be
challenged in detail.[5] What about the most numerous element, the
tenants? They remained available. Admittedly they were not insensitive
to hereditary loyalties, nor to the ties of allegiance, and could be
denied to their lords by disloyal or defaulting officers. Whatever loss of
support *may* have occurred amongst the gentry, the Courtenays
turned out *enough* men to win the fight at Clyst in 1455, committed
their connection to the Lancastrian cause in the north late in 1460
and in 1470–1 found their 'ancient' supporters awaiting them.
Moreover such interruptions were temporary. Dowagers, kinsmen,
executors, feoffees and central administrators represented the family
across minorities and even forfeitures.[6] Lords strove to mitigate the
worst scenarios through trusts. Testators minimised the dissolution of

households by allowing time for relocation and ordering continued payment of fees.[7] Speculative guardians who married their offspring to heirs were investing in continuity. Estate administration persisted, together with the tenants, the officers and any annuitants, ready for the next heir, who normally acceded peacefully and without difficulty to his predecessor's local standing. A dowager's longevity could not be counted on and was an unsound basis for planning the future. Nobody knew when she would die – some widowhoods were brief – and the heir always held the reversion. Even if lordship was temporarily exercised by others, they had no interest in dismantling rather than maintaining going concerns. Vacuums were most commonly filled by pre-existing networks, which outlived individual lords. On succession heirs were well placed to revive their predecessors' connections. Presumptions about precedence, service, lordship and loyalty need not be disturbed.

Outlying estates were not especially vulnerable. All magnates had them – the Beauchamp lands in Devon, the Percy lordship of Petworth (Sussex), a Neville manor in Essex – and transmitted them across the generations for centuries. Whatever rival protagonists claimed at the time, attacks on land without any title were rare, almost unknown. There was no need to be politically active everywhere to keep hold of land and revenues. It was sensible, perhaps, to latch on to existing power structures – to appoint local men of substance and standing as officers. Just as earls of Warwick appointed local notables to manage Barnard Castle in County Durham, so did the bishops of Winchester with their Somerset estates. Moreover power need not derive from men from lands in the immediate locality. Magnates brought in manpower from afar, yeomen from the north midlands being deployed by Buckingham both in Kent and Warwickshire and by the Percies from Cumbria.[8] A lord's household provided manpower enough for most purposes wherever he was. It was potentially a mobile hit-squad. In a classic instance in 1453, Warwick took Staffordshiremen first to determine the war in Glamorgan and then to the Neville–Percy feud in the north.[9]

Was local government really the key to local politics or to victory? There are almost no records. We know who held office and some of their bastard feudal connections. We seldom know why they were appointed – what lies behind the pricking of a sheriff or the commission of a JP. Were they appointed because *retained* by a great lord or retained because their local standing had brought them public office? What reflects what? Did lords put their men into office – seek to control office – or did they not care? Did gentry seek such office themselves? Occasionally we know the answer: in contested parliamentary elections and Sir William Plumpton's desire to be a JP. We cannot know if such instances were typical. Was it because he was Clarence's retainer that Sir John Stanley was appointed sheriff of Staffordshire? As this was his fourth term, surely not? What difference did the manner of appointment make to their conduct? Should we suppose that everything was political – that sheriffs, escheators and justices were uniformly partisan – or that only occasionally did such matters obtrude? If a county's officers are mainly connected to a particular lord, does this demonstrate that he inserted them with a view to 'dominance in county-wide politics'?[10]

That most JPs failed to attend quarter sessions and left business to professional lawyers implies an absence of excitement and controversial issues. Bar elections, generally uncontested, little of political interest happened at county courts. Historians have attributed to local government an improbable capacity to be decisive. If the sheriff and escheator were significant figures, the former as the hub of the legal system and the latter as holder of the inquisitions that determined succession to land, each could influence what passed through their hands, but they could never resolve it. No case could be confined to their year of office, every verdict could be overthrown, and losing sides could too easily invite royal intervention, by purchasing royal commissions for instance. In every major feud, they did.

Lords did *rule* their countries. It makes sense, therefore, that they wished to do so. Norfolk declared in 1451 that 'we will have the principal rule and governance through all this shire, of which we bear our name whilst that we be living'. Such rule was seldom unqualified or exclusive. Yet even Norfolk asserted the priority of royal rule, the king's 'good grace and licence' for his authority and only 'as far as reason and law requireth'.[11] The greatest connections contained other peers whose local rule was respected. If some strove to extend their power-base, self-evidently Gloucester in the 1470s and Bonville in the 1450s, this need not have been a universal trait. They could be content with the status quo and interact peacefully with their neighbours. They could agree on respective spheres of influence, as the 4th earl of Northumberland did with Gloucester in 1473–4.[12] To suppose that the nobility were never content with their lot and had constantly to extend their hegemony produces some strange history. 'By 1445 it was clear', concludes Castor,

> that despite all the advantages Buckingham enjoyed in the
> exercise of his local authority, his efforts to establish a

coherent affinity and to extend his rule across Staffordshire and Derbyshire were significantly flawed … Rather, it seems that he was failing to establish his lordship as an authority which could adequately claim to represent or to control the north midlands.[13]

That there is no evidence of effective rule is most probably because this was not Buckingham's objective. He contented himself with the income and patronage of the duchy of Lancaster honours in preference to constructing a temporary connection beyond his own country. His clash with Warwick immediately to the south is another historians' invention. The lack of evidence of how Hastings used the same offices two decades later arises from the same causes. Appointed first by Clarence to intercede for him at court and then by Edward IV to prevent other lords from filling a power vacuum, Hastings was content to delegate his authority to others, most explicitly at Derby.[14]

Underpinning all these propositions is a conflict model to which most current historians subscribe. Bastard feudalism did after all deliver the manpower for foreign and civil war, contesting elections, factional politics, disputes and feuds, whether national or local. Yet historians today accept on the national stage that co-operation rather than conflict characterised relations between crown and nobility. Is it not surprising that the reverse is presumed in the localities? Lords had an interest above all others in law and order. Is it not strange that they could not live at peace with one another? Ironically these paradoxes arise from our excessive expectations of seigneurial rule and improved research into legal records. Even though crime, lawsuits and anti-social behaviour escalate today, we hold fifteenth-century magnates at fault for failing to quell them. Legal records in all ages inevitably portray conflict, yet we extract from them an unrealistic polarisation of fifteenth-century politics. Any dispute, any crime, any lawsuit involving the aristocracy or the lord himself is interpreted to indicate that lords were failing to resolve differences and to impose order.

Any substantial landholder was drawn into litigation local and national about unpaid rents, disputed tithes, defaults by officers, poaching and so on. This is as true of the Yorkshire Plumptons as for dukes and earls. Probably many cases were initiated by officers and seigneurial councils rather than by lords themselves. Few concerned essential interests. Lords sued people who in other capacities were kinsmen, officers or friends. Every case could not determine a political stance. Litigation need not indicate a lord's authority had collapsed or that relations had broken down. It is the mark of a well-regulated and law-abiding society, in which lords employed royal justice to resolve disputes peacefully. Just as they resorted to the court of common pleas to convey land, to forfeit the sureties of defaulting officers or those repudiating arbitration awards and to prosecute trespasses, so they invoked royal justice against criminals and royal commissions against their rivals. Kings expected the king's peace to be implemented through royal courts and royal justice: peace-keeping out of court was supplementary and conformed to the same standards. Lords could not concern themselves with every issue in their locality amongst their inferiors unless explicitly invited to intervene. Such matters could be left to others or delegated. It was potentially disruptive cases involving retainers that they felt most bound to resolve peacefully whatever the wishes of participants.

Most disputes had specific contexts and did not interact. That Clarence prosecuted defaulting officers everywhere did not mean they combined against him. The inheritance disputes of the 1450s between Warwick, the Despenser heir and the Beauchamp co-heiresses, between the senior co-heiress, her Talbot stepson and her Berkeley cousins, remained separate and did not merge into one. It is far-fetched to originate the Percy–Neville feud in the north of the mid 1450s to a dispute about precedence in the house of Lords a decade earlier.[15] Precedence only mattered when the dukes or earls were together – who sat higher, processed first, deferred or condescended – and magnates of the same substantive rank rarely met away from the court and parliament. Lords could, must and did keep such issues separate. The 1450s were distinctive, not typical, when disputes escalated and merged into national sides. It was because William Tailbois' attempt to murder Lord Cromwell was unprecedented that the latter, quite exceptionally, backed the impeachment of Tailbois' master Suffolk.[16] Contested elections were also untypical, occurring at most in 2 per cent of cases. County communities normally agreed their representation unanimously and here peaceably, without recourse to voting.[17]

Communities rural and urban

Aristocratic society was a pyramid of lords, who were superimposed on their social inferiors – peasants and commons – and ruled them. Within their immediate compass, even the least of gentry were unrivalled. Domestics served them alone and their tenants could be retained by no one else, theoretically: they could hold land of other manors and other lords. Lords' influence, however, was not constrained by the boundaries of their estates, for parish gentry were members of their social circle and their local communities, within which they rubbed shoulders with their equals, inferiors and superiors. Landholding and rank gained them admittance: wealth, lifestyle, lineage, seniority, offices and track record determined their standing within those communities that they did not lead.

There were overlapping spheres of influence: that of the parish gentleman fell within that of his larger neighbour, an esquire or knight; the latter's within that of a peer; a mere baron's, within that of a magnate. 'The country gentry were the natural allies of the peerage.'[18] Subordination arose from attendance, deference, services and occasional patronage. It was perfectly possible to have an exclusive sphere, within which nobody wished to intervene, and to be comprehended in a larger one, established formally by retainer, estate or local government office, or informally by acceptance of the social superiority, precedence and leadership of a greater man. Although it was the 'great ease and quiet' of Richard Willoughby in 1449 'that no other person but he shall have interest in the said towns of Wollaton, Sutton and Willoughby' (Notts.), he nevertheless acknowledged the lordship of Cromwell as local magnate.[19] It is seldom obvious what capacity and degree of formality caused men to seek the Plumptons' intercession. The topmost sphere encompassed a whole region and might exclude any choice of patron or good lord. Northumberland under the Percies is a good example. In 1469 the Pastons would have served Norfolk if he had not attacked their interests:[20] their neighbour Lord Scales, though the king's brother-in-law, was no effective alternative.

Horizons varied, as two contemporary concepts – *country* and *rule* – demonstrate. 'Every great lord had "his country".'[21] Virgoe recorded 150 instances of the term. What it meant varied. Occasionally it related to a whole region – the north country or west country – more often to a shire. Many of the instances of country cited by Virgoe, however, relate to smaller areas: the district around Caister and Walsingham in Norfolk, for example.[22] 'Only exceptionally', notes Harriss, 'was an affinity co-extensive with the county community'.[23] Similarly rule could be applied to a particular place, such as the town of Derby, or to the whole north. Great variety is implied in 1482 by the king's despatch 'northwards [of] my lord of Gloucester and my brother Parr and such other folk of worship as hath any rule in the north parts'.[24] This is not surprising. Property might be located in just a few contiguous parishes or overrun county boundaries. Many Elizabethan county JPs attended quarter sessions only when held in their corner of the shire. Such men had limited horizons, their communities being strictly local, their acquaintance with the county and the wider world at one remove. Their country – and hence their community of neighbours, superiors, equals and inferiors – differed from the county elite, perhaps only encountered at parliamentary elections, from the fellow retainers of their lord recruited from catchment areas that did not coincide, from their blood kin and in-laws, from the fraternities to which they belonged, their friends and, perhaps also, from fellow soldiers, courtiers and MPs. Stonors, Pastons and Plumptons alike, with estates and interests dispersed in more than one shire, were more capable of perceiving a whole county as their country or even of taking a regional view. Every county contained communities with little sense of county but a pronounced sense of locality, towards which obligations and loyalty were due.

All aristocrats had contacts of diverse kinds with different categories of people: menials and tenants, kinsfolk, neighbours, trading connections, associates in business and local government, members of the same parish and gild, friends and boon companions, acquaintances and well-willers, lords and patrons, no less miscellaneous, overlapping, indefinable and varying in importance as today. Informal contacts for recreation and rites of passage are underdocumented and underplayed. Many Warwickshire gentry were brothers of gilds at Coventry, Stratford, Henley and Knowle, some of more than one. There were many communities with which each individual was identified or could choose to be identified. These different groupings were united by the individual, who might be associated with others in several contexts and who was linked to many others via mutual acquaintance. The web of relationships could embrace large numbers of people. Jessica Freeman has connected almost all the knights of the shire of fifteenth-century Middlesex within a single pedigree, and Professor Pollard has linked together many Richmondshire families.[25] It is unlikely that such inter-marriage and interrelationships were exceptional. It was only the uppermost level of society, courtiers and under-age wards, who married nationally. Before Earl Ralph (d. 1425), even the Nevilles of Raby had matched themselves within the north. Nobility, county and parish gentry alike married those whom they knew, those commonly therefore within their own communities. Professor Everitt has shown for the seventeenth century how many aristocratic societies were intermarried, from Cornwall to Cumbria and Kent, although Mary Honeywood's 367 living descendants c.1620 was exceptional by any standard.[26] Add to this all the other contacts, associations and relationships outlined above, and every aristocrat was enmeshed in a complex web of relationships with those about him. Reciprocal witnessing of deeds and co-membership of trusts and commissions are good examples.

No wonder historians have sometimes perceived these relationships as sufficient for social solidarity and the role of peers as superfluous, extraneous and intrusive. The horizontal ties of association, so it is argued, mattered more than the vertical ones of lordship. There is an illogicality to a society of lords, in which lordship is acknowledged up to the gentry but not above, yet fifteenth-century provincial society may have operated like that. To distinguish between Lords and lords appears unreal. More seriously, such an argument presumes the network of associations was strong enough to determine actions and that it endured across time. Do numerous routine interactions equate with fundamental decision-making?

Kinship is a bond that starts tight – what ties are closer or more crucial than those between parents and children? – and becomes progressively weaker as shared ancestors die, new nuclear families are formed and each collateral branch acquires its own interests. This can and has been presented schematically.[27] What united the 367 descendants of Mary Honeywood was their relationship to her: she however was one of two parents, four grandparents, eight great-grandparents of her descendants, always at least once through the female line at a time when the male line was more important. Her descendants were heads of separate nuclear families, first or more distant cousins, almost beyond the point where kinship could be acknowledged at all. All had their own priorities, unrelated to their common ancestry. Northumberland called Sir William Plumpton cousin. If the latter reminded the earl of their kinship, it may have predisposed them to co-operate, but it certainly did not override the earl's closer relationships with his mother, countess, siblings and offspring. Most quarrels occurred within families. If this was true even of kinship, how much less significant surely were other types of association sealed with less than blood.

Each family, estate and community is a continuum into which the individual fits. This is most obvious with the family. Everyone has a unique family, different from each sibling, which slowly evolves as mortality, family formation and fertility take effect, as the newest infant supplants his predecessors as head of the family. Each new member slots into communities that are already formed, generally senior in age, and with pre-existing hierarchies and associations. If there is a presumption of continuity, with heirs stepping into their father's shoes, and of stability, there is nevertheless constant movement as the personnel change and the connections require renewal or replacement. A network is only as strong as the weakest link. Even if each local community was cohesive and mutually supportive, whether confined to a vicinity or to the handful of county gentry, connections between associates of associates of associates can have had little force. If valuable in reconciling differences, such connections can seldom have over-ridden more personal and essential interests.

Did anything? Although anxious for Plumpton's good lordship, the prior of Newburgh warned that the abbey's rights took precedence.[28] How much more direct than a long chain of connections was the single link from a lord to each individual. It was through the power of the lords, in their capacities as king's officers, that kings looked to the rule of the localities, transmitting royal commands further down and acting as conduits upwards for petitions and grievances. This was the system in the palatinates of Lancaster and Chester, in the pockets of Richard II himself and the dukes of Lancaster up to 1399, and of Warwickshire and Devonshire when dominated by the earls of Warwick and Devon. Although grumbling and with prejudices to be flouted at one's peril, East Anglian electors *did* defer to their local dukes in 1472.[29] The apex of a host of local networks and communities, lords harnessed them into a 'single lineage' or 'single patronage system', not just temporarily, but for generations.[30]

Not all counties were ruled by peers. Nottinghamshire and Derbyshire, for instance, were run by groups of county families of gentry. It was they who ruled. Local lords did not have to be peers. If 'England was a federation of lordly spheres of influence', as Given-Wilson indicates,[31] the lords included many who were not peers. The Vernons traditionally were kings of the Peak (Derbys.), the economic equals of many a baron, and the Herons were rulers of Redesdale (Northumb.). Peers did have precedence socially over mere esquires and alone could retain outside their households – an indication that parliament considered peers better suited to rule. Many counties had no presiding peer, no dominant house of gentry, no recognisable oligarchy of gentry. Such communities should not be seen as essentially different: their leaders were lords too, if of inferior rank, perhaps infe-rior authority, a narrower geographical sway and lesser connections of their own. No single pattern of local politics applied everywhere and each county was different.

Historians have explained such differences in short sequences, in terms of the ebb and flow of particular families and estates, and have ignored the underlying structures. Staffordshire's political history has been recounted in twenty- or thirty-year chunks and Warwickshire's by generations of earls of Warwick. Provincial systems of landholding and hence provincial politics derive from the balance of landholding between the crown, peerage, gentry and Church, which changed very little over the centuries. This is most obvious when account is taken of the Church, which almost all fifteenth-century historians ignore: such neglect detracts from all published county and regional studies to date. There were counties such as Hampshire, Dorset, Kent and Hertfordshire where bishops and abbeys held the bulk of the land; in Suffolk it was not the dukes of Norfolk or Suffolk, but the abbey of Bury St Edmunds that was the greatest landholder. The Church held significant percentages of land everywhere. And they had done so for many centuries, the greatest accretions originating before the Norman Conquest, most of the rest no later than the thirteenth century. Such holdings constrained secular landholding and county politics. So too, more surprisingly, with the other categories of landholders. In the nine historic counties of southern England, Cornwall, Sussex and perhaps Devon were consistently dominated by the nobility, Somerset and Wiltshire by the gentry, and Dorset, Hampshire and Kent by the Church. This was as true in 1086, as in 1316, as in 1412.[32] Such structures imposed patterns, frameworks and limits to the politics of those counties. Most probably it was the lesser peerage and the gentry, greater in Wiltshire and Somerset, and ecclesiastical tenants elsewhere who ran affairs. Such variations were to be found everywhere. Where there was no great magnate, as in Derbyshire in 1433, it is no surprise that Grey of Codnor, the local baron, was outweighed by the leading gentry.[33] Only in eight counties between 1386 and 1421 was parliamentary representation controlled by a noble connection; it was 'the palpable strength of the gentry communities' that was decisive in another eight.[34] These variations need to be identified, charted, researched and compared.

It is therefore implausible that county politics was as kaleidoscopic as historians tend to suppose. They exaggerate what they find. What they record are, for the most part, minor shifts, adjustments temporary or occasionally permanent, within enduring structures. Minorities, dowagers and even temporary forfeitures were mere interruptions. Modern historians inevitably search for change, for the developments or beginnings of developments that inaugurate something new. The belief that the Beauchamp minorities of 1439–49 permanently weakened the earldom of Warwick is a fallacy easily exposed by reference to later evidence.[35] Historians dislike determinism, which robs them and past contemporaries of their free will. Of course there were changes. If the crown held the county of Chester, duchy of Cornwall and ancient queens' lands throughout, it nevertheless accrued the duchy of Lancaster in 1399, of York in 1461, the Warwick inheritance in 1487, and much else besides, not always permanently but with important impact in particular areas. Adjustments necessarily followed. Families added to their inheritances, failed in the male line, rose by inheritance as did the Talbots and by purchase as did Fastolf, and suffered partitions as did the Holland earls of Kent, without necessarily altering significantly the balance of landholding, power and politics within their shires. They were interchangeable over the *longue durée*. Which gentleman or family secured an estate, status, wealth and power was of course crucial to those involved. People thought that they mattered and generally behaved on the basis that they did.

Contemporaries, of course, did not perceive the underlying structures: they believed, rightly, that they were shaping events. They accepted political realities without reflecting on them and perhaps never perceived that contrasting patterns of landholding and power around them had developed long ago. Historians need to record their personal histories, but they should also understand the parameters within which they operated. Of course what happened at the time mattered, but it happened within structures that it did not change. National society and the national political system changed very little during the later middle ages.

Conflict and resolution

There is ample evidence of violent crime and perversion of justice for every decade and county in fifteenth-century England. Some aristocratic crimes were classics for any age. Most well-documented towns experienced friction between the elite and the rest, even the election of two rival mayors at Leicester in 1489, and conflict on taxation, grazing, precedence and with rival franchises. Historians deplore the lawlessness. So too did fifteenth-century parliaments. MPs blamed lawlessness on those responsible for enforcement. The most lurid *causes célèbres* were aristocratic. Arson, robbery and cold-blooded murder in the Radford case by a future earl in 1455 was actually exacerbated by perjury, perversion of justice and sacrilege. The judicial murder of Ankarette Twynho in 1477 by a royal duke abused almost every rule of due process. There were tit-for-tat killings. The Pastons suffered invasion of their lands, demolition of their house, a full-scale siege and fraudulent indictments.

Private wars in Devon, Yorkshire and Gloucestershire culminated in private battles. The Yorkists eliminated personal enemies at the battles of St Albans in 1455 and Northampton in 1460. Justice could not be done in relation to magnates, nor indeed many lesser aristocrats, or their lawsuits, because the whole judicial process was susceptible to perversion, which everybody exploited as and when advantageous.

Quarrels and abuses had identifiable roots. Urban issues are usually clear enough, though often mere symptoms of deeper problems. They have generally been regarded sympathetically by historians temperamentally inclined towards the oppressed. We cannot always establish what lies behind some aristocratic quarrels. M.E. James placed great stress on the concept of honour, which meant that 'silly quarrels' could not be resolved other than violently.[36] 'Gentlemen's wars' were equated with 'land wars' by Professor Bellamy, who perceived that almost all such quarrels arose from disputes over land.[37] Murders of individuals, forcible entries and disseisins, bastard feudal abuses and the transfer of private differences into national politics usually grew out of disputes about property, often provincial in origin and generally provincial in pursuit. Tenure of property embroiled any significant landowner in disputes about boundaries, rights of way, water-courses and the demolition of buildings, just as today, together with tithes, common pasture, wardship and villeinage, which are more distinctively medieval. Small matters could inflate and escalate, just as today, sucking in other parties, the legal system and self-help, costs out of proportion to the original offence, and even rights to the land itself. There were a great many such issues. Our letter writers had several such side-shows running at any particular time.

Disputes about land itself, about inheritance, were not silly. They were crucial to participants and threatened their whole fortunes. Though numerous, they were less universal than sometimes appear. There were four main categories. The two least important, perhaps, were short-term intergenerational disputes, such as those between dowagers and step-children, and disputes involving defaulting trustees. More significant were inheritance disputes and disputed titles. Most properties always descended by inheritance, succession normally being peaceful and automatic. Problems arose when inheritance was less than direct, from father to son, which McFarlane reckoned occurred in a quarter of cases every twenty-five years.[38] The other 75 per cent, therefore, posed no problems. Of those that failed, there were normally no difficulties when there was a single undisputed heir – the next brother, a daughter, or uncle – or even when there were co-heiresses. Difficulties arose with different titles: between the heirs male and heirs general, as in the Arundel–Warenne and great Berkeley inheritance disputes of 1417; when the half-blood came into play, a whole sister of a brother taking preference over a half-sister, as in the Beauchamp and Despenser disputes from 1449; and when property was transferred from a senior to a junior line, as in the

Neville–Neville, Talbot–Talbot and Mountford–Mountford cases. Whilst particularly large scale and high profile, there were less of these cases than of those in the fourth category, which arose from transfers from one family to another. Titles were always imperfect. The most secure title had proof of continuous occupation from time immemorial, since 1189, which was almost unattainable. That title could then be conveyed to the purchaser. Problems arose not so much in creating a new right as in extinguishing old ones. Childless sellers almost invariably had collateral heirs – siblings, uncles, cousins and very distant cousins – to be disadvantaged by a sale. Even if their rights were bought out and a raft of quitclaims secured, mortality could bring to the fore yet more distant claimants, perhaps unborn or under age at the time of the sale. The seller might not legally be free to sell: he could be a tenant-for-life constrained by an entail. Sale-prices took account of such problems, litigation adding significantly to the costs that Fastolf paid to acquire his estates. The Ogard purchasers of Buckenham Castle in Norfolk from the childless Sir John Clifton lost out to the rightful heirs, the Knyvets. The bastard John Hopton was fortunate indeed that no Swillington heir effectively challenged his right.

Fortunately and unfortunately such disputes are the principal subject matter of the Paston, Plumpton and Armburgh letter collections. Fortunately they cast a mass of light. Unfortunately they tempt us to see them as typical – whereas it may be that it was the dispute that caused the records to be created and kept – and we see events through the eyes of the authors.[39] John Paston I 'put his trust in an Englishman's right to law'[40] – he thought himself right and his historian agrees – but he could nevertheless have been mistaken. Distinguishing right from wrong may be an inappropriate approach. How can we tell? Alternative titles could legitimately exist. That the eldest son of the 1st earl of Westmorland remitted his claims to a younger sibling did not extinguish the rights of his offspring and intermediate brothers. Distinctions are needed between right and title. The Pastons bought at East Beckham and Gresham (Norf.) the titles of trustees to family lands that had not been quitclaimed by the heirs whose titles were being reasserted. Did the will declaring the trust override the residual hereditary rights of others? Whatever the Pastons and modern historians have said, Robert Lord Moleyns had an arguable claim to Gresham (Norf.).[41] Claimants were entitled to bide their time for generations, until the most propitious moment, and did so.

The law itself was uncertain. Were the titles of the duke of Warwick's Beauchamp half-sisters, who were excluded by their half-blood, different from his Despenser half-sister, who partitioned their heritage?[42] The common law did not recognise or understand trusts, nor did it accept chancery decrees as definitive. All cases could be overturned at least once. Inquisitions could be overthrown or new inquisitions could be held. And all stages of any dispute, at court, in the law courts and in the shires, were potentially affected by bastard feudal abuses – maintenance, embracery, champerty, bribery, of sheriffs, escheators, justices and jurors. Often, no doubt, the charges were untrue; more often, no doubt, there were abuses, but no surviving charges. The law offered no final solutions. Some cases rolled on and on, through lawsuits, arbitrations and violence, for generations or even centuries, with long lulls in between. Thirty years after losing their battles for their main inheritances, the Beauchamp co-heirs pursued the Beauchamp trust and the Despenser heir revived his claim. A precautionary quitclaim was still worth securing thirty years after the settlement of the Neville–Neville dispute.[43] It is actually quite reassuring that force seldom determined title, though it often conferred possession.

The flood of litigation in the central courts indicates both the amount of discord amongst the propertied and their pursuit of peaceful rather than (or besides) violent means. Such lawsuits demanded the interruption of possession and forcible entries, violent acts in contemporary parlance. The response might well be violent, the coercion of royal officers and courts, and an escalation might well ensue, the worst cases involving assaults, ambushes, murders, riots, skirmishes, battles and sieges. Such events happened. Violence was not however inevitable, nor was it the normal end result. Much supposed violence, indeed, never happened. As Maddern has shown, violence was the fiction necessary to qualify peaceful conduct for particular types of legal action:[44] a game that made sense to contemporaries, but one difficult for historians five centuries afterwards to fathom.

Much violence never happened because it was not allowed to happen. Self-discipline had its place. Medieval landholders were capable of swallowing trivial differences, of compromising, quit-claiming or selling disputed rights without recourse to force or the law. Lords refused to become embroiled. Only fools attacked more powerful opponents. There were powerful social pressures. The Plumpton correspondence contains examples of mediation before cases reached court. John Walker, for example, sought mediation on behalf of his mother, so 'that then you can bring him to *reasonable* end'; if not, he would sue.[45] That most court cases never reached a verdict was almost certainly because they were settled out of court. The result was unpredictable. Time, effort and costs expended were often more than the issue was worth: John Russe as early as 1465 begged the Pastons to settle with their opponents in the Fastolf inheritance dispute.[46] Society had an interest in the love, union, peace, accord, quiet and amity to which arbitration awards constantly appealed. So did lords: 'within the area of the lord's influence, the affinity was a powerful regulator of social behaviour'.[47] Discord was not only socially divisive, but was also discreditable to the causers, damaging both to those who refused mediation and those who rejected awards. Intransigence was deplorable. Even temporary respite was to be preferred. Arbitration offered a way out that was cheaper, an escape without dishonour and a compromise in which both parties saved something even if neither gained all as in litigation. If Amesbury Abbey was wrong to claim the Salisbury mayor John Hall as a serf, it was saved the full consequences of defamation and wrongful arrest.[48] Family, friends, neighbours, lords, bishops, kings and ministers constantly offered mediation, individually, successively, simultaneously and in concert. It was often almost irresistible. Society possessed homeostatic (self-righting) mechanisms to defuse disputes, to encourage compromise and to prevent disagreements getting out of hand. Once a remedy was reached, it was often reinforced by a public display of reconciliation – an act of contrition, apology and forgiveness, the holding of hands, a church service – that made the solution final and backsliding almost impossible. The Loveday at St Pauls (1458) conforms to type.

Some did reject such pressures: the Pastons were notorious examples. Undying ecclesiastical corporations found acceptance of any loss – the inevitable consequence of compromise – too much to stomach. Hence the bitterness of disputes with tenants or Crowland Abbey's disputes with its neighbours which laymen might have resolved. Some rejected the awards, despite the penalties which they sought to evade, often proceeding to further arbitrations, although the Catesby family's resort to five such panels in their search for a favourable award appears to be the record.[49] Rejection of an award might make enemies of the arbiters. Defaulters tended to allege bias by the arbiters, sometimes with justice. Arbiters were selected with as much care as jurors, to secure favourable verdicts, hence nomination by both sides. Often, apparently, arbiters moved from party lines to compromise in the arbitration chamber, but sometimes, unsurprisingly, they were unable to agree. Occasionally they – or the umpire – came down too firmly on one side, perhaps because their own interests were involved. Not to act justly was damaging to the worship of the arbiter. No lord could afford a track record of bad lordship. If some of the host of surviving awards are biased, most are meticulous and painfully fair, so that lords as seldom praised as the Kingmaker and Clarence emerge with credit.[50] Arbitration was approved by king, parliament and the judiciary. If it failed, king, judges or parliament might impose less palatable remedies. Authority at every level propelled those in dispute into peaceful channels and imposed order upon them.

10

INTERACTION

Centre and provinces

The revolution of 1399 changed little. The monarchy was unchallenged. The central machine maintained its prescribed procedures and timetables, amongst which the pricking and accounting of sheriffs, the issue and return of writs, the appointment of commissions, and the assizes calendared provincial societies everywhere. County courts, assizes and quarter sessions continued. Local elites, as royal officers, deployed their local standing on behalf of royal government and justice, ensuring both respect and implementation. Noblemen were expected to keep the peace and set good examples. The English governed themselves at the king's command. Inertia favoured the status quo.

Inertia by itself was never enough. Routine required constant reinforcement if it were not to be eroded in practice, not to decay through disuse, if it were to remain effective and to retain respect. Crown and order meant little when represented by neighbours no better than oneself, who were deputising for a king never seen and personally less than awesome. If Henry VI was indeed simple and child-like, it detracted in practice not only from his rule, but from that of his agents also. Royal power must be seen and exercised, must require attention and respect, and must be enforced. There was a voluntary element to the relationship of king and subject. Compliance could not be presumed and must sometimes be solicited.

All kings on occasion wanted action from their local officials, especially in wartime. Local commissioners and corporations arrayed the populace against threatened invasions and rebellions. Ships, billets, supplies and munitions were requisitioned. For foreign wars, in France or Scotland, requisitioning was on a larger scale for longer periods. Taxes were levied or anticipated by forced loans: instructions to a London alderman survive.[1] Local officers had to interview and pressure those of means.

Seen from the centre, local government was the king's instrument to command. Not so from the localities. Commands were despatched, but were they implemented? Governments 'still depended greatly on the co-operation of the so-called rulers of the countryside'.[2] Provincial societies had their own agendas. What they wanted, perhaps as communities and definitely as individuals, differed from the equitable imposition of centrally devised rules without regard to local circumstance. Royal office gave legitimacy to local rulers. It justified their local rule and enabled them to lord it over others' men in the king's name. Their standing as royal officers gave mayors much of their dignity and authority. Their wishes prevailed and victims were denied remedies. Bristol's corporation was able repeatedly to resist appeals to royal authority and impose obedience to itself.[3] Royal office-holding by provincial aristocrats and jurats was a compact of mutual advantage, rarely stated, but real nevertheless. Peers did not regard themselves as working justices and may seldom have sat, but they could do so if they wished. Some attended quarter sessions without actually officiating, such as Lord Stafford of Southwick at Exeter.[4] If monarchs did not yet demand of their officers personal attendance and excessive assiduity, in and out of court, the prestige and authority on offer was also less. Many JPs did not attend quarter sessions. JPs in the seventeenth century prioritised their pockets over their county and their county over the national interest.[5] Officers did not act against their own interests – the interests of their community and dependants, in this context, being their own. Their standing rested ultimately on consent from those below them. Villagers on occasion resisted distraints and refused to answer articles put to them or to indict neighbours.[6] The wishes of their constituency, electorate, fellow oligarch and communalty counted for more to mayors, if forced to choose, than any king's command. Even urban oligarchs, in the last resort, were chosen by their communities, 'and could, sometimes, be legitimately removed by them'.[7] Local elites sympathised with distinctive local crimes – social crime – and all officers (and even royal judges) sometimes abused the law, resorted to violence and practised aristocratic crimes. Governments had few alternatives of equal standing whose authority they could borrow. Reliance on lesser men, 'by whom the people would not be ruled' or whose relative necessitated extortion, or on outsiders, was counter-productive.[8] Passive resistance to royal decrees was normal.

The operation of royal justice illustrates many of these points. All officers swore oaths of office, promising to operate without fear or favour to great or humble. Frequently they lacked the power or more probably the desire to hold the powerful to account, so dozens of petitions to king, chancery and parliament, understandably partisan, allege. National eminence might count for little in the provinces, where national minnows could play the local shark. Some complaints against those locally irresistible emanate from national figures. However independent and impartial in theory, royal government and justice constantly failed to check the excesses, to try the crimes or to resolve the differences of the provincial aristocracy. Local government and justice were susceptible to abuse and were constantly abused, so it is argued, as everybody exploited the loopholes when advantageous and railed against them when not. Maintenance, the support of another man's suit, was legal, although certain aspects of it – the overawing of courts by force, for instance – were proscribed. Jurors were selected not from those who knew nothing about a case, as today, but from those in a position to know: they had therefore already made up their minds. It was perfectly legal to seek to influence them: paying them – embracery – was not. Hence the importance of having the right jurors and the efforts of parties to pressurise, influence or bribe the sheriff who empanelled them. It was again perfectly legal to select favourable commissioners or to influence and coerce them. Bribing and retaining judges was illegal, but nevertheless happened. And there were enormous opportunities besides to steal a march on one's opponents, legal or illicit, by making excuses (*essoins*) in court, by having writs delayed, by holding sessions in places favourable to one side and by suing plaintiffs in another court. Suits could be suspended, results biased and offences pardoned on royal intervention, which was itself to be solicited or bought. The judicial system was a morass, fraught with technicalities and demanding constant vigilance, always favouring those of rank, influence and wealth over the underdog, and constantly failed to fulfil its objectives.

This was not due to lack of central involvement in local justice. Government appointed sheriffs, JPs, justices of assize, ensured that the quorum was legally knowledgeable and placed judges on commissions, though it could seldom ensure actual attendance or that local lawyers rose above local society and politics. Assizes regularly reviewed local justice. The fruits of oversight and of local demands for oversight appear in the files of ancient indictments. Important cases finished at the centre, mainly because those involved, who may have been guilty, expected more sympathetic hearings away from their local peers. Many such cases ended *sine die* with royal pardons. The standard government response to local disorder was the commission of oyer and terminer. Accompanied and backed by the king himself, they were the solution to complaints of lawlessness at the parliament of 1472–5. Oyer and terminer commissions replaced the discontinued eyre and, after 1414, judicial progresses from king's bench. Chancery and later star chamber, king, council and parliament received many complaints of injustice, either trying or ruling them themselves or ordering others to arbitrate. Arbitration was a valuable complement to the common law. Kings settled in person disputes among those too powerful for their judges, such as the Warwick inheritance dispute between the king's brothers.[9] A stronger king could have prevented the escalation of feuds in the 1450s. Kings sometimes punished or imprisoned offending magnates. Peace, not justice, was the aim, for kings were liable to place political considerations first. Edward IV refused to protect the countess of Warwick against his own brothers or the Pastons against his brother-in-law.[10] He intervened in judicial processes on behalf of one party. When lawlessness was curbed, historians have been inclined to attribute it to other causes, such as the removal of offenders by military service in France.

Interaction: publicity and propaganda

Governments, their critics, individuals and pressure groups sought to influence public opinion. Governments had enormous advantages. All the symbolism of monarchy enhanced the presumption in the king's favour, asserted his authority, suspended scepticism and discredited critics. It 'was successful in putting across the king's role as head of the judicial system and ultimate earthly arbiter' even to those, such as peasants in revolt, who despised his judges and lawyers.[11] Kings had officers everywhere acting in their names. Every judicial session applied the king's laws and maintained his peace. Monthly county courts, quarter sessions, regular assizes and irregular commissions invoked his name and carried out his will. They offered opportunities to proclaim his wishes. Often church pulpits, ecclesiastical ceremonial, and the majesty of the law – executions and displays of quarters and heads not least – were enlisted in support. A host of personal messages emanated from the privy seal and signet office, such as the newsletters, explanations and instructions apparently accumulated by the London alderman Sir Thomas Cook.[12] If most such informal material is lost, we have the proclamations, both enrolled and often returned. Nor should we presume that official records resulting from formal official processes, such as the preambles to statutes and indictments of traitors, were any less partisan. A modern historian has found the case for a Southampton Plot (1415) to be unbelievable.[13] Indictments were the charges of enemies seeking the destruction of defendants – who had a vested interest in discrediting them – and sought to dissuade and deter potential opponents.

Government propaganda was seldom confronted. Most dissenters and disturbances were localised and raised purely local issues, that were resolved locally. Jack Cade's manifestos were exceptional in converting disparate and mutually contradictory woes into coherent programmes of general appeal. Local strikes, disputes, riots and insurrections could be restricted near their origins, tamed or repressed from purely local resources, without ever becoming dangerous movements. Protesters, rebels and critics never developed archives as complete as those of the crown. Yet some objections were recorded, insurrections aroused and complaints registered. Others broadcast their messages and invited support with propaganda. Aristocratic rebels always had to explain themselves, from the Percies in 1403 to the Yorkshiremen of 1469 and 1489, composing and circulating manifestos, exploiting the pulpit and issuing publicly what were ostensibly private letters. Commercial policies were advanced by *The Libel of English Policy*, and William Worcester's *Book of Noblesse* promoted intervention in France. Mirrors of Princes repeatedly addressed royal conduct. *Hardyng's Chronicle(s)* and Caxton's lament about the death of chivalry enshrined individual points of view.

Such material was always topical and biased. The most apparently conventional and innocuous statements were actually partisan, designed to appeal, influence, persuade and to impel to action. If all kings wished to maintain the status quo, to dispel opposition and to secure support, their critics sought to reach the aggrieved, to arouse anger, to encourage self-help and to recruit committed supporters to their cause. Exaggeration, distortion, misrepresentation, disinformation and character assassination all had a role.

No event invited more manipulation of opinion than 1399. The official Lancastrian *record and process* necessarily (if fictionally) portrayed Richard II's removal as a voluntary abdication with smiling face (*hilari vultu*). Entered on the parliament roll, it recurs in many London chronicles.[14] This was not merely because of its own intrinsic merits vis-à-vis rival alternatives, but rather because of the number of copies broadcast by the usurping regime. Similarly the proliferation in London chronicles of terms of surrender of so many Norman strongholds indicates how Henry V publicised his mundane campaign of attrition, fostered patriotism and loosened taxpayers' purse-strings;[15] his speeches, proclamations, processions, services of thanksgiving and official narratives are better known. Three well-known letters, in which Bedford presented the City corporation in 1422 with his right to rule, whereby Beaufort requested his (Bedford's) intervention in 1426, and whereby Gloucester in 1440 opposed the release of the duke of Orleans, were open letters addressing much wider audiences and seeking to win them over. How could Bedford (or any other reader) not 'desire the welfare of the king our sovereign lord and of his realms of England and France and ... of us all'?[16] Massive publicity presented the relief of Calais as a national crisis that was indeed successfully overcome.[17] Alternative, hostile, versions were also current, such as the French anti-Lancastrian accounts of 1399 by Creton and in the *Treason and Death of Richard II*. Manifestos justified the insurrections of the Percies in 1403 and Archbishop Scrope in 1405.[18] Rumour, prophecy and portents were the weapons of opposition. If never widely accepted, tales of Richard II alive in Scotland and attributions of Henry IV's maladies to divine punishment for the sins of usurpation, perjury and the sacrilegious murder of an archbishop were nevertheless current.[19] The legend of Joan of Arc, in France, counteracted that of Henry V, which nevertheless in England inspired his brother Gloucester to pose as his true heir in opposition to Henry VI's peace policy.[20] Defeat in conventional politics prompted Gloucester to go public; as, apparently, did York when charged with corruption.[21] The trials of Gloucester's duchess for sorcery and, potentially, Gloucester himself served propagandist purposes if nothing more.

Almost every variety of opinion-shaping literature survives for 1449–50 and 1459–61. We know that much more than what remains emanated from both the government and its critics. That there are fewer examples after 1471 is partly due to survival. Richard III's usurpation was coloured, so chroniclers report, by open and secret letters, political verses, dissident manifestos and proclamations, all of them now missing. Was it because the reformers in 1450–61 and the rebels of 1469–71 succeeded that their propaganda was retained, whereas the propaganda of the unsuccessful rebels of 1486–1504 was discarded and hence rarely survives?

Such attacks stimulated reactions from the crown, which exploited its normal channels to maximum effect. Following his failed coup in 1452, York had to swear an extremely explicit oath of allegiance that was published and repeatedly re-issued.[22] Cade's uprising was categorised as rebellion, he himself was (eventually) attainted and York's most trusted councillors were indicted as co-conspirators. All the formidable resources of the state were deployed against dissidents, who were disparaged in the historical record. The government's version of the Loveday at St Paul's was promulgated through several different media. In 1459 the whole decade was rewritten from a Lancastrian perspective. The acts of 1461 declaring Edward IV's title and attainting Henry VI reversed not only the revolution of 1399, but the public perception of the last sixty years.[23] *The Chronicle of the Lincolnshire Rebellion* and *The Arrival of Edward IV* are official accounts of Edward's victories in 1470 and 1471. The Tudor myth, first enunciated in 1485–6, boldly reinterpreted the whole century, from 1399 to 1485, as a single providential cycle of sin and punishment terminated victoriously by Henry VII. Rival interpretations had expired before Shakespeare's history plays imposed it on future generations for whom the original providential message has no meaning.

From 1450 onwards governments consistently lost the propaganda wars. Defeat in France, near bankruptcy and public disorder exposed successive regimes to assault from late medieval spin-doctors, who set the agenda. Typically regimes were held to account and charged with crimes that were really misdemeanours, mistakes or mere misfortunes. Accuracy and fairness were incidental. Reformers never took the defensive – neither the Yorkist earls of 1460 nor Warwick in 1470 confronted their previous offences – and they never answered responses directly. They asserted that they had been wronged and were believed. It was an error in 1460 for Queen Margaret to answer her critics when appealing for support against the perjured York.[24] Propagandists from York to the Tudors tailored their message to their target audience. Some of the most effective official propaganda dates from 1455 and 1460,[25] *after* governments had been captured by the opposition. Governments always had to react to opponents who had selected the topics at issue and had chosen their time to strike. They could not retort quickly or effectively. Henry VI's considered replies to York in 1450 were subverted in the duke's own propaganda.[26] A Yorkist view of the 1450s that ultimately derived from such partisan pieces as the *Parliamentary Pardon* of 1455 and York's claim in 1460 were incorporated into many contemporary chronicles.[27] The Lancastrian alternative was forgotten. King Edward's splendid *Lincolnshire Chronicle* and *Arrival* retrospectively stilled recriminations, shaped the future and informed foreign audiences. Fellow Englishmen needed to be convinced of Warwick's guilt in 1470 and in 1471, and foreign backers needed to be reassured that Edward's victory was complete.

Interaction: parliament

Parliament constituted the limbs of a body politic of which the king was the head. Henry VIII was never more a king, he flatteringly declared, than when knit with his members in parliament. Some powers had to be exercised with parliament. Most sessions were pacific, co-operative occasions and even joyous celebrations, but there were others that were not. Fifteenth-century kings commonly sat in the Lords, participated in discussions, and planned and orchestrated business out of hours. In 1465 King Edward took counsel in the lower council chamber and liaised with his chancellor and clerk of parliament in his chamber. Acts of resumption involved most wide-ranging reviews of patronage, which were serviced by the king's secretariat. Edward may always have interviewed those seeking exemptions. He definitely did in 1467 and 1473, when there were respectively 282 and 221 suitors, suggesting that he may have held respectively 564 and 442 interviews of a staggering number of hours with them.[28] Surely such contacts conferred on the king considerable personal ascendancy over his suitors?

Parliaments did not always do the king's bidding. The Lords had a right and duty to attend and personal axes to grind. Community of interest explains the occasional acquittal of royal scapegoats. Although conciliar colleagues and fellow landholders, lords temporal and spiritual often differed in outlook. Party politics had its place, as partisan interpretations of events were imposed by the Yorkists in 1455 and the Lancastrians in 1459, when Henry VI had difficulty in restraining the vengeance of some of his supporters.[29] Peers were mandated by nobody. They brought to parliament their concerns outside parliament: kinship and seigneurial ties; inheritance disputes and provincial rivalries; and personal expertise and preoccupations. Clashes on precedence, on inheritance and on national politics all occurred. It may have been Cromwell's decision to break ranks that opened the way to Suffolk's impeachment, the outraged honour and losses of an erstwhile lieutenant that set York against the vanquished Somerset, and it was certainly Cromwell in 1455 who pressed his rights to Ampthill (Beds.) against the absent duke of Exeter.[30] The Commons raised the petitions that constituted most parliamentary business. Often local in origin, they included many critical of royal actions and royal agents. The price kings paid for compliance was patient and sympathetic reception to Commons petitions, some of which always passed into law although seldom of interest either to king or government.

The Commons represented the local communities that elected them, or rather the propertied governing elites that were eligible to vote. That begs the question whether they sat on their own behalf, as representatives of their constituencies, or on behalf of the powerful people who put them in. Up until 1406, when election was first regu-

lated, it appears that shire elections were shaped by a few local notables: magnates or their attorneys, not necessarily even barons. Such
formal dominance had ended by the 1430s, when parliament had set a
franchise of 40s. corresponding to hundreds of voters per county.
Magnate dominance may have given way to genuine representation.
'The 1420s witnessed increasing incidents of disruption at elections',
writes Clark, 'again to all appearances with members of the gentry, not
the nobility, acting as prime movers.' Analysis of evidence beforehand
does not suggest that many magnate retainers sat in parliament: only
14 per cent have been identified. In localities, such as the north and
Devon, where those elected correlate closely to the principal aristocratic connections,[31] it does not follow that their lords placed them
there. If lords were any good at recruitment, their men should have
been sitting in parliament anyway. That king and lords had retainers in
parliament need not imply that they had placed them there or even
cared about their election. It may be more significant that all knights
of the shire and most burgesses were aristocrats, themselves lords and
dependants of lords. Burgesses from seigneurial boroughs did not need
pressing to represent their lords and their mutual interests. Kings occasionally sought to pack in their men – or were credited with doing so –
and succeeded in 1478, when fifty royal servants were elected. Peers
sometimes tried to place their men, for example the earl of
Westmorland at Grimsby in 1470 and the dukes of Norfolk on several
occasions,[32] but normally, it seems, did not. External interference,
royal or noble, might be resented, but was not always effectively
resisted.

Those seeking election, more probably for personal reasons than a
desire to serve their constituents, maximised their connections, mobil-
ising friends and kin, tenants, clients and neighbours, and paid for their
service as well. It was the men of Bassetlaw who secured Sir John
Stanhope's election for Nottinghamshire in 1460 and perhaps Bishop
Morton's tenants who decided the 1482 Norfolk election.[33] Elections
reflected the local balance of power. Contested elections surely indicate
the rifts that divided counties or developed them, as in the contest
between Sir John Ormond and Sir John Tiptoft in Cambridgeshire in
1439.[34] Apparently contests were uncommon. To the handful explicitly recorded may perhaps be added a few others suggested by
exceptional crowds of attestors. Perhaps there were no contests before
1406, when there were no rules, or perhaps no grounds for complaint.
Maybe the hordes of voters that parliament deplored in 1430 were
confined to a few counties. Yet the number of contests is unimpressive.
A maximum of 5 out of 548 elections in 1406–30 and 28 out of 557

in 1430–78 (2 per cent) attracted a hundred attestors. Almost all elections, by implication, were uncontested, consensual and unanimous, as under Elizabeth I and during the early seventeenth century.[35] Perhaps elections did not matter much. Those who cared almost always agreed. MPs could therefore represent everybody with full authority. We cannot know whether they did.

Proceedings appear always dominated by legislation arising mainly from petitions. It was an important constitutional safety valve that parliament could redress grievances and that all such grievances were received. 'Every person high and low suing to this high court of parliament of right must be heard', though not necessarily answered 'without the king's commandment'.[36] Whereas the receivers and triers of petitions had often diverted complaints to the courts or council, they no longer monopolised access for bills to parliament. Many petitions were presented without reference to them. In 1461 bills were presented directly to the Lords and in 1485 to the Commons.[37] Parliament was an important last resort to those unable to obtain justice: occasionally it humbled the powerful.[38] The lobbying of parliament by cities and livery companies can sometimes be connected to specific legislation. Suitors were not always right and those seeking new laws were not always seeking the common rather than their own private good. Many bills were never enacted, from the Lollard disendowment bill (1410) and John Rows' depopulation bill (1459), to the countess of Warwick's two bills of 1472–85. Most petitions were concerned with particular individuals, families, corporations and locations.[39] Some certainly originated with MPs, who may have been performing a genuinely representative role, but this can only rarely be demonstrated from references in urban archives. Contemporaries supposed that lawyer MPs often acted for clients. Most bills originated with vested interests and aimed to remedy specific ills or to advantage individuals or groups. Increasingly they purported to come from the Commons as a whole, but this can seldom be the case. All reached the Commons already cast into the correct format as parliamentary bills. On the evidence of the two fruitless commonwealth debates of 1485, the Commons itself was ill equipped to devise its own legislation.[40]

The Lords in 1461 was surprisingly advanced procedurally. The Commons did not develop over the century and was less sophisticated in 1485 than it appears. Procedures for debating, vetting and tracking bills were undeveloped. Many bills made no progress. There was no provision for separate consideration in committee. As no bills were read more than once, any amendments must have been made at the first reading. Many of the acts in 1485 appear not to have been discussed by the Commons.[41] Commons bills were sometimes treated with scant respect by king and Lords. If amended, they might not have to be returned to the Commons or might even be consolidated, rewritten and enacted without further reference to them. Henry IV's promise not to alter acts after they were passed was not operational eighty years later.[42] Bills were still being enacted without Commons participation in 1485. Twenty-one Lords bills were apparently nodded through. The attainder bill, which was grossly unjust, was passed because the king insisted. This picture of a subservient house, that deferred to its social superiors in the Lords and the king, exaggerates somewhat. There are well-known instances when the Commons were more assertive: Henry IV was sorely tested by Speaker Savage.

Yet kings could not do as they pleased. Special political reasons always brought them to parliament. Parliament was a political occasion, often the venue for set-piece political drama, sometimes of major political crises. These were of four principal types: parliaments summoned as the forum for state trials; the first parliaments of usurping kings; parliaments dominated by financial considerations, especially taxation; and parliaments where criticism of the regime became acute or even overpowering. The categories overlap. Taxation has already been discussed. The most major crisis is discussed below. The first two categories follow.

Trials of great magnates were scheduled for 1447, 1459 and 1478. In 1447 Gloucester died before the form of his trial was revealed. Bury St Edmunds in Suffolk was chosen as venue to distance him from sympathisers in London. Likewise London was avoided in 1459 when Coventry, where the king was strong, was preferred. York and his fellow rebels, most of whom were in exile, were attainted. If electors were indeed encouraged to elect committed Lancastrians, it was not so stated in the actual writs of summons.[43] Parliament was more hostile to the Yorkists than the king, insisting on attainting some who had submitted and obliging the king to exercise his veto.[44] The third instance, the trial of Edward IV's brother Clarence at Westminster in 1478, was combined with a royal wedding. Extremely carefully prepared, the spoils being distributed in advance, it had the highest representation of royal servants among the Commons of the century; the court nobility were also well represented and an unusually large number of MPs were in the service of court nobles. That such precautions were deemed necessary even when the king was leading for the prosecution – the king's testimony was taken as record in his own courts – indicates how little parliament could be taken for granted.[45]

Too much hung on such trials for kings to rely on the presumption being in their favour.

Six usurpers held parliaments to approve their titles, to resume the grants of their predecessors, proscribe their foes and vote them the revenues with which to rule. In 1399 Richard II was set aside in favour of Henry IV and the decision had to be justified: Richard's supposed abdication annulled oaths of allegiance and eased tender consciences and Henry IV was acclaimed and approved. Richard was unquestionably a legitimate king, so his acts remained valid except those from his last years of tyranny. His favourites were demoted, from dukes to earls, but not persecuted, prosecuted nor proscribed. Further appeals were quashed. Reconciliation was preferred. The year 1399 was the model for two subsequent Yorkist usurpations, those of Edward IV in 1461 and Richard III in 1483. Events were orchestrated as an election and were ratified retrospectively by later parliaments.[46]

When York claimed the throne in parliament in 1460, the Lords – although mainly his partisans and sympathisers – declined. They settled instead for the *Accord*, which was never formally submitted to parliament for enactment. The *Accord* acknowledged his hereditary right, which peers found undeniable, but postponed his actual accession until Henry VI's death. York was to rule. Following York's death his son was obliged to bid for the throne on the pretext that Henry had broken the *Accord* and had thus forfeited his throne. Two sermons set out his title, he was invited and repeatedly acclaimed by 'the people', and was formally elected by the great council and acknowledged by the Lords. Donning the cap of estate, he seated himself on the throne at Westminster Hall, attended services both at St Paul's and Westminster Abbey, where he received the royal sceptre and swore the coronation oath. Participants were a limited group of his adherents.

Victory at Towton and a proper coronation changed him from an aspirant pretender well before the assembly of the parliament that recognised him as King Edward IV. It confirmed his hereditary title and the myth that Henry had forfeited his crown. It had to overturn the Lancastrian title approved by parliaments in and since 1399 and substitute a Yorkist orthodoxy of recent upheavals. Rebels against earlier Lancastrians in 1400 and 1415 were rehabilitated: Warwick twice turned this to advantage.[47] Henry VI himself became a traitor, his duchy of Lancaster remaining annexed to the crown, Lancastrian partisans at all the battles since the *Accord* (which they had never accepted) were attainted and Henry VI's own patronage since 1422 was resumed into the king's hands. Since 1422, not since 1399. It was not possible to turn the clock back sixty years, nor indeed wholly to 1422. Even a sympathetic parliament, from which Edward's enemies were excluded, could not be expected to agree to that. Most of their own creations as peers dated since then. What of the laws of Henry IV, Henry V and Henry VI, the judgements and sentences deriving from them? What of liberties and franchises confirmed since then, town charters, alienations in mortmain and religious foundations? Were they all void? Were all assignments of dower, pardons, presentations to church livings, appointments of judges, liveries of temporalities to bishops and grants of wardships to be annulled? Obviously they could not be, if chaos was to be avoided. Hence the protracted and delicate discussions of the Lords, agreeing the terms of exemptions amongst themselves and in some instances with the Commons, whilst accommodating Edward's unwillingness to concede authority to parliament. In several instances, he refused the phrase by 'authority of parliament', substituting 'the king's pleasure' that left him free to revoke, whilst promising verbally not to do so.[48] Blanket proscription of the Lancastrians was politically unwise. Edward IV had no desire to create opposition through excessive rigour, wished indeed to persuade his opponents to come to terms, and needed indeed, if his regime were to endure, to become king to more than a faction. Only 113 suffered attainder or were threatened with it if they did not submit. Some escaped attainder or were fined. Individual provisos exempted 186 corporations and individuals. The Lords understood the delicacy of the situation, shared the king's intentions and imparted the message to the Commons.[49]

The Readeption parliament of 1470–1 annulled the title of Edward IV in favour of Henry VI and attainted at least some of his partisans, whilst allowing many of his actions to stand. The model was 1461. The partial restoration of proscribed Lancastrians who expected blanket restitution was a delicate issue, since many of their properties had passed to the turncoat Yorkists on whom the new regime depended. Compromise failed and assisted Edward's destruction of a patchwork regime.[50] The opening parliament of Edward's second reign, in 1472–5, was able to disregard the Readeption and continue as before.

Richard III made himself king by disqualifying the titles of his rivals and through his staged election by Londoners, his troops, the rump of the superseded parliament, quickly sealed by his coronation and backed by his northern army. Insurrections against him postponed for the year parliamentary confirmation of *Titulus Regius* – the supposed 'petition' that set out his fictional claims. Rebels from the autumn were attainted. No more was needed, since Richard – unlike his brother in 1461 – accepted the legitimacy of the previous regime, to which he posed as heir. There was not even an act of resumption.

Henry VII, like Edward IV, made himself king in battle rather than by inheritance and by blackening his predecessor, but the precedent of 1461 saved him from experimentation. Naturally parliament repealed *Titulus Regius*, but it had no need to upset any other Ricardian arrangements. Reversing recent and more ancient attainders posed few problems as most recipients were dead and the lands in royal hands. As in 1471 and 1484, it was business as usual. Only once his authority was secure did King Henry wed Elizabeth of York.

Common purposes in 1450

The fourth type of parliamentary crisis was when all sections of society – commons, Commons and Lords – united in criticism of the government. In a hierarchical era it was extremely rare, occurring only thrice in the later middle ages: in 1297, 1376 and 1450. From 1450 it inspired a reforming movement that sought to keep the issues alive and which was a major component in the upheavals of the Wars of the Roses. In 1450 enough peers supported the impeachment of the king's principal councillor by the Commons for the result to be in doubt. London and the south-east were swamped by popular insurrection. Suffolk's murderers, mere mariners, arrogated to themselves sovereign power and spoke for the community of the realm,[51] as did indeed Cade's rebels as they overran London and the south-east. Ministers were assassinated. A royal duke asserted the validity of the rebel programme in parliament to almost universal acclaim. The shipmen who murdered Suffolk thought that they were acting for the community of the realm and applying its sovereign power. Cade's rebels also perceived themselves as the community of the realm. They believed that the king – indeed all kings – needed their goodwill. To them the Peasants' Revolt of 1381 was a precedent and an inspiration. Their cause was limited neither socially nor geographically. Building on a pre-existing popular culture and fund of latent constitutional principles, they rationalised their grievances in their manifestos into constitutional issues recognisable to the elite and broadly defined, to which manifestos could appeal and elicit a response. The people shared the constitutional ideas and expectations of the elite.

Not all the issues of 1450 were of equal interest to the Kentishmen. Their manifestos devote little attention to commerce, which may have mattered more to rebels in London, to the liberties of the Church or to dynasticism. They lamented the loss of Lancastrian France, the parlous counsel and counsellors that had brought these disasters about, domestic abuses and the king's finances. What they deplored, so they supposed, were unquestionable matters of fact:

> Item, we say that our sovereign lord may well understand that he hath had false counsel, for his lands are lost, his merchandise is lost, his commons destroyed, the sea is lost, France is lost, himself so poor that he may not [pay] for his meat nor drink; he oweth more than ever did king in England.

By focusing on counsellors, the king was exempted from responsibility. If he levied money illegally, without the authority of parliament, or mistakenly claimed to be above the law, this was not his own fault, but that of his counsellors. If he had not heard and remedied complaints, it was because he did not know of them, because his counsellors restricted access to him or charged for access. Also above criticism were those royal dukes, supposedly the king's natural councillors, who had been excluded from government in favour of 'persons of lower nature', for whom covetousness was an identity card. 'And if there were no more reason to know a friend by, he may be known by his covetousness'. Greed, rather than the public good or the king's interests, governed their actions and advice. They had robbed the king of his estates, so that he could not live as he ought. Therefore he lived off the commons, taxing them, taking what he needed by purveyance, which remained unpaid, and from other levies and abuses.

Embedded in these rebel articles was thus a respect for the office and person of the king, the real head of government and fount of justice, whose role it was to receive petitioners, to hear complaints and to right wrongs. It was not cheese-paring that was expected of him, but a regal lifestyle. Kings should live like kings. Their grievances remedied, the commons looked forward to a time when

> our sovereign lord shall reign with great worship, love of God and his people, that he shall be able with God's help to conquer where he will ... He shall then reign like a king royal as he is born our true Christian king anointed ...[He] shall be the richest king Christian.

They accepted and indeed respected the social hierarchy and 'desireth the welfare ... of all his true lords spiritual and temporal', especially the royal dukes, whose great wealth implicitly freed them from the search for profit that motivated lesser men and made them into disinterested councillors. The commons wanted to live in harmony with the king:

not only was he unable to stand against them, but he needed their love. His duty to advance the commonweal debarred him from living off the commons. Rather, he should manage on his own income, his own livelihood, which he should rebuild by resuming grants made to unworthy favourites. He would thus have enough for his needs.[52] Government, finance and justice should operate in the interests of all. The prosperity and the protection of the commons, their lives and property, were the proper business of the crown.

Removing evil counsellors was the route to reform and to re-establish good governance. The loss of did not result from the strength of the French and the king's debts were unrelated to military expenses and reduced income. What went wrong was the fault of individual Englishmen, who were neither unlucky, incompetent, negligent nor injudicious, but rather malicious, self-interested and culpable. As in 1376, scapegoats were sought. The worst of motives were attributed. Ministers and diplomats behind the loss of France were guilty of treason. So too were those who counselled the king to break the law and go against the commonweal, and likewise those who peculated and bent the law in Kent. Resumption was the panacea: to resist it was another crime. Those who had lost France, badly counselled the king or ran Kent corruptly should suffer the penalties of treason.[53] A cocktail of naive idealism, snobbish trust, assumption and prejudice informed rebel assessments of constitutional propriety and impropriety.

Criticisms of the regime ahead of Suffolk's impeachment in December 1449 emerge from seditious bitterness in the preceding decade.[54] It was on the basis of public opinion – rumour and *notoriety* – that the house of Commons first impeached the duke. Charges principally of deliberate betrayal of the king's interests in France were found insufficient by the Lords. Supplementary articles developed the original counts and added many domestic offences 'against your royalty, honour, estate and [the] prosperity of your most noble person and the weal of all your true subjects of your realms'. Suffolk's impeachment and hence criticisms of the government with which he was associated thus enjoyed majority or unanimous support in the Commons, the representatives of the community of the realm. The duke was behind grants of land that the king could not afford, new franchises that impeded the operation of the law, lavish rewards for himself and subversion of the law. He encouraged lawlessness and disorder. Not only had he destroyed Duke Humphrey and abridged the lives of other royal princes, but he had 'estranged from your good grace, favour and conceit full great lords to you right nigh. And was ever the most damaging counsellor and unprofitable person to your high estate and your said realms that can be remembered of in days past'.[55] Suffolk's decision to submit to the king and suffer exile rather than await judgement by the Lords to which he was entitled suggests that he feared that they might convict him.[56] A plethora of satirical verses and bills tracing his fall stage by stage indicate how public opinion was informed and orchestrated against him and how parliament was pressurised. Such publications and the sentiment of both houses of parliament justify his murderers' claim to represent the community of the realm.[57] When York's royal blood and claim to the crown became a distracting issue, Cade denounced it as a slander devised by those about the king.[58]

Of course Cade's rebellion had its own distinctive regional origins and complaints. Its manifestos were angled to a more plebeian audience than the articles of impeachment. Many specific charges against Suffolk were ignored though the duke's guilt was taken as read. Others recurred. Allegedly Cade saw himself as fulfilling the wishes of the Commons. His manifestos justify that belief. Appeals were made to the authority of parliament and Suffolk's impeachment was attributed to 'all the communalty of England'. That Suffolk escaped condemnation and that resumption was still being resisted was blamed on 'false traitors'. Cade sought to 'void all the false progeny and affinity' of Suffolk, to try and punish them. 'Item', he explained, 'we will it be known that we blame not all the lords nor all that been about the king's person, nor all gentlemen, nor all men of law, nor all bishops, nor all priests, but such as may be found guilty by a just and a true enquiry by law'. Some 'true judge' held sessions at which courtiers were indicted and ministers were summarily slain. Cade believed that he was acting in concert both with the Commons and the 'true' lords, the royal dukes and those unfortunate enough to have been serving in France.[59]

Although the rebellion was repressed, the reform programme with which it was identified and of which it was a component was not thereby discredited. Many continued the campaign. Those about the king feared a dynastic revolution and resisted York's return from Ireland. York's earlier bills from Ireland and Wales exonerated himself and declared his loyalty. That acknowledged, York took up the issues of Cade against the leftovers of Suffolk's regime. 'Please it unto your highness', commenced his second bill, 'tenderly to consider the great grudging and universal rumour in this realm of the justice not yet duly administered to such as trespass and offend against your laws and especially of them that [have] been indicted of treason and others being openly noised of the same.' He regarded Cade's indictments as valid and offered to imprison the accused pending trial. King Henry declined, referring such matters to a council to include York. Ostensibly to this council, but actually to a more general audience, York pressed for the trial of the accused, assumed there were others 'about the king's person' guilty of treason and crime, and ascribed once more the betrayal of Lancastrian France, the non-enforcement of the law and the procuring of grants from the king to counsellors who were covetous, cowardly and 'brought up of nought'. His bill was highly rhetorical, echoed many aspects of Cade's manifestos, construed misgovernment as treason and thus greatly enlarged those at risk of punishment. Like Cade, York addressed the 'true' lords, councillors and princes of the blood royal. Though negligent in the past and unmindful of perjury, they were urged henceforth to 'think on your oath what you owe to [our] sovereign lord and live not in perjury but give true counsel'.[60] He tailored his message to a pre-existing public mood. His stance was widely appreciated and appealed alike to local elites and commons. Although the Commons were not those who had impeached Suffolk, they took up the torch of reform, electing York's own retainer as speaker and urged a further resumption of royal grants, Suffolk's attainder and the exclusion from the king's company of thirty named individuals 'misbehaving about your royal person'. The latter had impoverished the king and subverted the law and one of them, Edmund Duke of Somerset, now the king's right-hand man, had been the unsuccessful (in their eyes, traitorous) commander in France. 'Universal noise and clamour ... [against] the said misbehaving', states the bill, 'runs openly through all this your Realm....' A great shout was raised against traitors in Westminster Hall and Somerset himself was lucky to escape the mob.[61] In the autumn and winter of 1450, as in the spring, the Commons and commons were at one. They were supported by York and an incalculable, probably varying, but substantial proportion of the Lords. That the court was able to hold out was due to Henry's obstinate refusal in the face of overwhelming odds to give way. That he retained his throne is ample testimony to the allegiance of the political nation – Lords, Commons and commoners alike – to whom a change of king was unacceptable.

The Reform Movement after 1450

After 1450 ministers and councillors feared being held to account. The Reform Movement inspired political action for the next thirty years. It was a crucial new element in politics. Reform was the clarion call of subsequent appeals to force in 1452, 1455, 1459, 1460, 1469–70 and even 1483. York as lord protector could not carry out his programme in full. Evil councillors, especially the 'traitor' Somerset, the loss of France, full resumption and subversion of the law were recurring themes. Some temporary factors disappeared from the reformist agenda: Suffolk's reputation; the betrayal of France after the death of Somerset, the prime villain, in 1455; and the list of Kentish grievances. New griefs arose. One of Cade's manifestos was re-issued, presumably to the men of Kent, in 1460. His vision of what ought to be was properly articulated in new Yorkist manifestos. Warwick issued them on his march to the midlands, the former addressed perhaps initially to the citizens of London, the latter certainly to those of Canterbury. Both were loyal protestations, acknowledging Henry VI as king and invoking religion and divine law. They sought the honour, safety and worship of the king, who should neither be impoverished nor live off the commons, but ought instead to maintain his royal state from his own resources. Each promoted the commonweal, politic laws, justice and trade. Evil councillors kept the king in ignorance and pursued their own covetous advantage. The manifestos looked backwards, to precedent and to absolute standards of law, and decried all innovation. It was the message of 1450 all over again.

It was also a winning formula. Just as 1450 was the model for 1459 and 1460, so Warwick adapted the latter for his coup in 1469. He signed the covering letter to a set of articles and petitions ostensibly from Robin of Redesdale and the 'true and faithful subjects and commons of this land', and was most probably behind the rest of the text as well. If the commons did not write them, they were certainly targeted as the audience, specifically those of Kent and London and those with mercantile and maritime interests. The subject matter was commonplace. King Edward had failed to fulfil his own reforming programme: charges of lawlessness, financial stringency, excessive impositions and a diminished household were easy to make. He too had excluded princes of the blood from his council in favour of evil councillors, in particular the Wydeville family of his queen, whom he had deliberately built up and who (as in 1450) had engineered convictions for treason to their own advantage. To endow them was to disendow the crown. He had broken his promise of 1467 to live of his own. The heir to York's reforming cause had breached it himself. To be a ruler or a king, with financial and political responsibilities, was very different from leadership of the opposition. Complaints were backed in 1469 not just by force, but by ominous comparisons with the discredited regimes of the deposed monarchs Edward II, Richard II and Henry VI.[62]

The appeals to Kentish audiences of 1459, 1460 and 1469 curtailed the specifically Kentish grievances of 1450. They may have been redressed. More probably this was because Warwick represented not only the ideals of Jack Cade, but had succeeded to the corrupt administrators of 1450 and had allied himself to county and urban elites as captain of Calais, keeper of the seas, warden of the Cinque Ports and constable of Dover. There was no mileage in reviving many of the earlier complaints. Local animosities were again invoked in 1469 by including the Wydevilles of Maidstone and Sir John Fogge of Ashford among the evil councillors and their supposed oppression of Alderman Cook among the griefs. Warwick's maritime and mercantile activities – he was the darling of the staplers, of xenophobes and of pirates! – secured him the backing of the City mob and Kentishmen in 1459–61 and of his own mariners and the Kentishmen again in 1470–1.[63]

The years 1460 and 1469 were the models in 1483 for Gloucester, who presented himself also as the protagonist of reform, this time against the regime of his late brother. The letters that Gloucester circulated in London before his protectorate 'had a great effect on the minds of the people, who, as they had previously favoured the duke in their hearts from a belief in his probity, now began to support him loudly and aloud: so that it was commonly said by all that the duke deserved the government'.[64] Once protector, his conduct in public, and once king, his professed intentions and declaration of title (*Titulus Regius*), all explicitly sought popular support. 'By these arts Richard enjoyed the favour of the people.' Richard explicitly identified himself with good governance on behalf of the commonweal, with public-spirited councillors, impartial justice, flourishing commerce and adequate livings for the poor. His stance recalls those reforms implied in 1450, 1460 and 1469. He made much of subversion of the law and property rights, 'all politic rule was perverted', in defiance of God's law and his Church. He dwelt on the oppressions of the poor. Edward himself escaped the blame which befell his evil councillors, again the family of his queen, who had excluded Gloucester and Buckingham, 'the old royal blood of the realm', from the royal court. These councillors had amassed patronage and seized the royal treasure.[65] Gloucester professed himself as concerned about evil counsellors, the king's livelihood and worship, the subversion of the law, commerce and the commonweal like Cade, York and Warwick, and used such issues to mobilise public opinion. He reshaped his earlier career along the lines of earlier overmighty subjects and idols of the multitude, exaggerating and reinterpreting his northern focus as exclusion from court and hence from the decisions and mistakes of his brother's offending regime.[66] He modelled his actual usurpation, which included a form of election, on that of his brother in 1461.[67]

The grandeur of Richard's coronation, coronation oaths in English which all could understand, and subsequent progresses appealed beyond the political nation he had cultivated before his accession. Richard genuinely tried to execute the reform programme that he had initiated. He presented himself as genuinely interested in justice for all regardless of rank and set himself against the worst financial excesses, and forced gifts from towns and benevolences.[68] He placed more emphasis on the poor and cultivated them more directly than his predecessors. Adverse circumstances impeded his programme, driving him into expedients similar to those he had denounced, for which he was exposed by More.[69]

We cannot tell whether Henry Tudor as pretender claimed to be a reformer or a bringer of good governance, nor whether reform was a serious platform for his rivals. A hostile paraphrase of the 1489 manifesto obscures as much as it reveals.[70] A manifesto of Perkin Warbeck survives from the Cornish Rising of 1497. Perkin's denunciation of 'the outrageous and importable sums' imposed upon the whole body of the realm to the great hurt and impoverishing of the same' befitted a tax revolt, but also appears the most effective charge that he could make. Whilst Henry's arrest, disinheritance and execution of traitors and claimants were condemned, Perkin appears short of concrete crimes with which to charge his Tudor rival or indeed his advisers: the 'caitiffs and villains of simple birth', who predictably 'by subtle inventions and pilling of the people have been the principal finders, occasioners and counsellors of the misrule now reigning in England'. Styling himself already as king, Perkin appealed to allegiance, promised to rule with the 'great lords of our blood with the counsel of other sad persons of approved policy, prudence and experience', offered 'indifferent administration of Justice and the public weal of the land' and to rule according to the 'good laws and Customs heretofore made by our noble progenitors Kings of England'. His case enshrined traditional notions of justice, counsel, hierarchy and public probity.[71]

By 1509, however, there were many financial and legal oppressions that recall the more general charges of earlier manifestos to which Edmund Dudley admitted. Others were condemned at Henry VIII's first parliament. Polydore Vergil and others were critical of Henry VII's avarice and oppressions. A commission was appointed by Henry VIII to inquire into things done 'to the subversion of his laws and good governance of his said realm', but came up with very little. The commission and legislation, Professor Elton argued, were the price necessary for taxation to be voted rather than evidence of wrongdoing. What is recorded, in terms of offences and grievances, relates mainly to the aristocracy – to lots of the aristocracy – and is highly specific rather than expressed as the cogent constitutional complaints of earlier reformers.[72] The recovery of the economy and consequent alleviation of suffering, attested also by a greater willingness to provide financial support, suggests that well before 1509 the old reforming programme had lost its justification and had run out of steam.

Reform aroused substantial and even overwhelming responses from the commoners of London (1460, 1483), the south-east (1460, 1471), the south-west and perhaps the midlands (1470), from at least some towns, possibly more widely and perhaps on other occasions too. It appealed in the south, most probably the midlands, but apparently never the north. The manifesto supposedly of Robin of Redesdale in 1469 may not have reached his followers: it has a southern audience in mind.[73] The same principles impelled the commons decisively into politics even when nothing much was wrong. Governments were understandably apprehensive. In 1475 his peace with France, towards which much taxation had been raised, caused Edward IV to defuse public anger by not collecting one instalment and despatching pre-emptive commissions to the provinces. It was actually the dynastic appeal of Henry VI that was genuinely popular and addressed in a manifesto in 1470, when Warwick swallowed his pride to secure a Lancastrian alliance.[74] It died with Henry himself: Henry Tudor's appeal in 1483–5 owed little to his Lancastrian title. The capacity of constitutionalism to bring the southern commons into national politics had apparently ebbed by the mid 1480s, when aristocratic outrage against Richard III was not accompanied by significant popular support, and subsequent pretenders stressed legitimacy rather than reform. The regional uprisings of 1489 and 1497, in contrast, were provoked by oppressive taxation: re-direction of insurgents into national politics was unsuccessful. Renewed prosperity may explain why the commons by the 1480s again left high politics to natural rulers. If there was indeed 'no articulate voice of revolt' in the sixteenth century,[75] it appears that the precocious sophistication of popular politics during the Wars of the Roses was a passing phase and not the lineal ancestor of the popular radicalism of the seventeenth and subsequent centuries.

The unity between reformers, parliament and commons in opposition to the government that was so apparent in 1450 was unprecedented and was not to endure. How far aristocratic backers of successive political revolutions were moved by reforming programmes rather than pre-existing ties and personal motives cannot be accurately assessed. Certainly the great proved less susceptible. Whilst most magnates accepted York as protector when the king was indisposed, a mere handful rebelled with him in 1452, 1455, 1459 or 1460. Only a few more peers backed his son in 1461 – Edward IV notoriously was made king by a faction – or Warwick, Clarence and Henry VI in 1469–71, Gloucester in 1483, Henry Tudor in 1485, or later rebels thereafter. For this group, the bond of allegiance that they had sworn in person may have too strong. Maybe, rather better informed than the commons, they could see through calls for reform that had been fulfilled and were governmentally impracticable. In practice the king *de facto* invariably secured more support from the peerage; the turnout was especially impressive when the result was already clear. York found the Lords reluctant to condemn Somerset or to approve his draconian act of resumption in 1456. If many in both houses were unhappy about endorsing the Yorkist version of events in 1455 and the attainders of Richard III's supporters in 1485, they nevertheless acquiesced; great councils and parliament repudiated at the king's command the pretensions of York in the 1450s, Warwick in 1467–70 and Clarence in 1478. Maybe popular politics did frighten away aristocratic support. Only the most sympathetic peers attended parliament in 1460 to find York's title irrefutable. Although backed by the commons, Warwick secured little support from the elite at the Readeption, even from some whose sufferings ought to have driven them into his arms. A unity of constitutional outlook, focusing on support *for* rather than opposition *to* the government *de facto*, returned in or before Henry Tudor's accession.

11

CIVIL WAR

Categories and causes

 Civil war occurred because subjects could not achieve their ends by constitutional means and rebellion had a chance of success. When one side was definitely the stronger, with the king in command or bereft of support, differences had to be resolved peacefully. The fifteenth century witnessed more than its share of civil war. Civil war made Henry IV into a king and repeatedly threatened to unseat him. Conflict in 1403–8 was largely confined to Wales and the north-east. The Wars of the Roses (c.1452–97) were brief and decisive campaigns separated by long tracts of peace. There were few sieges and little devastation: continuous hostilities were confined to the peripheries, to Northumbria, north Wales and Jersey. Popular insurrections occurred in every century until alternative modes of protest become effective. There were rebellions against every king. Yet civil war was always unnatural and unusual. Exceptional circumstances precipitated it.

Civil wars can be categorised into five principal types. Popular strikes, riots and demonstrations seldom grew into full-scale revolts of the populace. If not defused with concessions or nipped in the bud quickly, they could outgrow the capacity of any government to control or withstand them: the rebellions of Archbishop Scrope (1405), Jack Cade (1450) and the Cornishmen (1497) are striking examples. Such insurrections were always regional in origin and generally remained so. Secondly, there were the Lollard uprisings of 1414 and 1431, which were predominantly popular, but with some aristocratic and clerical stiffening and leadership. Lollards were concentrated in a few areas, but combined into an uprising that was national in scope. A third variety was the private war between aristocrats, also geographically focused, such as those in 1470 fought between Berkeley and Lisle in Gloucestershire and Norfolk versus the Pastons in Norfolk. Such feuds in concert with other irritants could produce more general conflict as happened in the 1450s. Fourthly, political insurrections or *coups d'état*

by great magnates, such as York's Dartford (1452) and St Albans (1455) campaigns, sought to change the personnel of the government and/or its policies. Force was applied unexpectedly against a regime too powerful to engage in open conflict. No effective resistance was possible when York ambushed the court in 1455 or for Gloucester's seizure of Edward V in 1483. Fifthly, the largest and most formidable rebellions, those that threatened to overthrow not merely councillors, but king and dynasty, combined features of all others. Such attacks had to overcome the allegiance owed by all subjects to the crown, the presumption in its favour and its consequent massive advantage in resources. Surprisingly many uprisings achieved their objectives in the fifteenth century. Most failed. Rebellion was a high-risk strategy to be attempted only as a last desperate fling.

Rebellions were never irrational. Participants decided to rebel. Rebellions always had causes. Whenever historians investigate rebellions, they invariably uncover grievances and frictions in the preceding years. Harvey tracked Cade's Rebellion back to causes twelve years old; Henry VII's Yorkshire and Cornish uprisings, like the Peasants' Revolt itself, were precipitated by national taxation. Albeit false, fears of afforestation in 1450 and of a judicial eyre in 1470 were incentives to rebel. Such problems were known to the authorities, so action could be taken to remedy grievances, dispel misapprehensions or to suppress protests before they expanded into insurrection. Such causes did not make conflict inevitable. Disputes about land, labour and taxation occurred at all times and in all areas. Special combinations of circumstances caused them to outgrow their origins and develop into something else.

Every rebellion arose from grievances and frictions that were fundamental and unresolved. The Percies were aggrieved by failure to pay their wages as wardens or compensation due for captives taken over by the king. Poverty or fear of impoverishment actuated many popular insurgents. They were confident in their own rightness and undeterred by verdicts against them. Many rebels first tried helping themselves, making illegal entries, perverting justice and assaulting their opponents. Remedies were sought through established channels. All to no avail. Perhaps their claims were unjust, perhaps they were on the wrong side of bastard feudal lordship and could not obtain a fair hearing (or thought they could not), or maybe their enemies denied them access to the king. Suffolk, the Tuddenham and Heydon gang and their associates may sometimes have stood for justice, but they were not perceived as such within the Paston circle. Supposedly the Percy–Neville dispute was settled in 1456 by the courts, but the verdicts and sentences could not endure: intended as exemplary, they appeared partisan and the ruinous fines could not be collected.[1] Another supposed compromise, the 1460 *Accord*, failed because it disregarded the essential interests of Queen Margaret, Prince Edward and other magnates absent from parliament. These were not battles that they could afford to lose. Henry VI's family, the Percies and the tax rebels had either to accept defeat, disinheritance, impoverishment and ruin, or resort to violence.

Causes and motives mattered, but by themselves were never enough. A variety of private reasons explain the participation of many individuals in political movements overtly about constitutional and dynastic principles. Grievances had to be shared with enough others for violence to be a feasible option. Because resentment against taxation was widespread, it generated rebellions that the authorities had to take seriously. The sufferings of the Yorkshiremen in 1461 confronted Edward IV with hostility on his landing in 1471.[2] York's calls for reform were much more formidable in 1450 and 1460 when his message was widely shared than in 1452, when he failed to get it across. If the complainant was alone or almost alone, he must submit and perhaps bide his time for changed circumstances. Norfolk exploited royal weakness to besiege Caister in 1469. His death in 1476 enabled the Pastons to retrieve it. A coincidence of grievances, like the three separate disputes which aligned Warwick and the Nevilles with York against Somerset, Exeter and the Percies, could create a coalition of national significance. York's rule as protector enabled him to decide both Warwick's inheritance dispute and the Percy feud in favour of his Neville allies. Neville backing for York at St Albans (1455) not coincidentally eliminated *their* rivals.

For private grievances to provoke public rebellion they had to have a public dimension. The Berkeley–Lisle and Norfolk–Paston feuds of 1469–70 ended before such issues arose: might proved right. Local grievances, against rival magnates or oppressive landlords, could affect the crown when it failed to provide remedies. It was the absence of relief for the maladministration and injustice of local rulers that brought Cade's men out against the regime. Denunciations of corruption against the Suffolk regime were constantly recycled and adapted. Broader issues appealed more widely and subsumed original narrower grievances into larger and more extensive movements. Most leaders blended public principles, private grievances and aspirations, in varying proportions. They could be used to discourage recruitment: surely Richard III's poor turnout in 1485 owed something to the moral disapproval heaped on him by Tudor propaganda? Many, of course, had no such choice on the issues, but merely followed where lords, towns and commissioners of array commanded or led.

Violence was not the only possible consequence of civil wars and rebellions. Popular rebellions, in particular, drew forceful attention to unremedied grievances and could often be curbed by conceding the essential points. Prince John conceded Scrope's demands and the rebels dispersed. Popular rebels had limited objectives best satisfied by negotiation with the government in being. Henry VII's refusal to negotiate contributed to the death of Northumberland and left the rebels with nothing to achieve. Whether ascendant or at a disadvantage, York's rebellions in the 1450s were all accompanied by negotiations. Even in 1471 Edward IV offered terms to Warwick.[3] The implications of armed protests and demonstrations sometimes only became clear as events moved on. Lincolnshiremen in 1470 and Yorkshiremen in 1489 found that their grievances did not justify death in battle. The government sought to make the choice starker through warnings, threats and exemplary executions. Lessons were learned: Edward IV and Henry VIII withdrew exactions to still dissent.

Preconditions for revolution

Any rebellion, whatever its type, had to draw itself to the attention of government and demand its intervention and countermeasures, including concessions. These were enormously formidable tasks. Many succumbed to local resources and never got off the ground. In 1400 three Ricardian earls were lynched almost before their rebellion started. Northumberland was defeated by the sheriff of Yorkshire at Bramham Moor in 1408, Robin of Holderness by Montagu in 1469, and the tax-rebels at Ackworth in 1492. In 1471 Edward IV found the coastal defences too strong for him at Cromer and was at great risk in Holderness. Success at the start was necessary even to compete nationally.

It was to the advantage of such rebels that England, unlike the strongest contemporary states, had no professional military machine: no standing army, no committed garrisons in mainland England and scarcely any navy. Defence against enemies, domestic or foreign, depended primarily on the voluntary support of local elites and their bastard feudal levies which, moreover, were geographically dispersed. The king needed time to assemble troops, over whose quality, equipment and training he had no control and which were no better than those of his adversaries. He could not maintain defences indefinitely. Impressed levies had to be fed and could not abandon their livelihoods indefinitely. Seamen recruited to resist Warwick's invasion in 1460 mutinied because they could not be paid.

Every government held the initiative. Its manpower, financial resources and credit rating far exceeded those of any contemporary magnate. Local government everywhere was the king's to command. The central machine was a uniquely valuable source of information, communication, coercion and command. The presumption of allegiance preconditioned everyone in its support, whether noblemen and gentry with their connections or individual citizens, and deterred recruitment by the rebels, who had everything to fear from commitment and failure. Edmund Mortimer, Earl of March, whose royal blood and unparalleled resources made him the obvious figurehead for every anti-Lancastrian rebellion, found the stakes too high and always failed his backers. Government was a formidable obstacle to overcome.

Popular rebellions seldom broke out of their regions of origin. Though attracting large numbers of participants, which gave them immunity from attack, they lacked other resources necessary for the battlefield or campaigns of attrition. Typically slow-moving, unwilling to strike at the jugular or to remain at arms for long, such risings were more anxious to negotiate remedies with the regime than to overthrow it. Popular rebels looked loyally to the king to remedy their grievances in preference to substituting another. They wanted peaceful rather than violent solutions. Tudor observers coined a phrase for such revolts: they were 'inkennelled', camp-bound,[4] voluntarily placing physical limits on their movements because they had limited themselves intellectually to loyalty to the regime. Uprisings in Yorkshire, whether in 1489 or 1536, transcended local control and could not safely be confronted on the battlefield, yet they failed to force national governments to back down. A threat to London, by the Peasants in 1381 and Cade in 1450, demanded greater respect. However terrifying locally, whilst confined to the west country, the Cornish rebels were a source of governmental concern rather than alarm; once at Blackheath, their suppression became the regime's top priority. To take such a step, popular rebels needed the political realism, the awareness of what was possible, of practical objectives and of how to pressurise the regime, that was provided by aristocratic leadership. Nevertheless all ultimately failed.

Aristocratic rebels deployed their connections. Even in combination, they could not usually match the king, still less the additional resources slowly unrolled by obligations of allegiance and commissions of array across the country as a whole. A royal victory in the field was the most likely outcome. Hence York's humiliating flight from

Ludford in 1459. Hence in part the speed of many campaigns, as the aggressors dispensed with dispersed supporters to forestall full deployment of the king's loyal subjects. Why pursue a course so likely to fail? Attempts were made to short-circuit the system. More limited resources, deployed unexpectedly against the king and those in his company, offered greater chance of success. The 1st battle of St Albans (1455), the Edgecote campaign (1469) and Gloucester's Stony Stratford coup (1483) were conspicuous successes, but failures are easier to list: Oldcastle's Rebellion (1414), the Southampton Plot (1415), Dartford (1452), the Lincolnshire Rebellion (1470) and the Yorkshire rising of 1486.

The most striking success was the first, the usurpation of Henry IV. Backed by the duke of Orleans and accompanied by 300 men on three ships, he was able to select his bridgehead and survive the first crucial days. He was joined by his own Lancaster connection, such noble allies as the Percies, and the populace. 'Everywhere the tenants of Lancaster crowded to join him while the common people welcomed him, poor fools that they were, as a deliverer.'[5] His disinheritance was undeniably unjust and his objective, avowedly mere restoration, was both limited and justified. It won support and disarmed resistance. The ruling regime was denied the moral authority of the king, absent in Ireland, and included his most unpopular agents. Victory was won before King Richard returned and unwisely placed himself in his cousin's hands. Once in control, public opinion, the political nation and parliament could be manipulated. No fighting was needed. The three Ricardian earls rose too late. But had Richard evaded capture, how different the tale might have been!

Even without Richard, the new king was strained to keep his throne. The Glyndŵr rebellion was a national conflict of Welsh versus English, with mass popular support in Wales but (partly in consequence) little in England. It received some foreign support, too little to be decisive. The Percies were regionally important, though less powerful even in the north than King Henry as duke of Lancaster and his brother-in-law Ralph Neville, Earl of Westmorland. The coalition was formidable.

The battle of Shrewsbury was as serious a threat to Henry IV as that at Stoke to Henry VII. He could have lost, but did not. Thereafter the wars against the Glyndŵr and the Percies were regional rather than national and were isolated geographically. Although strained and indeed seriously overstretched, royal resources were never so attenuated as to suspend the military effort and were repeatedly replenished by (grudging) parliamentary grants. Most people accepted Henry IV as king. The chosen figurehead of so many rebels, Edmund Mortimer, was unwilling and uninspiring. The presumption of allegiance to the king *de facto* was never overturned.

Between Shrewsbury (1403) and Blackheath (1497) lay forty years of relative domestic peace and a further forty when rebellions were more commonly successful. This was the Wars of the Roses. England experienced three regional revolts, a host of private feuds, skirmishes and sieges, thirteen full-scale battles, ten *coups d'état*, more than a score of invasions including four that succeeded, five usurpations, five kings and three changes of dynasty. Each war had causes specific to it, albeit vigorously debated by historians, which made conflict arise and repeatedly resume. There could have been no Wars of the Roses without the many-sided crisis of 1450, which brought down Suffolk's ministry without removing any of the underlying problems. The Wars could not however have persisted, nor could rebellions have been so frequently successful, if the circumstances had not been propitious for them: quite exceptionally propitious to produce such remarkable results. What made them so is the thrust of what ensues.

The Wars of the Roses

The presumption and initiative of the crown and the nobility's bastard feudal access to manpower are constants, everywhere and at all times. The Wars of the Roses were initially no different from other conflicts. Four factors made them distinctive. First of all, this was an era when the people were brought into politics as active players. Secondly, there was an international dimension: the Wars can be seen as part of the struggle between France and Burgundy that was fought on English soil. It was external intervention, not internal divisions, that unseated Henry VI (twice) and Edward IV. Both these factors also applied, to lesser degrees, in 1399–1408. The Wars occurred, thirdly, when the English crown was exceptionally short of resources. And finally the dynastic theme increasingly removed the presumption in favour of the king *de facto*, undermined loyalty and encouraged resistance almost in defiance of logic and self-interest. If there came to be 'an entrenched moral and ideological malaise' as Gross has claimed, it was a result not a cause of the Wars of the Roses and proved to be within the capacity of Henry VII to rectify.[6]

The Wars of the Roses brought the people into politics as active participants. Every civil war required their unthinking numbers. Opposition leaders in the Wars of the Roses required them to make up their other deficiencies. They were used to coerce, overawe and even

incumbency and
women

sweep away governments. Carefully targeted propaganda was
composed and distributed that informed, consulted and courted them
and enlisted them in their cause. It was the overwhelming numbers of
the commons and their receptiveness to constitutional issues that gave
York such political clout in the decade after 1450 when he had less
support among the Lords. He invoked popular support for coups in
1452 and 1460, alleged such backing in 1459, and used the Commons
to pressurise the Lords in 1455–6. In apparent defiance of the progressive recovery from the nadir of 1450 by successive governments, the
myths of evil governance and evil counsel endured and were repeatedly
invoked. Long-lasting and progressive economic discontent (the 'Great
Slump' c.1440–80) predisposed the commons towards criticism of
government and forceful support for such self-styled reformers as York,
Warwick and Richard III. The people, so McFarlane observed, held all
governments responsible for their ills and could be aroused against any
government. He even suggested that it was the people who were most
politically committed.[7]

The commons injected a new element of instability. Hitherto
nobody had wished to mobilise the strength revealed by the Peasants'
Revolt. *Now*, however, the people were the objects of publicity
distributed to the localities and designed to appeal to their emotions,
interests and principles. *Now* they were urged to participate in politics
by high-ranking and politically mature leaders, who not only had political objectives, but knew also how to attain them. *Now* they were
reassured that their insurrection was neither criminal nor treasonable,
but instead that it was permissible, legitimate and indeed in the public
interest. Whatever may have been the case under the Tudors, magnates
initially suffered no loss of reputation by being rabble-rousers. If
bastard feudal power alone resourced some coups and rebellions, it was
the management of public opinion by self-proclaimed reformers that
placed successive governments on the defensive and only the mobilisa-
tion of the people made other coups possible. Though determined to
be loyal, the populace once at arms could be diverted into other channels. Warwick and Clarence, in particular, applied force recruited for
one cause in support of another.

Yet the popular will prevailed only twice, in 1460 and 1470, and
never was it sufficient on its own. Noble leaders and noble retinues
were always required. In 1459 and 1469 popular participation was
orchestrated from Calais by Warwick in support of noble insurrections.
In 1460 and in 1470 it was exiles invading from abroad that the
people were induced to join. Incursions across the Scottish borders
were encouraged by Queen Margaret in the 1460s, Louis XI in the

early 1480s and by Perkin Warbeck in the 1490s. Harlech was the entry for at least two Lancastrian invasions in the 1460s and Ireland for two Yorkist pretenders against Henry VII. It was safer for the principals to operate outside their opponents' realm. Much diplomatic effort was devoted to dislodging such pretenders and conspirators, sometimes successfully; foreign powers recognised accordingly their potential to neutralise successive kings and to re-align English foreign policy. The Wars of the Roses were not merely a domestic contest and cannot be explained in purely indigenous terms. There was an international aspect to the Wars of the Roses that distinguished them from others among England's civil wars and that was often decisive. It added an important dimension to the conflict. In particular there had been no depositions or usurpations until foreign powers became involved.

Late-fifteenth-century Englishmen did not recognise that England's ascendancy over France during the Hundred Years War had been a passing phase, the consequence as much of temporary French weaknesses as English strength, and that the resurgent France of Charles VII had become too strong to fight on equal terms. English kings called themselves kings of France, new triumphs were demanded and periodic invasions were made of the continent. Never successful, none were disastrous, because France had higher priorities in its rivalry with Burgundy and the Italian wars. It was never admitted at home that England was now merely one element in an inward-looking north European political system dominated by France and Burgundy. These rival states looked to England as an ally against the other. Each in turn sought to negate England's hostility by invoking Scottish pressure on the north or by backing conspirators, rebels or invaders to undermine, destabilise, or even overthrow the government of the day. Full-scale invasion was never necessary to keep England in a ferment and effectively neutralised.

The Yorkists initiated seaborne interventions from their bases in Calais and Ireland. At least twenty invasions across the seas reached England and Wales of which those of 1460, 1470, 1471 and 1485 were successful in overthrowing the government, king *de facto* and incumbent dynasty. Among the dozen that did not, several like Oxford's in 1472–4 were mere raids designed to embarrass rather than to unseat the regime. Political rivals were always being harboured abroad outside the power of the current king from 1459, when the Yorkists fled to Calais and Ireland, and 1525, when Richard de la Pole fell at Pavia. All the diplomatic efforts of Edward IV, Richard III and Henry VII served only to move on their rivals, never to isolate them completely; only Edmund Earl of Suffolk was surrendered into English hands. From refuges in foreign countries, in Calais and in Ireland, English exiles were able to regroup, re-plan and prepare their propaganda. Louis XI repeatedly stimulated incursions across the borders by the Scots in the early 1460s, sometimes stiffened with the Frenchmen of Pierre de Brezé, then permitted and subsidised Jasper Tudor's attacks through Wales, next harboured the exiled Warwick and launched his successful invasion in 1470, before finally despatching Oxford to Essex and St Michael's Mount (Corn.). Henry Tudor in 1485 brought substantial French and Scottish companies with him and Martin Swart's Burgundians were the kernel of Lambert Simnel's defeated army at Stoke in 1487. Edward IV's sister Margaret of Burgundy was only one of the foreign backers who sustained Perkin Warbeck through most of the 1490s.

Foreign troops were never in sufficient numbers to be decisive by themselves. They were important qualitatively as well as in quantity, those of De Chandée in 1485 and Swart in 1487 constituting the trained nucleus of rather small armies. Forces a few hundred strong defended bridgeheads long enough for recruitment to commence. Foreign forces were intended to *supplement* domestic rebels. No expedition was intercepted before arrival by sea. Governments were more successful in uncovering and destroying networks of spies and conspirators in England. It was impossible to guard every landfall. Whereas Scottish attacks had to commence in the borders and were thus relatively predictable, those across the sea could be (and were) directed to any part of the long coastline of England and Wales. Britain's geography had not changed. What was new was that now there were enemies anxious to exploit it and less capacity to defend it. Kings could no longer divine where the blow would fall and guard effectively against it. It was the aggressors who chose the time and place to maximise their resources, prepared their supporters on shore and executed a preconceived plan.

Such international threats were the more dangerous because of exceptional English weaknesses. The problem was one of resources. The income of the English crown that had been about £110,000 as late as 1400 fell to half or even a third of that level in the mid-century depression. The ordinary business of government, the royal household, the defence of Calais and the northern borders, all cost more than everything that the king received. Henry VI's debts of £372,000 were unmanageable.[8] He could not afford to live like a king, to fund any military or diplomatic initiatives, and his credit was understandably bad. His Yorkist successor struggled to find the money to resist Scottish invasions, abandoned Berwick as financially unattainable and had to use war-taxation to fund his sister's marriage. Resumption of grants and living of one's own was no panacea. 'Dramatic windfalls ... which vastly increased the extent of royal holdings and enhanced the role of land as a source of revenue' nevertheless left royal income diminutive by French standards.[9] They improved solvency and credit-worthiness rather than funding enhanced military expenditure. Even after his vaunted recovery, Edward IV's revenues were only about £65–70,000: he could not really afford his newly recovered fortress of Berwick and died with insufficient cash for his funeral. His foreign policy was unduly influenced by a paltry French pension.[10] None of these kings could afford fleets or armies in being to prevent or defeat invasions. They had almost no spare cash in hand in emergencies. It was difficult to borrow because their credit was so poor.

Kings also became more dependent on the bastard feudal retainers of their greater subjects, whose much smaller resources compared not unfavourably with what was uncommitted from royal revenues ten times the size. Fiscal realities enabled such men as York and Warwick to exercise more influence than was appropriate to a subject. They were indeed overmighty.[11] Propitious circumstances permitted them to overthrow several of their kings. They were able to justify rebellion to themselves (and indeed to others) and evade the stain of treason that befell lesser men.

York regarded himself as acting for the common good and above the law of treason. Unquestionably one of those great lords of the blood entitled to counsel the king, he constantly pressed his advice, if necessary by force, in the interests of the commonweal and common profit of the realm, to which kings were also bound to subscribe. He regarded his stance as compatible with his allegiance. The duke never considered himself perjured when he broke his oaths not to take direct action. 'True lords of the royal blood of his realm', of 'old ancestry of great might and strength', the king's natural councillors, could not be disloyal. It was presumptuous of lesser men 'to call him and these other lords traitors'; they should not utter 'such language of lords being of the king's blood'.[12] Their assertion of birth above merit, their denial of equality before the law' and their notions of faith and allegiance, which seem to us so eccentric and peculiar, seem not to have affected York's reputation. Warwick took the same line late in the 1460s, negotiating with the king as an equal, demanding the removal of evil councillors, attending councils in strength, imposing his own counsel and executing evil councillors. There are obvious parallels in 1483 with Gloucester, who flouted most standards of political behaviour. No king accepted their case, not even Henry VI, who was

214

reluctant nevertheless for York to suffer the penalties of treason. Subsequent kings were less charitable. Royal dukes and princes of the blood, even the king's brother, were summarily executed in 1464, 1471, 1478 and 1483.

Such attitudes were restricted to very few. More important from 1461 was the dilution of the obligation of allegiance by the emergence of alternative claimants for the crown. No king *de facto* accepted the title of his rival or hesitated to treat his adherents as traitors, but to individuals it offered private justification for not supporting or opposing them. If dynastic legitimacy could now be denied, no king could count on his subjects' allegiance. The king's moral superiority was removed. Without it, current kings lost their principal advantage over their rivals and were more readily challenged. There was always a king *de iure* to set against the king *de facto*. Dynasticism made credible claimants of the de la Poles, who were never magnates, of Henry Tudor, whom nobody knew, and of pretenders like Simnel and Warbeck. Dynastic figureheads could be used to buttress every rebellion. Kings responded by punishing those guilty only of misprision, such as Alderman Cook and Sir William Stanley, but they could not control their subjects' minds. The last battles of the Wars of the Roses were the worst attended on either side. If dynasticism failed to generate opposition as reform had done, kings regnant were just as vulnerable.

The unmaking of civil war

The Wars of the Roses did not end in 1485. The battle of Stoke in 1487 could have reversed the verdict of Bosworth. Like Henry IV, with whose early years his reign had many parallels, and as befitted a usurper with a substandard title, the first Tudor king had to expend much effort merely to survive. He too had to overcome rebellions and pretenders. Potentially dangerous in-laws, representing the white rose of York, multiplied. Henry VII also required international recognition to deny foreign refuges and support to rival claimants. Like Henry IV, he retained his throne, and after 1487 never again had to hazard everything in battle.

Henry VII has traditionally been credited with his own success. He rebuilt the authority of the monarchy. He was the Yorkist candidate to the throne, selected by a Yorkist establishment disgusted by Richard III and assured by his marriage to Elizabeth of York, and was acceptable also to any remaining battered Lancastrians. From the moment of his accession, he mobilised propaganda on his own behalf, enhancing and publicising Richard's crimes and laying claim to the Arthurian legend. Securing the succession in the male line in 1486 was a priceless asset. He compensated for the absence of collateral Tudor magnates, at least at first, by binding the noblest houses to his own through marriage to his sisters-in-law of York. Rather than courting the nobility, whose upbringing he had not shared, he coerced them, insisting on their compliance and obedience as Edward IV had seldom dared. Instead of dissipating his wealth through patronage, he restored the gap in resources that differentiated the crown from its greatest subjects. He settled aristocratic feuds before they got out of hand. His reliance on trusted officials of undistinguished birth (again like Henry IV) did not backfire during his own lifetime; afterwards they were repudiated and punished. His decisive leadership also helped. He paralleled the first Lancastrian's decisive countermeasures in 1403 with his own against the Yorkshire rebels in 1489.[13] His authority grew the longer he reigned, just as the Lancastrians and Edward IV had found.

Mere recovery from weakness insufficiently explains the end of the Wars of the Roses. Unpleasant and constraining though they were, King Henry's 'bonds, coercion and fear' were merely deterrents, threats no more awesome than the penalties of treason that so many had braved before. All Henry's rebuilding did no more than reconstitute the resources that Richard II and the early Lancastrians had enjoyed. Local government and defence were still essentially voluntary, delegated, and at the king's request. Had Henry been faced by the overwhelming popular hostility, overseas invasions and bastard feudal might of 1460 or 1470, orchestrated for a dynastic rival by overmighty subjects, why should he have withstood it more successfully than Henry VI or Edward IV? He encountered no such combination. The propitious circumstances that facilitated rebellion and dynastic revolution disappeared and the opportunities ceased to justify the risks.

Popular rebellion did not end. Future revolts were characteristically popular in origin, intent and scope. They were responses to economic (and later religious grievances), legalistic in their justifications, limited in their desire for relief, less violent and essentially loyal to the king. Even if taken over by aristocratic leaders they were neither fomented by them nor merged with conventional bastard feudal retinues. What Edward IV feared in 1475 did not materialise. The aristocratic rebellions of the 1480s and 1490s attracted little popular support. The commons had ceased to intervene in national politics and were no longer tools for aristocratic demagogues. Perhaps aristocrats had forgotten the knack. One essential factor was the end of the mid-century recession, the recovery of the economy and the relief (albeit temporary) of economic discontent. A contented populace could not be aroused by dynasticism alone. Hordes of commons could no longer be conjured up by claimants, reformers, disgruntled magnates or idols of the multitude. The best hope for Egremont in 1489 and Warbeck in 1497 was to hijack existing revolts.

Opportunities in Europe shrank decisively. The great powers lost interest in fomenting disorder and dynastic upheavals in England. The treaty of Arras (1482) and the minorities of both French and Burgundian monarchs suspended the intense Franco–Burgundian rivalry. The backing of Margaret of York, Dowager-Duchess of Burgundy did not equate to that of Burgundy itself and was curtailed diplomatically before her death. The outbreak of the Italian Wars in 1494 and the subsequent Habsburg–Valois rivalry distracted French attention from English power politics for half a century. French resources so far outstripped those of England that it was fortunate that defeat of the fruitless invasions of north-eastern France by the first two Tudors was never the highest French priority. It was cheaper to buy the Tudors off with trivial pensions than to destabilise their realm.

The prevailing ideology also changed. Although refuted by the *Somnium Vigilantis*, York's brand of forceful counselling and loyal rebellion was in vogue in 1450–60 and as late as 1483. Henry IV and VI at first found no consensus that such actions were treasonable or that everyone, even magnates, had a duty of obedience. Yet these became the winning arguments. Edward IV was the poacher turned gamekeeper. Dating his accession from 4 March 1461, he had his opponents at Towton (29 March) and even his those of his father at Wakefield (31 December 1460) attainted and subsequent conspirators executed. 'Nighness of our blood' and 'old love and affection' tempered his justice with favour and pity in 1470, yet he refused to offer sureties and pardons to his brother Clarence. Edward's dignity as sovereign made no distinction between his subjects, however great or royal.[14] That great lords and royal princes were no different was demonstrated by him and his successors with the execution of princes of the blood in 1471, 1478 (his own brother), 1483, 1499, 1513 and repeatedly thereafter. Magnates henceforth had no privileged right to coerce, counsel forcefully or rebel, and were as liable to execution and corruption of blood as anyone else. Gloucester, so far as we know, was the last to follow York's example.

Not only were such actions breaches of allegiance, but the practical penalties were excessive. Henry VII was always harsh and his restorations only partial. It is not surprising if magnates became fearful and anxious to avoid sedition and its disastrous penalties. Not that this was new in 1485. Many earlier peers quailed from assuming royal authority. Rebellions took the name of shadowy front-men. Simnel and Warbeck had forerunners in the Yorkshire Robins and the pseudo-Richard II. Without high-ranking leaders and without their visible involvement, popular uprisings became less focused and less threatening to the political establishment.

However disgruntled they may have been, the early Tudor nobility were no longer interested in destabilising the political system or in seizing power. Over for a third time, the Wars of the Roses were not to resume. Henry VII's blatant pretext in 1485, that his reign began a day before Bosworth, which allowed him to attaint King Richard's supporters, was much resented by the Commons, but the king got his way. If the support for a legal king could carry the same penalties as rebellion, it is not surprising that subjects stood aside. It was obedience and non-resistance to the king *de facto*, not dynasticism, that the Tudor concept of order was to teach. Allegiance was paramount, other loyalties being purely secondary; indeed for those to whom the secondary loyalty was also to the crown, the king's household and officers, service to others was forbidden. These messages, developed under Henry VII and VIII, broadcast and internalised thereafter, affected not only aristocrats but also the people, who henceforth conducted all their protests within the framework of allegiance. The evolution from familiar late medieval notions to Tudor commonplaces has yet to be convincingly traced.

12

CONCLUSION

Times had changed. Fifteenth-century political culture was the culmination of what preceded and caused it and was itself the foundation of what followed. The ideas of the Wars of the Roses, themselves the results of evolution, slowly evolved into something new. Old notions of treason were passing their sell-by date. New ideas, momentarily fashionable, new movements and new institutions failed to survive. The decisive involvement of the commons in fifteenth-century politics proved premature, dwindled into tax revolts and had to be revived in later centuries. Fortescue's impractical recipes for political reform became prophetic after his death. Every age is an age of transition and the fifteenth century is no different in this respect from any other. Evolution was slow. The fifteenth-century kings, their constitution and principles appeared so familiar to Shakespeare and his audiences that they overlooked the nuances and read their own age into the past. Much more of the fifteenth century endured essentially the same into subsequent centuries than was changed. Transformations so obvious with hindsight to modern historians occurred at rates too slow for contemporaries to perceive, experience or explain. History comprises a series of successive states, each of which is deserving of study, in context. To understand the context – the pressures, assumptions, prejudices and principles – we need to appreciate the constituent institutions and ideas. Fifteenth-century political culture, this book reiterates, witnessed no fundamental turning points. It was amazingly complex, rich and worthy of historical study. All classes at all times and in all regions subscribed to a common core of standards and values on which they had their own slant and by which they lived predominantly peaceful lives. Much less is known than we need to know. Much we cannot know or coherently intermesh. This book summarises much that is known, and contributes and indicates (often by implication) what remains to be done. It brings out what the author finds significant, intriguing and exciting about English political culture in the fifteenth century.

NOTES

1 PARAMETERS

1 J. Hatcher, 'The Great Slump of the Mid-Fifteenth Century', *Progress and Problems in Medieval England*, ed. R.H. Britnell and J. Hatcher (Cambridge, 1996), ch. 12.
2 L. Stone, *Crisis of the Aristocracy 1558–1641* (Oxford, 1965), p. 5; P. Laslett, *The World We Have Lost Further Explored* (1983), ch. 8 at p. 208; C. Hill, 'A One-Class Society?', *Change and Continuity in Seventeenth-Century England* (1974), pp. 214–17.
3 M.A. Hicks, *Bastard Feudalism* (Harlow, 1995), pp. 2–4.

2 POLITICAL CULTURE

1 Myers, p. 1.
2 Ibid.
3 C.F. Richmond, 'Patronage and Polemic', *The End of the Middle Ages?*, ed. J.L. Watts (Stroud, 1998), p. 77.
4 C. Carpenter, 'Political and Constitutional History: Before and After McFarlane', *McFarlane Legacy*, p. 178.
5 Green, *Truth*, pp. xiv, 295.
6 R. Eccleshall, *Order and Reason in Politics* (Oxford, 1979), p. 5.
7 Myers, p. 1.
8 L. Stone, *Crisis of the Aristocracy 1558–1641* (Oxford, 1965), p. 6; M.H. Keen, *Chivalry* (New Haven, 1984), p. 1; C.F. Richmond, '1485 And All That, or what was going on at the Battle of Bosworth?', *Richard III: Loyalty, Lordship and Law*, ed. P. W. Hammond (1986), p. 196; C.F. Richmond, *The Paston Family in the Fifteenth Century. Endings* (Manchester, 2000), pp. 227, 249.
9 Myers, p. 1.
10 Carpenter, *McFarlane Legacy*, p. 187.
11 T. Jones, 'History as I invented it', *Sunday Times* (20 Aug. 2000); but see also G. de la Bédoyère, 'Vicious Circles', *Heritage Today* (Dec. 2001), p. 16.
12 N. Orme, 'The Culture of Children in Medieval England', *Past and Present* 148 (1995), pp. 49–88.
13 A. Musson, *Medieval Law*, p. 5, emphasis added.

14 A. Macfarlane, *Marriage and Love in England: Modes of Reproduction 1300–1840* (Oxford, 1986), passim.

15 P. Laslett, *The World We Have Lost Further Explored* (1983), pp. 12–13, 82–4, 100.

16 *Fifteenth-cent. Attitudes*, passim.

17 As demonstrated by Orme, 'The Culture of Children'.

18 S.K. Walker, 'Political Saints in Later Medieval England', *McFarlane Legacy*, p. 88; P. Morgan, 'Henry IV and the Shadow of Richard II', *Crown, Government and People in the Fifteenth Century*, ed. R.E. Archer (Stroud, 1995), p. 27; Green, *Truth*, pp. 50–9; A.J. Gross, *The Dissolution of the Lancastrian Kingship* (Stamford, 1996), p. 24.

19 Musson, *Medieval Law*, pp. 1–2.

20 *Crowland*, pp. 125, 181.

21 A. Hudson, 'The Examination of the Lollards', *BIHR* 46 (1973), pp. 145–59, at pp. 147–8, 152.

22 G.L. Harriss, 'Introduction: An Exemplar of Kingship', *Henry V*, p. 25; *Crowland*, pp. 150–1.

23 James, pp. 24–5.

24 C. Rawcliffe, 'The Great Lord as Peacekeeper: Arbitration by English Nobles and their Councils in the Later Middle Ages', *Law and Social Change in British History*, ed. J.A. Guy and H.G. Beale (1984), pp. 34–53, esp. pp. 34–7.

25 James, p. 17.

26 Musson, *Medieval Law*, pp. 50–2; Green, *Truth*, pp. 64, 106; Harriss, *Henry V*, p. 11; E. Powell, *Kingship, Law and Society* (Oxford, 1989), pp. 129–30; and see ch. 3 below.

27 A.J. Pollard, *Late Medieval England 1399–1509* (Harlow, 2000), p. 192.

28 P. C. Maddern, 'Honour among the Pastons: Gender and Integrity in English Provincial Society', *Journal of Medieval History* 14 (1988), p. 365.

29 R.E. Archer, 'Rich Old Ladies: The Problem of Late Medieval Dowagers', *Property and Politics*, ed. A.J. Pollard (Gloucester, 1984), pp. 15–31, esp. pp. 22, 24–5; T.B. Pugh and C.D. Ross, 'The English Baronage and the Income Tax of 1436', *BIHR* 26 (1953), pp. 9, 23–5.

30 Queen Joan of Navarre, Eleanor Cobham, Jacquetta of Luxemberg and Queen Elizabeth Wydeville.

31 Vale, p. 207.

32 J.T. Rosenthal, 'Other Victims: Peeresses as War Widows', *History* 72 (1987), pp. 213–30; *Parliamentary Texts of the Later Middle Ages*, ed. N. Pronay and J. Taylor (Oxford, 1980), p. 186; Hicks, *Rivals*, pp. 178, 296–316, 329–33.

33 J.G. Bellamy, *Bastard Feudalism and the Law* (1989), p. 95.

34 C. Phythian-Adams, 'Ceremony and the Citizen: The Communal Year at Coventry 1450–1550', *The Medieval Town: A Reader in English Urban History 1200–1500*, ed. R. Holt and G. Rosser (Harlow, 1990), pp. 240, 245; C. Rawcliffe, ' "That Kindliness Should be Cherished More, and Discord Driven Out": The Settlement of Commercial Disputes by Arbitration in Late Medieval England', *Enterprise and Individuals in Fifteenth-Century England*, ed. J.I. Kermode (Stroud, 1991), pp. 106–7; P. Lee, *Nunneries, Learning and Spirituality in Late Medieval English Society* (Woodbridge, 2001), p. 29.

35 Myers, pp. 63–4, 67, 83, 92, 96, 107, 115, 130, 146–7, 149–50, 156, 162–3.
36 Vale, pp. 187, 191, 194, 199, 210, 212, 233; *Original Letters*, p. 6; *RP*, vol. 5, p. 462.
37 Vale, p. 194.
38 Harriss, 'Political Society', p. 53.
39 Maddern, 'Honour and Gender', esp. p. 361; A.E. Curry and E. Matthew, 'Introduction', *Concepts of Service*, pp. xv–xvi.
40 Vale, p. 214.
41 *Concepts of Service*, p. 2.
42 Myers, pp. 144, 147.
43 For example, McFarlane, *England*, p. 34.
44 Hicks, *Rivals*, p. 374.
45 *Concepts of Service*, p. xv; *Stonor L & P*, vol. 2, pp. 70, 93.
46 R.E. Horrox, 'Service', *Fifteenth-cent. Attitudes*, p. 61.
47 J.T. Rosenthal, *Nobles and the Noble Life 1295–1500* (1976), p. 154.
48 *Concepts of Service*, pp. xvii–xviii.
49 M.A. Hicks, *Bastard Feudalism* (Harlow, 1995), p. 1.
50 Horrox, *Fifteenth-cent. Attitudes*, p. 78.
51 Chrimes, pp. 4, 16.
52 Ibid., p. 185.
53 S.H. Rigby, 'Urban "Oligarchy" in Late Medieval Towns', *Towns and Townspeople in the Fifteenth Century*, ed. J.A.F. Thomson (Gloucester, 1988), p. 64; see also P. Fleming, 'Telling Tales of Oligarchy in the Late Medieval Town', *Revolution and Consumption*, pp. 180–1.
54 Vale, pp. 223, 241.
55 Myers, pp. 67–8.
56 Eccleshall, *Order*, p. 16.
57 *Harl 433*, vol. 3, pp. 173–82 at p. 175; Myers, pp. 67–8, 142–50.
58 C.D. Ross, *Richard III* (1981), p. 174; *Parliamentary Texts*, p. 189.
59 Watts, *Henry VI*, p. 17.
60 G.L. Harriss, 'Aids, Loans and Benevolences', *Historical Journal* 6 (1963), pp. 1–19.
61 Lander, p. 16.
62 Eccleshall, *Order*, pp. 19, 60, 69.
63 S. Payling, 'The Widening Franchise – Parliamentary Elections in Lancastrian Nottinghamshire', *England in the Fifteenth Century*, ed. D. Williams (Woodbridge, 1987), p. 171.

3 MONARCHY

1 Chrimes, p. 6; A.J. Gross, *Dissolution of the Lancastrian Kingship* (Stamford, 1996), p. 37.
2 A.J. Pollard, *Late Medieval England 1399–1509* (Harlow, 2000), p. 232.
3 *The Coronation of Richard III*, ed. P.W. Hammond and A.F. Sutton (Upminster, 1983).
4 Chrimes, p. 7.
5 *Travels of Leo Rozmital*, ed. M. Letts (Hakluyt Society 2nd series, 108, 1957), pp. 46–7. Accounts of many of these ceremonies are being systematically edited by Dr A.F. Sutton and Mrs L. Visser Fuchs in *The Ricardian*.

6 Vale, p. 234.
7 L. Visser Fuchs, 'Laments for the Death of Edward IV', *The Ricardian* 145 (1999), pp. 506–24.
8 Myers, pp. 48, 63–5, 69.
9 Ibid., p. 48; *Crowland*, pp. 148–51.
10 Chrimes, pp. 41–3; Watts, *Henry VI*, p. 17.
11 T. Smith, *De Republica Anglorum*, ed. M. Dewar (Cambridge, 1982), p. 87.
12 Vale, p. 207.
13 Hicks, *Rivals*, pp. 419–33, esp. p. 429.
14 Lander, ch. 11; M.A. Hicks, *Bastard Feudalism* (Harlow, 1995), pp. 127, 204–5.
15 H. Castor, *The King, the Crown, and the Duchy of Lancaster* (Oxford, 2000), p. 30; Hicks, *Bastard Feudalism*, p. 135.
16 *Paston L & P*, vol. 2, p. 71; M.A. Hicks, 'The 1468 Statute of Livery', *HR* 64 (1991), p. 26; C.L. Scofield, *The Life and Reign of Edward the Fourth*, vol. 2 (1923), p. 373; G.L. Harriss, 'Preference at the Medieval Exchequer', *BIHR* 30 (1957), pp. 17–40.
17 Chrimes, pp. 9, 16, 42, 47–9.
18 *Harl 433*, vol. 3, p. 180; M.A. Hicks, *Richard III* (2nd edn, Stroud, 2000), p. 143.
19 *Plumpton L & P*, p. 26.
20 Hicks, *Rivals*, p. 225.
21 Lander, p. 27.
22 Dunham, *Hastings*, p. 133; 'Private Indentures', pp. 164–5; *RP*, vol. 6, p. 194.
23 J.G. Bellamy, *The Law of Treason in England in the Later Middle Ages* (Cambridge, 1970), p. 106.
24 Vale, p. 185.
25 Lander, ch. 5.
26 Castor, *Duchy of Lancaster*, p. 259; D.A.L. Morgan, 'The King's Affinity in the Polity of Yorkist England', *TRHS* 5th series 23 (1973), p. 18n.
27 *Harl 433*, vol. 3, p. 180.
28 J.T. Rosenthal, *Nobles and the Noble Life, 1295–1500* (1976), p. 42.
29 B. Wilkinson, *Constitutional History of England in the Fifteenth Century* (1964), p. 43.
30 R. Eccleshall, *Order and Reason in Politics* (Oxford, 1978), p. 70.
31 J.L. Kirby, *The Reign of Henry IV of England* (1970), p. 119.
32 *Crowland*, pp. 150–3.
33 P. W. Hammond and A.F. Sutton, *Richard III: The Road to Bosworth Field* (1985), p. 209.
34 G.L. Harriss, 'Introduction: The Exemplar of Kingship', *Henry V*, p. 11.
35 B.P. Wolffe, *The Royal Demesne in English History* (1971), esp. p. 105.
36 *RP*, vol. 5, p. 290.
37 Given-Wilson, *Chronicles*, p. 179.
38 Wilkinson, *Constitutional History*, p. 54.
39 For example, Griffiths, 'King's Council', pp. 318–19.
40 A.G. Dickens, *The Courts of Europe* (1977), pp. 34–5.
41 *Harl 433*, vol. 3, pp. 173–4.
42 Vale, p. 223; E. Talbert, *The Problem of Order* (Chapel Hill, 1962), p. 16.
43 Chrimes, p. 74.

NOTES TO PAGES 40-51

44 Chrimes, pp. 47–9, 55, 56, 58, 72.
45 M. Bennett, 'Edward III's Entail and the Succession to the Crown, 1376–1471', *EHR* 113 (1998), pp. 580–609.
46 Ibid., p. 581; P. McNiven, 'Legitimacy and Consent: Henry IV and the Lancastrian Title 1399–1406', *Medieval Studies* 44 (1982), pp. 470–85.
47 M.A. Hicks, 'Richard III, the Great Landholders, and the Results of the Wars of the Roses', forthcoming.
48 G.L. Harriss, *Cardinal Beaufort* (Oxford, 1988), p. 40.
49 E. Powell, 'The Strange Death of Sir John Mortimer: Politics and the Law of Treason in Lancastrian England', *Rulers and Ruled*, pp. 83–97; T.B. Pugh, *Henry V and the Southampton Plot* (Gloucester, 1988).
50 Harvey, *Cade*, p. 189.
51 Chrimes, p. 30; Vale, pp. 197–8.
52 Vale, p. 203.
53 Hicks, *Clarence*, pp. 85–6, 145–8; Lander, ch. 10; see also Bennett, 'Entail', p. 604.
54 Dockray, p. 149.
55 Pollard, *Late Medieval England*, p. 332.
56 E. Kantorowicz, *The King's Two Bodies* (Princeton, 1957), p. 7.
57 Chrimes, p. 14.
58 *Certain Sermons or Homilies*, ed. R.B. Bond (Toronto, 1987), pp. 161–70; J. Walter and K. Wrightson; 'Dearth and the Social Order in Early Modern England', *Past and Present* 71 (1976), pp. 108–28; E.P. Thompson, 'The Moral Economy of the English Crowd in the Eighteenth Century', *Past and Present* 50 (1971), pp. 76–136 ; James, chs 6, 7.
59 'Financial Memoranda of the Reign of Edward V', ed. R.E. Horrox, *Camden Miscellany* 29 (1987), p. 209.
60 Carpenter, *Wars*, p. 205.
61 Chrimes, p. 21; Wilkinson, *Constitutional History*, p. 248.
62 *RP*, vol. 5, p. 242.
63 Kantorowicz, pp. 403–4; *Harl 433*, vol. 2, p. 3; Hicks, 'Richard III and Landholding'.
64 Griffiths, 'Kings Council', p. 317; Wilkinson, *Constitutional History*, p. 66.
65 Wilkinson, *Constitutional History*, pp. 14, 124.
66 Ibid., pp. 252–3; Watts, *Henry VI*, pp. 133sqq.
67 Vale, pp. 222–5; Hicks, *Clarence*, pp. 78–82; but see Griffiths, 'For the might of the land', pp. 80–98, for a more optimistic interpretation.
68 Griffiths, *Henry VI*, *passim*; B.P. Wolffe, 'The Reign of Henry VI', *Fifteenth-cent. England*, pp. 29–48; R. Lovatt, 'A Collector of Apocryphal Anecdotes: John Blacman Revisited', *Property and Politics*, ed. A.J. Pollard (Gloucester, 1984), pp. 172–97, esp. pp. 182–90; Carpenter, *Wars*, esp. p. 93; Watts, *Henry VI*, *passim*, esp. pp. 108–9; Castor, *Duchy of Lancaster*, pp. 47–50.
69 Hicks, *Warwick*, pp. 75, 133–8, 187; 'Propaganda and the First Battle of St Albans, 1455', *Nottingham Medieval Studies* 44 (2000), p. 177.

4 ARISTOCRACY

1 J.K. Powis, *Aristocracy* (1984), p. 11
2 V.H. Galbraith, 'A New Life of Richard II', *History* 26 (1942), p. 227, as amended by McFarlane, *England*, p. 19; J.T. Rosenthal, *Nobles and the*

Noble Life 1295–1500 (1976), p. 20; Powis, p. 30; C.F. Richmond, *The Paston Family in the Fifteenth Century. Endings* (Manchester, 2000), p. 201. For other extreme examples, see Richmond, *Endings*, pp. 248–9.

3　M.L. Bush, *The English Aristocracy: A Comparative Synthesis* (Manchester, 1984), p. 4.

4　Chrimes, pp. 170, 172.

5　Powis, p. 2.

6　*The Poll Taxes of 1377, 1379 and 1381*, I, ed. C.C. Fenwick (British Academy Records of Economic and Social History, new series 7, 1998), p. xv.

7　Myers, pp. 94–9, 101–3.

8　'Private Indentures', pp. 150, 152, 162.

9　R.A. Allmond and A.J. Pollard, 'The Yeomanry of Robin Hood and Social Terminology in Fifteenth-century England', *Past and Present* 170 (2001), p. 76.

10　F. Heal, *Hospitality in Early Modern England* (Oxford, 1990), pp. 24, 26.

11　Hicks, *Rivals*, pp. 390–4.

12　N. Saul, *Death, Art and Memory in Medieval England* (Oxford, 2001), p. 176.

13　Given-Wilson, *Nobility*, pp. 56–7.

14　J.E. Powell and K. Wallis, *The House of Lords in the Middle Ages* (1968), pp. 427n, 464–5, 468n, 474, 477, 601; R.E. Archer, 'Parliamentary Restoration: John Mowbray and the Dukedom of Norfolk in 1425', *Rulers and Ruled*, pp. 99–116; Hicks, *Warwick*, p. 31 ; J. Smyth, *The Lives of the Berkeleys*, ed. J. Maclean, vol. 1 (1883), p. 110; M.W Warner and K. Lacey, 'Neville vs. Percy: A Precedence Dispute *circa* 1442', *HR* 59 (1996), pp. 211–17.

15　Chrimes, pp. 147–51

16　Mertes, 'Aristocracy', *Fifteenth-cent. Attitudes*, p. 42; F. Heal and C. Holmes, *The Gentry in England and Wales 1500–1700* (Basingstoke, 1994), p. 15; P. Laslett, *The World We Have Lost Further Explored* (1983), ch. 2.

17　J.R. Lander, *The Limitations of English Monarchy in the Later Middle Ages* (Toronto, 1989), pp. 15–16.

18　M.H. Keen, *Chivalry* (New Haven, 1984), p. 2.

19　Myers, p. 126; Bush, *English Aristocracy*, p. 2.

20　Richmond, *Endings*, p. 234.

21　Rosenthal, *Nobles*, p. 20; Mertes, 'Aristocracy', pp. 53–4; Myers, pp. 126–7.

22　Myers, pp. 126–7.

23　*The Rous Roll*, ed. W.H. Courthope (1859), no. 50.

24　Mertes, 'Aristocracy', p. 55.

25　Given-Wilson, *Chronicles*, pp. 194–5; R.L. Storey, *End of the House of Lancaster* (1966), p. 168; *Paston L & P*, vol. 1, p. 340.

26　Keen, *Chivalry*, p. 175; Hicks, *Rivals*, p. 51.

27　Warner and Lacey, p. 214.

28　Given-Wilson, *Chronicles*, p. 212.

29　For what follows, see Hicks, *Rivals*, pp. 48–51. Vale, pp. 262–4; Smyth, *Berkeleys*, pp. 109–11.

30　*Crowland*, pp. 144–7. Those on trial for treason were not allowed legal representation; the king's testimony was taken as record.

31 M.K. Jones, 'Somerset, York and the Wars of the Roses', *EHR* 104 (1989), pp. 285–307.
32 Powis, p. 9.
33 Ibid. p. 26; Heal, *Hospitality*, p. 11; Saul, *Death, Art and Memory*, pp. 96–7; *The Great Chronicle of London*, ed. A.H. Thomas and I.D. Thornley (1938), p. 207; Hicks, *Warwick*, pp. 230–1. C.M. Woolgar provides a guide to the norm and exceptions, 'Fast and Feast: Conspicuous Consumption and the Diet of the Nobility in the Fifteenth Century', *Revolution and Consumption*, pp. 7–25.
34 T. More, *History of King Richard III*, ed. R.S. Sylvester (New Haven, 1963), p. 8.
35 Powis, p. 4; Mertes, 'Aristocracy', p. 51; Heal and Holmes, *Gentry*, p. 51.
36 *Stonor L & P*, vol. 1, p. 117.
37 Mertes, 'Aristocracy', p. 51.
38 Hicks, *Rivals*, pp. 171, 339; *Rous Roll*, no. 50.
39 Lander, *Limitations*, p. 6.
40 McFarlane, *Nobility*, pp. 172–6; see also S.J. Payling, 'Social Mobility, Demographic Change, and Landed Society in Late Medieval England', *Economic History Review*, 2nd series 45 (1992), pp. 51–71.
41 *CCR 1468–76*, nos 936, 1026; Hicks, *Rivals*, ch. 19; H. Castor, *The King, the Crown, and the Duchy of Lancaster* (Oxford, 2000), p. 138.
42 As spelt out for each property on PRO SC 11/ 947.
43 J.M.W. Bean, *The Estates of the Percy Family 1416–1537* (Oxford, 1958), p. 120; Hicks, *Rivals*, p. 174; Virgoe, pp. 166–70; C.F. Richmond, *John Hopton* (Cambridge, 1981), p. 2.
44 *CCR 1468–76*, nos 221–40.
45 *Armburgh, passim.*
46 Castor, *Duchy of Lancaster*, p. 128.
47 For example, Hicks, *Rivals*, pp. 22–3 (citing Carpenter), 333.
48 For example, M.A. Hicks, 'Cement or Solvent? Kinship and Politics in Late Medieval England: The Case of the Nevilles', *History* 83 (1998), pp. 35–8.
49 McFarlane, *Nobility*, p. 250.
50 Heal and Holmes, *Gentry*, p. 44.
51 Hicks, *Rivals*, ch. 19; Castor, *Duchy of Lancaster*, p. 138; *CCR 1468–76*, no. 1026.
52 Bean, *Estates*, pp. 119–20.
53 Hicks, *Rivals*, chs 4–6, 8–10.
54 M.A. Hicks, *Richard III* (2nd edn, Stroud, 2000), p. 104.

5 CLASS PERSPECTIVES

1 B. Wilkinson, *Constitutional History of England in the Fifteenth Century* (1964), p. 88.
2 R.L. Storey, 'Episcopal King-makers in the Fifteenth Century', *The Church, Politics and Patronage in the Fifteenth Century*, ed. R.B. Dobson (Gloucester, 1984), pp. 82–3, 87–94.
3 E. Mason, 'The Role of the English Parishioner 1100–1500', *Journal of Ecclesiastical History* 27 (1976), pp. 17–29.
4 *The Medieval Town: A Reader in English Urban History 1200–1500*, ed. R. Holt and G. Rosser (Harlow, 1990), pp. 13–14.
5 *Ingulph*, pp. 367–8.

6 *RP*, vol. 5, pp. 475–6.

7 *Crowland*, p. 151.

8 A.H. Thompson, *The English Clergy and their Organisation in the Later Middle Ages* (Oxford, 1947), p. 292; J.S. Roskell, 'The Problem of the Attendance of the Lords at Medieval Parliaments', *Parliament and Politics in Late Medieval England* (1981), vol. 1, pp. II 174–5.

9 *Ingulph*, pp. 357–61, 391–2.

10 Ibid., pp. 356–7, 364.

11 R.B. Dobson, 'The Residentiary Canons of York in the Fifteenth Century', *The Church and Society in the Medieval North of England* (1993), pp. 195–204 at p. 204.

12 H.M. Jewell, 'English Bishops as Educational Benefactors in the Later Fifteenth Century', *Church, Politics and Patronage in the Fifteenth Century*, ed. R.B. Dobson (Gloucester, 1984), pp. 146–67.

13 Hicks, *Rivals*, p. 83n.

14 V. Davis, 'Preparation for Service in the Late Medieval English Church', *Concepts of Service*, p. 51.

15 P. Fleming, 'Telling Tales of Oligarchy in the Late Medieval Town', *Revolution and Consumption*, pp. 187–93.

16 B. McRee, 'Religious Gilds and the Regulation of Behavior in Late Medieval Towns', *People, Politics and the Community in the Later Middle Ages*, ed. J.T. Rosenthal and C.F. Richmond (Gloucester, 1987), pp. 113–15; Holt and Rosser, *The Medieval Town*, p. 12.

17 Holt and Rosser, *The Medieval Town*, p. 12; S. Rigby, 'Urban "Oligarchy" in Late Medieval Towns', *Towns and Townspeople in the Fifteenth Century*, ed. J.A.F. Thomson (Gloucester, 1988), p. 67.

18 C. Phythian-Adams, 'Ceremony and the Citizen: The Communal Year at Coventry 1450–1550', *The Medieval Town*, ch. 12.

19 Fleming, 'Telling Tales', pp. 180–1.

20 Rigby, 'Urban Oligarchy', p. 64.

21 C. Rawcliffe, ' "That Kindliness Should be Cherished More and Discord Driven Out" ': The Settlement of Commercial Disputes by Arbitration in Later Medieval England', *Enterprise and Individuals in Fifteenth-Century England*, ed. J.I. Kermode (Gloucester, 1991), pp. 104–5.

22 Fleming, 'Telling Tales', pp. 180–5, 188–94; D. Palliser, 'Urban Society', *Fifteenth-cent. Attitudes*, p. 147; Rigby, 'Urban Oligarchy', pp. 68, 70, 74; Holt and Rosser, *The Medieval Town*, p. 15.

23 R.B. Goheen, 'Peasant Politics? Village Community and the Crown in Fifteenth-Century England', *American Historical Review* 96 (1991), pp. 42–61 at p. 51.

24 R. Faith, 'The "Great Rumour" of 1377 and Peasant Ideology', *The English Rising of 1381*, ed. R.H. Hilton and T.H. Aston (Cambridge, 1984), ch. 2, esp. p. 47.

25 M. Mate, 'The Economic and Social Roots of Medieval Popular Rebellion: Sussex 1450–1', *Economic History Review* 45 (1992), pp. 661–76.

26 S. Payling, 'The Widening Franchise – Parliamentary Elections in Lancastrian Nottinghamshire', *England in the Fifteenth Century*, ed. D. Williams (Woodbridge, 1987), pp. 174, 183–5; 'County Parliamentary Elections in Fifteenth-Century England', *Parliamentary History* 18 (1999), pp. 251–7.

27 Hicks, *Warwick*, pp. 300, 303, 311–12.
28 Ibid., pp. 176–9; *Paston L & P*, vol. 1, p. 259.
29 D.A. Carpenter, 'English Peasants in Politics 1258–67', *Past and Present*, 167 (1992), pp. 11–12; Harvey, 'Popular Politics', p. 169.
30 Harvey, 'Popular Politics', pp. 156–7.
31 M. Cherry, 'The Struggle for Power in Mid-fifteenth Century Devonshire', *Patronage, The Crown, and the Provinces in Later Medieval England*, ed. R.A. Griffiths (Gloucester, 1981), p. 143 at n88; R.A. Griffiths, 'Local Rivalries and National Politics: The Percies, the Nevilles, and the Duke of Exeter 1452–4', *King and Country*, p. 330 .
32 As Harvey makes clear, *Cade*, appendix B, pp. 193–4.
33 C.L. Scofield, *The Life and Reign of Edward IV*, vol. 1 (1923), pp. 36, 37n; C.F. Richmond, 'Fauconberg's Kentish Rising of May 1471', *EHR* 85 (1970), pp. 683–6; I. Arthurson, 'The Rising of 1497: A Revolt of the Peasantry?', *People, Politics and Community in the Later Middle Ages*, ed. J.T. Rosenthal and C.F. Richmond (Gloucester, 1987), ch. 1, pp. 12–14.
34 Richmond, 'Fauconberg's Rising', pp. 684–9; Arthurson, 'Cornish Rising', pp. 5–9.
35 Harvey, 'Popular Politics', p. 171.
36 Ibid., p. 161; *Cade*, pp. 77, 186, 190–1.
37 Harvey, *Cade*, p. 105.
38 K. Dockray, 'The Yorkshire Rebellions of 1469', *The Ricardian* 83 (1983), pp. 249–52.
39 Harvey, *Cade*, pp. 80, 186–7; Vale, pp. 208–9.
40 Hicks, *Warwick*, pp. 177–8; *English Chronicle*, p. 107.
41 Mate, 'Medieval Popular Rebellion', p. 672.
42 A.J. Pollard, *The Wars of the Roses* (2nd edn, Basingstoke, 2001), pp. 80–5.
43 Harvey, *Cade*, pp. 187–9.
44 Harvey, 'Popular Politics', p. 158.
45 Harvey, *Cade*, pp. 188–91.
46 R.A. Allmond and A.J. Pollard, 'The Yeomanry of Robin Hood and Social Terminology in Fifteenth-century England', *Past and Present* 170 (2001), p. 76.
47 Harvey, 'Popular Politics', p. 156.
48 Harvey, *Cade*, p. 32. Compare Fulke Greville's famous observation of 1593 that 'if the feet knew their strength ... they would not bear as they do', C. Hill, 'The Many-Headed Monster', *Change and Continuity in Seventeenth-Century England* (1974), ch. 8, p. 187.
49 J.L. Watts , 'Ideas, Principles and Politics', *The Wars of the Roses*, ed. A.J. Pollard (Basingstoke, 1995), pp. 110–11.
50 C.F. Richmond, 'Patronage and Polemic', *The End of the Middle Ages?*, ed. J.L. Watts (Stroud, 1998), pp. 86–7.

6 GOVERNMENT

1 Myers, pp. 104–5, 142.
2 Griffiths, 'For the might of the land', p. 94.
3 Myers, pp. 105, 142.
4 D.A.L. Morgan, 'The King's Affinity in the Polity of Yorkist England', *TRHS* 5th series 23 (1973), pp. 2–5, 11.

5 Ibid., p. 2; M. Richardson, *The Medieval Chancery under Henry V* (List and Index special series 30, 1999), p. 50.

6 M. Hawkins, 'The Government: Its Role and Aims', *The Origins of the Civil War*, ed. C. Russell (Basingstoke, 1973), pp. 37–8.

7 B.P. Wolffe, *The Royal Demesne in English History* (1971), chs 6 and 7.

8 J.L. Kirby, 'The Issues of the Lancastrian Exchequer and Lord Cromwell's Estimates of 1433', *BIHR* 24 (1951), pp. 121–51.

9 M. Blatcher, *The Court of King's Bench, 1450–1550* (1978), preface.

10 N. Pronay, 'The Chancellor, the Chancery, and the Council at the End of the Fifteenth Century', *British Government and Administration*, ed. H. Hearder and H.R. Loyn (Cardiff, 1974), pp. 85, 89. For arbitration, see especially Hicks, *Rivals*, ch. 7; E. Powell, 'Arbitration and the Law in England in the Later Middle Ages', *TRHS* 5th series 33 (1983), pp. 49–67.

11 Brown, *Governance*, p. 3.

12 A.R. Myers, 'Parliament 1422–1509', *English Parliament*, pp. 144–6.

13 G.O. Sayles, *The King's Parliament of England* (1975), p. 116.

14 Myers, 'Parliament', p. 180.

15 J.S. Roskell, 'The Problem of the Attendance of the Lords in Medieval Parliaments', *Parliament and Politics in Late Medieval England*, vol. 1 (1981), pp. II 190–1, 194.

16 *HPT*, vol. 1, p. 39.

17 Ibid., p. 53.

18 *Plumpton L & P*, p. 63.

19 *Parliamentary Texts of the Later Middle Ages*, ed. N. Pronay and J. Taylor (Oxford, 1980), pp. 185–9; *Fane Fragment, passim*.

20 *Historical Studies in the English Parliament*, vol. 2, *1399–1603*, ed. E.B. Fryde and E. Miller (Cambridge, 1970), p. 4; Myers, 'Parliament', pp. 171, 174; *HPT*, vol. 1, pp. 78n, 129, 170, 171.

21 H.G. Richardson, 'The Commons in Parliament', *TRHS*, 3rd series 28 (1946), p. 29.

22 This is fully discussed in M.A. Hicks, 'King in Lords and Commons', forthcoming.

23 *Crowland*, pp. 146–7 ; W.H. Dunham, ' "The Books of Parliament" and "The Old Record", 1396–1504', *Speculum* 51 (1976), p. 707; *CPR 1461–7*, p. 63; *1476–85*, p. 63.

24 Chrimes, p. 152.

25 G.L. Harriss, 'The Formation of Parliament', *English Parliament*, p. 28.

26 L. Clark, 'The Benefits and Burdens of Office: Henry Bourgchier, Viscount Bourgchier and Earl of Essex and the Treasurership of the Exchequer', *Profit, Piety and the Professions in Later Medieval England*, ed. M.A. Hicks (Gloucester, 1990), p. 128; Hicks, 'King in Lords and Commons', forthcoming.

27 G.L. Harriss, 'Preference at the Medieval Exchequer', *BIHR* 30 (1957), pp. 17–40.

28 Wolffe, *Royal Demesne*, p. 157; Hicks, *Rivals*, p. 71.

29 R.E. Horrox, 'Introduction', *Fifteenth-cent Attitudes*, p. 19.

30 T.B. Pugh, 'The Magnates, Knights and Gentry', *Fifteenth-cent. England*, pp. 92–3; but see also Hicks, *Rivals*, pp. 214–16.

31 PRO C 49/54/35, 56.

32 A.G. Dickens, *The Courts of Europe* (1977), p. 35.

33 T. Walsingham, *Annales Ricardi Secundi et Henrici Quarti*, ed. H.T. Riley (Rolls Series, 1866), p. 403; Harvey, *Cade*, p. 189.
34 *Paston L & P*, vol. 1, p. 617; Myers, 'Parliament', p. 170; *Plumpton L & P*, p. 52.
35 Hicks, 'King in Lords and Commons', forthcoming.
36 Vale, p. 223.
37 Lander, pp. 191–220, 309–320.
38 'Financial Memoranda of the Reign of Edward V', ed. R.E. Horrox, *Camden Miscellany* 29 (1987), pp. 200–44.
39 *CPR 1467–77*, p. 583.
40 Griffiths, 'King's Council', pp. 318–19; Hicks, *Warwick*, pp. 109–10.
41 Griffiths, 'King's Council', p. 311.
42 Hicks, *Warwick*, pp. 132–5, 151–4, 156–8; Hicks, *Clarence*, pp. 41–2, 48, 131.
43 Vale, p. 244.
44 *Plumpton L & P*, pp. 51–2.
45 Vale, p. 244.
46 *HPT*, vol. 1, pp. 20–4; Hicks, 'King in Lords and Commons', forthcoming.
47 *Fane Fragment*, pp. 20, 25; Griffiths, *King and Country*, pp. 261–2.
48 *Fane Fragment*, p. 12.
49 Griffiths, 'Wales and the Marches', *Fifteenth-cent. England*, pp. 160–5.
50 N.B. Harte, 'State Control of Dress and Social Change in Pre-Industrial England', *Trade, Government and Economy in Pre-Industrial England*, ed. D.C. Coleman and A.H. John (1976), pp. 134–46; M.A. Hicks, *Richard III* (2nd edn, Stroud, 2000), p. 52.
51 *Harl 433*, vol. 3, p. 176.
52 Musson, *Medieval Law*, p. 16; C. Rawcliffe, 'The Great Lord as Peacekeeper: Arbitration by English Nobles and their Councils in the Later Middle Ages', *Law and Social Change in British History*, ed. J.A. Guy and H.G. Beale (1984), pp. 323–4; I. Rowney, 'Arbitration in Gentry Disputes of the Later Middle Ages', *History* 67 (1982), p. 368; Powell, 'Arbitration', p. 51; Hicks, *Rivals*, pp. 145–8 .
53 Rawcliffe, 'Great Lord', p. 411.
54 Rowney, 'Arbitration', p. 371.

7 ALTERNATIVE PERCEPTIONS

1 G.L. Harriss, 'The Dimensions of Politics', *McFarlane Legacy*, p. 15.
2 Harvey, *Cade*, p. 191.
3 *Armburgh*, p. 130; *EHD*, p. 265; B. Wilkinson, *Constitutional History of England in the Fifteenth Century* (1964), pp. 38n, 318.
4 *Chronicle of Adam of Usk 1377–1421*, ed. C. Given-Wilson (Oxford, 1997), pp. 90–1.
5 *Crowland*, pp. 120–1, 128–9.
6 *Death and Dissent*, pp. 97, 100, 102, 105; *Crowland*, pp. 120–1, 128–9, 137–8, 190–1; Chrimes, pp. 169–73 as modified by J.T. Rosenthal, *The Nobles and the Noble Life 1295–1500* (1976), p. 122; Hicks, *Warwick*, p. 303.
7 C. Hill, 'The "Many-Headed Monster"', *Change and Continuity in Seventeenth-Century England* (1974), ch. 8.

8 But see *EHD*, p. 264.

9 *Paston L & P*, vol. 1, p. 279.

10 C. Given-Wilson, 'Service, Serfdom, and English Labour Legislation 1350–1450', *Concepts of Service*, pp. 23–37.

11 'The Siege of Calais', *Historical Poems of the Fourteenth and Fifteenth Centuries*, ed. R.H. Robbins (New York, 1959), pp. 78–83; see also J.A. Doig, 'Propaganda, Public Opinion and the Siege of Calais in 1436', *Crown, Government, and People in the Fifteenth Century*, ed. R.E. Archer (Stroud, 1995), pp. 79–106.

12 Wilkinson, *Constitutional History*, pp. 114–15.

13 Doig, 'Siege of Calais', pp. 99, 101.

14 Wilkinson, *Constitutional History*, p. 115.

15 Hicks, *Warwick*, p. 195.

16 *A Relation or True Account of the Island of England*, ed. C.A. Sneyd (Camden Society 37, 1847), p. 21.

17 Griffiths, *Henry VI*, pp. 154–77, 551–61; *The Alien Communities of London in the Fifteenth Century*, ed. J.L. Bolton (Stamford, 1998), p. 55n; A.J. Pollard, *Late Medieval England 1399–1509* (Harlow, 2000), pp. 173–6, 194–8.

18 Pollard, *Late Medieval England*, p. 173.

19 P. Fleming, 'Telling Tales of Oligarchy in the Late Medieval Town', *Revolution and Consumption*, pp. 182–3.

20 S.J. Payling, 'The Widening Franchise – Parliamentary Elections in Lancastrian Nottinghamshire', *England in the Fifteenth Century*, ed. D. Williams (Woodbridge, 1987), pp. 183–4.

21 *Paston L & P*, vol. 2, pp. 120–1.

22 Virgoe, ch. 6.

23 A.J. Pollard, *The Worlds of Richard III* (Stroud, 2001), ch. 3; M.A. Hicks, *Richard III* (Stroud, 2000), pp. 169–70.

24 Green, *Truth*, p. 48.

25 Vale, p. 198; Chrimes, pp. 26, 78; A.R. Myers, 'Parliament 1422–1509', *English Parliament*, pp. 145–6.

26 The fullest recent discussion is in M.A. Hicks, *Bastard Feudalism* (Harlow, 1995), ch. 4.

27 Chrimes, p. 74.

28 Dunham, *Hastings*, pp. 91–2.

29 *Harl 433*, vol. 3, pp. 174–5.

30 Ibid., p. 175.

31 Musson, *Medieval Law*, *passim*, esp. ch. 3; Harriss, 'Political Society', p. 53.

32 A. Harding, 'The Revolt against the Justices', *The English Rising of 1381*, ed. T.H. Aston and R.H. Hilton (Cambridge, 1984), pp. 165–93 at p. 165.

33 R. Faith, 'The "Great Rumour" of 1377 and Peasant Ideology', *English Rising*, ch. 2.

34 Green, *Truth*, pp. 19–73.

35 Brown, *Governance*, p. 138; Musson, *Medieval Law*, pp. 108, 115.

36 R. Allmond and A.J. Pollard, 'The Yeomanry of Robin Hood and Social Terminology in Fifteenth-century England', *Past and Present* 170 (2001), p. 58.

37 E. Powell, 'Law and Justice', *Fifteenth-cent. Attitudes*, p. 35; *Kingship, Law and Society* (Oxford, 1989), pp. 89, 170, 193n, 201, 204.
38 B.A. Hanawalt, 'Fur-collar Crime: The Pattern of Crime among the Fourteenth-Century English Nobility', *Journal of Social History* 8 (1974), pp. 1–17.
39 C.T. Allmand, *Henry V* (1992), p. 306; H. Kleineke, 'Why the West was Wild', paper at the fifteenth-century conference on authority and subversion, Bristol 2000.
40 Lander, p. 10.
41 For the remedies, see J.G. Bellamy, *Criminal Law and Society in Late Medieval and Tudor England* (Gloucester, 1984); for implementation see P. C. Maddern, *Violence and the Social Order* (Oxford, 1992), ch. 6, esp. p. 174.
42 Carpenter, *Wars*, p. 53.
43 Kleineke, 'Why the West was Wild'.
44 *Parliamentary Texts of the Later Middle Ages*, ed. N. Pronay and J. Taylor (Oxford, 1980), pp. 186–7.
45 W.R.D. Jones, *The Tudor Commonwealth, 1529–59* (1970).
46 Watts, *Henry VI*, pp. 39, 45.
47 Dockray, pp. 69, 70, 72–3, 78–80.
48 P. W. Hammond and A.F. Sutton, *Richard III: The Road to Bosworth Field* (1985), pp. 104, 146, 161; D. Mancini, *The Usurpation of Richard III*, ed. C.A.J. Armstrong (2nd edn, Oxford, 1969), pp. 80–2; Hicks, *Richard III*, pp. 102–10.
49 *Parliamentary Texts*, p. 186.
50 Harvey, *Cade*, p. 191; Vale, p. 188.
51 Vale, pp. 187–8.
52 Griffiths, 'King's Council', pp. 318–19.
53 Vale, p. 223.
54 Most recently Griffiths, ''For the might of the land', *Concepts of Service*, ch. 6.
55 Watts, *Henry VI*, p. 79.
56 M.A. Hicks, 'Lord Hastings' Indentured Retainers?', *Rivals*, pp. 229–46.
57 C.J. Harrison, 'The Petition of Edmund Dudley', *EHR* 87 (1972), pp. 87–90.
58 E. Powell, 'After "After McFarlane": The Poverty of Patronage and the Case for Constitutional History', *Trade, Devotion and Governance*, ed. D.J. Clayton, R.G. Davies and P. McNiven (Stroud, 1994), p. 6.
59 J. Hurstfield, *Freedom, Corruption and Government in Elizabethan England* (1973), p. 77.
60 C.F. Richmond, 'Patronage and Polemic', *The End of the Middle Ages?*, ed. J.L. Watts (Stroud, 1998), p. 69.
61 Carpenter, *Wars*, p. 43.
62 B.P. Wolffe, 'Acts of Resumption in Lancastrian Parliaments 1399–1456', *EHR* 73 (1958), pp. 583–616; Hicks, *Rivals*, pp. 71, 73–4; Vale, p. 224.
63 M. Jurkowksi, C.L. Smith and D. Crook, *Lay Taxes in England and Wales 1188–1688* (PRO Handbook 31, Kew, 1998), p. 36.
64 *RP*, vol. 5, p. 572.
65 J.R. Lander, *The Limitations of English Monarchy in the Later Middle Ages* (Toronto, 1989), p. 11.

66 Jurkowski, *Lay Taxes*, pp. 122–4, 127–8; Hicks, *Rivals*, pp. 406–9; I. Arthurson, 'Cornish Rising', ch. 1; M.L. Bush, 'Tax Reform and Rebellion in Early Tudor England', *History* 76 (1991), pp. 379–400.
67 G.L. Harriss, 'Introduction: The Exemplar of Kingship', *Henry V*, p. 16.
68 Dockray, pp. 72–3.
69 Jurkowski, *Lay Taxes*, p. 124; Hicks, *Rivals*, pp. 406–9; Arthurson, 'Cornish Rising', pp. 4–5.
70 Arthurson, 'Cornish Rising', p. 26; Hicks, *Rivals*, p. 404.
71 Bush, 'Tax Reform', pp. 379–400.
72 J.G. Bellamy, *The Law of Treason in England in the Later Middle Ages* (Cambridge, 1970), pp. 116, 145.
73 Powell, *Kingship, Law and Society*, pp. 170, 206; 'The Strange Death of Sir John Mortimer: Politics and the Law of Treason in Lancastrian England', *Rulers and Ruled*, pp. 87–97; Pollard, *Late Medieval England*, p. 48.
74 Harvey, *Cade*, p. 189; Vale, pp. 193–4; *Paston L & P*, vol. 1, p. 162.
75 T. More, *History of King Richard II*, ed. R. Sylvester (New Haven, 1963), p. 7.
76 Harvey, *Cade*, p. 187.
77 *Paston L & P*, vol. 1, p. 162.
78 A.E. Curry, *Agincourt* (Stroud, 2000), pp. 62–3.
79 Virgoe, p. 254 ; Harvey, *Cade*, pp. 186–91; Vale, pp. 187–8.
80 Green, *Truth*, pp. 6, 214.
81 Vale, p. 188.
82 Ibid.
83 Hurstfield, *Freedom*, pp. 140–2.
84 Ibid., pp. 137–62, esp. pp. 142–3.
85 L. Clark, 'The Benefits and Burdens of Office: Henry Bourgchier (1408–83), Viscount Bourgchier and Earl of Essex, and the Treasurership of the Exchequer', *Profit, Piety and the Professions in Later Medieval England*, ed. M.A. Hicks (Gloucester, 1990), pp. 121–2.
86 Vale, pp. 180–3; McFarlane, *Nobility*, p. 26.
87 *Harl. 433*, vol. 3, p. 175.
88 For example, C.L. Scofield, *Life and Reign of Edward IV*, vol. 2 (1923), p. 373; M.A. Hicks, 'The 1468 Statute of Livery', *HR* 64 (1991), p. 26.
89 For example, Hicks, *Rivals*, p. 147n. Early fourteenth-century legislation limited rather than terminated retaining: J.R. Maddicott, *Law and Lordship: Royal Justices as Retainers in Thirteenth- and Fourteenth-Century England*, Past and Present Supplement 4 (1978), p. 83.
90 *Harl 433*, vol. 3, p. 174.
91 Harvey, *Cade*, pp. 190–1.

8 BASTARD FEUDALISM

1 Myers, p. 98.
2 C. Carpenter, 'Law, Justice, and Landowners in Late Medieval England', *Law and History Review* 1 (1983), esp. p. 206n; C.F. Richmond, *John Hopton* (Cambridge, 1981), pp. 29–30; C.F. Richmond, 'When did John Hopton become blind?', *HR* 60 (1987), pp. 102–6; see also Carpenter, *Wars*, p. 58; D.A.L. Morgan, 'The Individual Style of the English Gentleman', *The Gentry and Lesser Nobility in Late Medieval Europe*, ed. M. Jones (Gloucester, 1986), p. 27.

3 *Marcher Lordships of South Wales 1415–1536. Select Documents*, ed. T.B. Pugh (Cardiff, 1963), pp. 227–32.
4 J.K. Powis, *Aristocracy* (1984), p. 5.
5 *Plumpton L & P*, p. 89.
6 Given-Wilson, *Nobility*, p. 93.
7 McFarlane, *England*, pp. 234–5.
8 Hicks, *Clarence*, p. 169.
9 *EHD*, p. 272.
10 M.E. James, 'The Murder at Cocklodge', *Durham University Journal* 57 (1964–5), pp. 80–7.
11 'Private Indentures', pp. 163–71, 178–9; Dunham, *Hastings*, p. 133.
12 McFarlane, *England*, pp. 27–8; J.M.W. Bean, *The Estates of the Percy Family 1416–1537* (Oxford, 1958), pp. 91–4; A.J. Pollard, 'The Northern Retainers of Richard Nevill Earl of Salisbury', *Northern History* 11 (1976), pp. 64–6.
13 Hicks, *Rivals*, p. 147 & n.
14 P. Lee, *Nunneries, Learning and Spirituality in Late Medieval English Society* (Woodbridge, 2001), p. 54.
15 R.E. Horrox, 'The Urban Gentry in the Fifteenth Century', *Towns and Townspeople in the Fifteenth Century*, ed. J.A.F. Thomson (Gloucester, 1988), p. 29.
16 R.H. Hilton, 'Towns in English Medieval Society', *The Medieval Town*, ed. R. Holt and G. Rosser (Harlow, 1990), pp. 26–7.
17 Dunham, *Hastings*, p. 127.
18 R.E. Horrox, 'Urban Patronage and Patrons in the Fifteenth Century', *Patronage, The Crown, and the Provinces in Later Medieval England*, ed. R.A. Griffiths (Gloucester, 1981), pp. 148–61.
19 A. Cameron, 'The Giving of Livery and Retaining in Henry VII's Reign', *Renaissance and Modern Studies* 18 (1974), p. 29.
20 'Private Indentures', p. 151.
21 Pollard, 'Northern Retainers', pp. 67–8.
22 'Private Indentures', pp. 146, 149, 151, 156–7, 162; Dunham, *Hastings*, p. 124.
23 Green, *Truth*, p. 159; 'Private Indentures', pp. 160–1, 163, 165, 171; Dunham, *Hastings*, p. 124.
24 Dunham, *Hastings*, p. 27.
25 I disagree with Prof. Richmond's assertions to the contrary conveniently collected in Hicks, *Rivals*, pp. 30–2.
26 T.B. Pugh, 'The Magnates, Knights and Gentry', *Fifteenth-cent. England*, pp. 101–4.
27 L. Clark, 'Magnates and their Affinities in the Parliaments of 1386–1421', *McFarlane Legacy*, pp. 134–5.
28 D.A.L. Morgan, 'The King's Affinity in the Polity of Yorkist England', *TRHS* 5th series 23 (1973), p. 7; *Paston L & P*, vol. 1, p. 595; Powis, p. 51.
29 M.A. Hicks, *Bastard Feudalism* (Harlow, 1995), pp. 97–9.
30 *Plumpton L & P*, p. 25.
31 McFarlane, *England*, pp. 234–5; P.J.C. Field, *The Life and Times of Sir Thomas Malory* (Cambridge, 1993), pp. 100–1.
32 'Private Indentures', pp. 160–1.
33 Dockray, p. 114.

34 Hicks, *Rivals*, pp. 365–418; *The Reign of Henry VII from Contemporary Sources*, ed. A.F. Pollard, vol. 1 (1913), pp. 72–6.
35 *Paston L & P*, vol. 1, p. 595.
36 This is discussed below, see ch. 9.
37 *Plumpton L & P*, pp. 54, 56, 70, 77, 78, 128–9.
38 *The Rous Roll*, ed. W.H. Courthope (1859), nos. 51, 54; T. More, *Utopia*, ed. P. Turner (1965), p. 45.
39 E. Powell, 'Law and Justice', *Fifteenth-cent. Attitudes*, p. 35; C. Rawcliffe, 'The Great Lord as Peacekeeper: Arbitration by English Nobles and their Councils in the Later Middle Ages', *Law and Social Change in British History*, ed. J.A. Guy and H.G. Beale (1984), p. 37; W.H. Dunham, 'The "Books of Parliament" and "The Old Record" 1396–1504', *Speculum* 51 (1976), p. 707; More, *Utopia*, p. 45.
40 *Stonor L & P*, vol. 2, p. 70.
41 Rawcliffe, 'Great Lord', p. 51.
42 *Plumpton L & P*, p. 28.
43 Ibid., pp. 24, 45–6, 48, 51–2, 55, 59, 60, 76, 82, 83, 103–4, 115, 133, 134.
44 *Stonor L & P*, vol. 2, p. 83.
45 *Plumpton L & P*, pp. 30, 44; Rawcliffe, 'Great Lord', p. 39.
46 *Plumpton L & P*, pp. 47, 52, 80.
47 Ibid., pp. 37, 109, 184; *Armburgh*, pp. 178–9; Rawcliffe, 'Great Lord', pp. 41, 51; S. Payling, 'Law and Arbitration in Nottinghamshire 1399–1461', *People, Politics, and the Community in the Later Middle Ages*, ed. J.T. Rosenthal and C.F. Richmond (Gloucester, 1986), p. 154.
48 Rawcliffe, 'Great Lord', pp. 38, 44–5; *Plumpton L & P*, p. 58; Hicks, *Clarence* (1st edn, Gloucester, 1980), p. 181.
49 *Plumpton L & P*, pp. 45–7, 74, 117; *Armburgh*, pp. 92, 97, 100, 114–16, 175, 177, 192.
50 *Plumpton L & P*, p. 131.
51 M.A. Hicks, 'The 1468 Statute of Livery', *HR* 64 (1991), pp. 18–21.
52 *Plumpton L & P*, pp. 102, 105–8.
53 Rawcliffe, 'Great Lord', p. 38; *Plumpton L & P*, pp. 51–2.
54 Vale, p. 247.
55 A. Gundy, 'The Earl of Warwick and the Royal Affinity in the Politics of the West Midlands, 1389–99', *Revolution & Consumption*, pp. 57–70; S. Mitchell, 'The Knightly Household of Richard II and the Peace Commissions', in ibid., pp. 45–56.
56 This is the central theme of H. Castor, *The King, the Crown and the Duchy of Lancaster* (Oxford, 2000).
57 Myers, pp. 108, 127; *Crowland*, pp. 146–7.
58 *Plumpton L & P*, pp. 82, 87, 161.
59 Dunham, *Hastings*, pp. 119–34; Hicks, *Rivals*, pp. 238–46.
60 *Harl 433*, vol. 2, p. 81.
61 *Plumpton L & P*, pp. 44–5.
62 Hicks, *Bastard Feudalism*, pp. 39–40.
63 *Plumpton L & P*, pp. 69, 73.
64 Ibid., p. 87.
65 R.E. Horrox, *Richard III: A Study of Service* (Cambridge, 1989), p. 16.

9 PROVINCIAL COMMUNITIES

1 M.A. Hicks, 'The Sources', *The Wars of the Roses*, ed. A.J. Pollard (Basingstoke, 1995), p. 37.
2 Hicks, *Rivals*, p. 333; Carpenter, *Wars*, p. 44; H. Castor, *The King, the Crown, and the Duchy of Lancaster* (Oxford, 2000), p. 174.
3 Castor, *Duchy of Lancaster*, pp. 78, 100, quoting Watts, *Henry VI*, p. 67.
4 Castor, *Duchy of Lancaster*, pp. 84–5; C. Carpenter, *Locality and Polity* (Cambridge, 1992), chs 11–13; 'The Duke of Clarence and the Midlands: A Study in the Interplay of Local and National Politics', *Midland History* 11 (1986), pp. 22–48; M. Cherry, 'The Struggle for Power in Mid-fifteenth Century Devonshire', *Patronage, The Crown, and the Provinces in Later Medieval England*, ed. R.A. Griffiths (Gloucester, 1981), pp. 123–44 at p. 137.
5 For the West Midlands, see Hicks, *Clarence*, esp. ch. 5; Hicks, *Warwick*, esp. ch. 3; Hicks, 'Between Majorities: The "Beauchamp Interregnum" 1439–49', *HR* 72 (1999), pp. 27–43.
6 For example, Hicks, 'Between Majorities', pp. 31–42; *Warwick*, pp. 31–6; *Rivals*, chs 9–10.
7 M.A. Hicks, *Bastard Feudalism* (Harlow, 1995), p. 97.
8 McFarlane, *Nobility*, pp. 234–5; P.J.C. Field, *The Life and Times of Sir Thomas Malory* (1993), pp. 100–1; R.L. Storey, *The End of the House of Lancaster* (1966), p. 130.
9 M.A. Hicks, *Warwick*, pp. 85, 89.
10 Given-Wilson, *Nobility*, p. 175.
11 Castor, *Duchy of Lancaster*, p. 169.
12 Hicks, *Rivals*, pp. 370–6.
13 Castor, *Duchy of Lancaster*, p. 266.
14 Hicks, *Rivals*, ch. 12; Dunham, *Hastings*, p. 127. For an alternative interpretation, see E. Westervelt, 'The Changing Nature of Politics in the Localities in the Later Fifteenth Century: William Lord Hastings and his Indentured Retainers', *Midland History* 26 (2001), pp. 96–106.
15 As suggested by M.W. Warner and K. Lacey, 'Neville vs. Percy: A Precedence Dispute c. 1442', *HR* 59 (1996), p. 214.
16 Virgoe, p. 291.
17 S. Payling, 'County Parliamentary Elections in Fifteenth-Century England', *Parliamentary History* 18 (1999), pp. 247–51.
18 Given-Wilson, *Nobility*, p. 80.
19 S. Payling, 'Law and Arbitration in Nottinghamshire 1399–1461', *People, Politics and the Community in the Later Middle Ages*, ed. J.T. Rosenthal and C.F. Richmond (Gloucester, 1987), pp. 151–3.
20 C.F. Richmond, *The Paston Family: Fastolf's Will* (Cambridge, 1996), p. 212.
21 Given-Wilson, *Nobility*, p. 160.
22 Virgoe, p. 98.
23 G.L. Harris 'Introduction', McFarlane, *England*, p. xv.
24 Dunham, *Hastings*, p. 127; *Stonor L & P*, vol. 2, p. 150.
25 J. Freeman, 'Middlesex in the Fifteenth Century: Community or Communities?', *Revolution and Consumption*, p. 97; A.J. Pollard, *The Worlds of Richard III* (Stroud, 2001), chs 4 and 5.
26 A. Everitt, *The Community of Kent and the Great Rebellion 1640–1660* (Leicester, 1960), esp. p. 36.

27 M.A. Hicks, 'Cement or Solvent? Kinship and Politics in Late Medieval England: The Case of the Nevilles', *History* 83 (1998), pp. 31–46.

28 *Plumpton L & P*, p. 82.

29 McFarlane, *England*, p. 11.

30 Given-Wilson, *Nobility*, pp. 75–7.

31 Ibid., p. 1.

32 T.S. Purser, 'The Hampshire Community of Gentry c. 1300–1540' (unpublished Southampton University PhD thesis, 2001).

33 Payling, 'County Parliamentary Elections', p. 246.

34 L. Clark, 'Magnates and their Affinities in the Parliaments of 1386–1421', *McFarlane Legacy*, p. 133.

35 See n5 above.

36 James, p. 308.

37 J.G. Bellamy, *Criminal Law and Society in Late Medieval and Tudor England* (Gloucester, 1984), pp. 70–84.

38 McFarlane, *Nobility*, pp. 175–6; *England*, p. 257.

39 Castor, *Duchy of Lancaster*, pp. 128–55, esp. pp. 128–9.

40 C.F. Richmond, *The Paston Family in the Fifteenth Century. Endings* (Manchester, 2000), p. 197.

41 For details, see Castor, *Duchy of Lancaster*, pp. 138–9; C.F. Richmond, *The Paston Family in the Fifteenth Century: The First Phase* (Cambridge, 1990), pp. 47–59, 74–82.

42 The fullest recent discussion is in Hicks, *Warwick*, ch. 3.

43 Hicks, *Rivals*, p. 273.

44 P.C. Maddern, *Violence and the Social Order* (Oxford, 1992).

45 *Plumpton L & P*, p. 104.

46 *Paston L & P*, vol. 2, pp. 307–8.

47 Harriss, 'Introduction', McFarlane, *England*, p. xv.

48 Hicks, *Rivals*, pp. 142–3.

49 C. Rawcliffe, 'The Great Lord as Peacekeeper: Arbitration by English Noblemen and their Councils in the Later Middle Ages', *Law and Social Change in British History*, ed. J.A. Guy and H.G. Beale (1984), p. 47.

50 Hicks, *Rivals*, ch. 7; *Warwick*, pp. 222–5.

10 INTERACTION

1 Vale, pp. 135–8.

2 G.R. Elton, 'Tudor Government: The Points of Contact', *TRHS* 5th series 24 (1974), p. 183.

3 P. Fleming, 'Telling Tales of Oligarchy in the Late Medieval Town', *Revolution and Consumption*, pp. 183–5.

4 Exeter RO, receivers' rolls 1–9 Edward IV.

5 C. Russell, *Parliament and English Politics 1621–1629* (Oxford, 1979), p. 8.

6 Musson, *Medieval Law*, pp. 108–9.

7 Fleming, 'Telling Tales', p. 178; S.H. Rigby, 'Urban "Oligarchy" in Late Medieval Towns', *Towns and Townspeople in the Fifteenth Century*, ed. J.A.F. Thomson (Gloucester, 1988), pp. 65–6.

8 J.R. Lander, *The Limitations of English Monarchy in the Later Middle Ages* (Toronto, 1989), pp. 31–2.

9 Hicks, *Clarence*, pp. 100–4, 108–11.

10 Ibid., p. 110; *Paston L & P*, vol. 1, pp. 544–5.
11 Musson, *Medieval Law*, pp. 224, 254.
12 For example, Vale, pp. 135–8, 148–52, 154–5.
13 T.B. Pugh, *Henry V and the Southampton Plot of 1415* (Gloucester, 1988), pp. 124, 129.
14 Given-Wilson, *Chronicles*, pp. 168–89. See also Vale, p. 176; *The Great Chronicle of London*, ed. A.H. Thomas and I.D. Thornley (1938), pp. 51–83; *Chronicles of London*, ed. C.L. Kingsford (1905), pp. 19–62.
15 Vale, pp. 176–7 & sources there cited.
16 Vale, pp. 139, 170, 175; *EHD*, p. 240.
17 J.A. Doig, 'Propaganda, Public Opinion and the Siege of Calais in 1436', *Crown, Government, and People in the Fifteenth Century*, ed. R.E. Archer (Stroud, 1995), pp. 91–103.
18 Given-Wilson, *Chronicles*, p. 192; *Annales Ricardi Secundi et Henrici Quarti*, ed. H.T. Riley (Rolls Series, 1866), p. 403.
19 P. Morgan, 'Henry IV and the Shadow of Richard II', *Government, Crown and Community*, pp. 8–31; S.K. Walker, 'Rumour, Sedition and Popular Protest in the Reign of Henry IV', *Past and Present* 166 (2001), pp. 37–44; A.J. Gross, *The Dissolution of the Lancastrian Kingship* (Stamford, 1996), pp. 15–18.
20 *Letters and Papers illustrative of the Wars of the English in France*, ed. J. Stevenson (2 in 3 vols, Rolls Series, 1861–4), vol. 2(2), pp. 440–51; Vale, p. 170. A new version is being investigated by Dr M.K. Jones.
21 Vale, pp. 170, 180–3.
22 Ibid., pp. 193–4.
23 *RP*, vol. 5, pp. 224, 346–9, 462–7.
24 Vale, p. 142. The attributed date 1461 is probably erroneous.
25 M.A. Hicks, 'Propaganda and the First Battle of St. Albans, 1455', *Nottingham Medieval Studies* 44 (2000), pp. 167–83; Hicks, *Warwick*, pp. 179–202.
26 Vale, pp. 186–7, 190; M.A. Hicks, 'From Megaphone to Microscope: The Correspondence of Richard Duke of York with Henry VI in 1450 Revisited', *Journal of Medieval History* 25 (1999), pp. 243–56.
27 For example, *English Chronicle*, pp. 71–2, 81–106; Vale, pp 178–80; Dockray, pp. 33–4; see also Hicks, *Rivals*, pp. 57–8.
28 Hicks, *Rivals*, p. 71; M.A. Hicks, 'King in Lords and Commons', forthcoming.
29 For example, Lord Stanley, *RP*, vol. 5, pp. 369–70.
30 Virgoe, p. 291; M.K. Jones, 'Somerset, York and the Wars of the Roses', *EHR* 104 (1989), pp. 290–1, 300–7; S. Payling, 'The Ampthill Dispute: A Study in Aristocratic Lawlessness and the Breakdown of Lancastrian Government', *English Historical Review* 104 (1989), pp. 897–8, 903.
31 L. Clark, 'Magnates and their Affinities in the Parliaments of 1386–1421', *McFarlane Legacy*, pp. 127, 53, esp. pp. 127, 134.
32 Hicks, *Clarence*, p. 140; Virgoe, ch. 3; M. McKisack, *The Parliamentary Representation of the English Boroughs during the Middle Ages* (Oxford, 1932), pp. 62–3.
33 S. Payling, 'County Parliamentary Elections in Fifteenth-century England', *Parliamentary History* 18 (1999), pp. 237–57, esp. p. 249; 'The Widening Franchise – Parliamentary Elections in Lancastrian Nottinghamshire', ed. D. Williams (Woodbridge, 1987), pp. 182–4; Virgoe, p. 348.

34 Virgoe, ch. 2.
35 D. Hirst, *A Representative of the People?* (Cambridge, 1975), pp. 4, 12–13.
36 *RP*, vol. 5, p. 375.
37 *Parliamentary Texts of the Later Middle Ages*, ed. N. Pronay and J. Taylor (Oxford, 1980), p. 186; *Fane Fragment*, p. 18.
38 C. Rawcliffe, 'Parliament and the Settlement of Disputes by Arbitration in the Later Middle Ages', *Parliamentary History* 9 (1990), pp. 316–42.
39 For example, *Parliamentary Texts*, p. 186.
40 Ibid., pp. 186–7. The next paragraph is based on ibid., *passim*; Hicks, 'King in Lords and Commons', forthcoming.
41 This suggests little development since the early fifteenth century, *HPT*, vol. 1, pp. 79–82.
42 Ibid., vol. 1, p. 103.
43 S. Payling, 'The Coventry Parliament of 1459: A Privy Seal Writ concerning the Election of Knights of the Shire', *HR* 60 (1987), pp. 349–52.
44 *RP*, vol. 5, pp. 369–70.
45 Hicks, *Clarence*, ch. 3.
46 C.A.J. Armstrong, 'The Inauguration Ceremonies of the Yorkist Kings', *England, France and Burgundy in the Fifteenth Century* (1983), ch. 2.
47 Hicks, *Rivals*, pp. 359–62; M.A. Hicks, 'An Escheat Concealed: The Despenser Forfeitures 1400–61', *Hampshire Studies* 53 (1998), pp. 183–9.
48 *Fane Fragment*, pp. 8–25; see also Hicks, 'King in Lords and Commons', forthcoming.
49 *Fane Fragment*, p. 12.
50 For the Readeption, see especially Hicks, *Clarence*, pp. 73–91; *Warwick*, p. 302.
51 Virgoe, p. 253.
52 Harvey, *Cade*, pp. 187, 189–91.
53 Ibid., pp. 187, 189, 191.
54 Ibid., pp. 31–2.
55 *Report from the Lords' Committees Touching on the Dignity of a Peer*, vol. 5 (1829), p. 286.
56 Griffiths, *Henry VI*, p. 684.
57 Virgoe, pp. 248–9.
58 P.A. Johnson, *Duke Richard of York 1411–60* (Oxford,1988), pp. 79–81; Harvey, *Cade*, p. 189; Virgoe, pp. 251, 253
59 Harvey, *Cade*, pp. 187, 189–91.
60 Vale, pp. 187–9.
61 *RP*, vol. 5, p. 216; Vale, pp. 210–12; see also Vale, pp. 208–10.
62 Dockray, pp. 68–73.
63 Dockray, pp. 68, 70, 71, 179–85; Hicks, *Warwick*, pp. 177–8, 298–300, 303
64 D. Mancini, *The Usurpation of Richard III*, ed. C.A.J. Armstrong (2nd edn, Oxford, 1969), pp. 72–3.
65 Ibid., pp. 64–5, 80–95; P. W. Hammond and A.F. Sutton, *Richard III: The Road to Bosworth Field* (1985), pp. 155–6; *The York House Books 1461–90*, ed. L. Attreed (Stroud, 1991), vol. 2, p. 714; M.A. Hicks, *Richard III* (2nd edn, Stroud, 2000) , pp. 102–7.
66 Compare M.A. Hicks, 'Bastard Feudalism, Overmighty Subjects, and Idols of the Multitude', *History* 85 (2000), pp. 386–403; *Richard III*, p. 123.

67 Armstrong, 'Inauguration Ceremonies', pp. 73–5.
68 Hicks, *Richard III*, pp. 143–53.
69 T. More, *History of King Richard III*, ed. R. Sylvester (New Haven, 1963), p. 8.
70 *The Reign of Henry VII from Contemporary Sources*, ed. A.F. Pollard, vol. 1 (1913), p. 70.
71 Ibid., pp. 150–5.
72 C.J. Harrison, 'The Petition of Edmund Dudley', *EHR* 87 (1972), pp. 87–90; *The Anglica Historica of Polydore Vergil*, ed. D. Hay (Camden 3rd series 74, 1950), pp. 146–7; G.R. Elton, *Studies in Tudor and Stuart Government and Politics*, vol. 1 (Cambridge, 1974), chs 3 and 4.
73 Dockray, pp. 68–73.
74 Vale, pp. 220–1; Hicks, *Warwick*, pp. 299–301.
75 *Rebellion, Popular Protest, and the Social Order in Early Modern England*, ed. P. Slack (Cambridge, 1984), p. 10.

11 CIVIL WAR

1 R.L. Storey, *The End of the House of Lancaster* (1966), pp. 149, 185.
2 Dockray, pp. 152–3.
3 Ibid., p. 158.
4 D. MacCulloch, 'Kett's Rebellion in Context', *Rebellion, Popular Protest, and the Social Order in Early Modern England*, ed. P. Slack (Cambridge, 1984), p. 47.
5 K.B. McFarlane, *Lancastrian Kings and Lollard Knights* (Oxford, 1972), p. 48.
6 A.J. Gross, 'K.B. McFarlane and the Determinists: The Fallibilities of the English Kings, c. 1390–1520', *McFarlane Legacy*, p. 68.
7 McFarlane, *England*, p. 255.
8 G.L. Harriss, 'Marmaduke Lumley and the Exchequer Crisis of 1446–9', *Aspects of Late Medieval Government and Society*, ed. J.G. Rowe (Toronto, 1986), esp. pp. 150, 164, 171.
9 Gross, 'K.B. McFarlane', p. 58.
10 C.D. Ross, *Edward IV* (1974), pp. 250, 286, 290, 385–6, 416; 'Financial Memoranda of the Reign of Edward V', ed. R.E. Horrox, *Camden Miscellany* 29 (1987), pp. 203, 209.
11 M.A. Hicks, 'Bastard Feudalism, Overmighty Subjects, and Idols of the Multitude', *History* 85 (2000), p. 403.
12 *Paston L & P*, vol. 1, p. 162; see also Hicks, *Warwick*, pp. 199–200.
13 M. Bennett, 'Henry VII and the Northern Rising of 1489', *EHR* 105 (1990), pp. 34–55.
14 Dockray, pp. 115, 117.

SELECT BIBLIOGRAPHY

Primary sources

The Alien Communities of London in the Fifteenth Century: The Subsidy Rolls of 1440 and 1483–4, ed. Bolton, J.L. (Richard III and Yorkist History Trust, Stamford, 1998)

The Anglica Historica of Polydore Vergil, ed. Hay, D. (Camden 3rd series 74, 1950)

The Armburgh Papers: The Brokholes Inheritance in Warwickshire, Hertfordshire and Essex, c. 1417–c.1453, ed. Carpenter, C. (Woodbridge, 1998)

British Library Harleian Manuscript 433, ed. Horrox, R.E. and Hammond, P.W. (4 vols, Upminster, 1979–83)

Calendar of the Close Rolls

Calendar of the Patent Rolls

Calendar of the Signet Letters of Henry IV and Henry V, ed. Kirby, J.L. (1978)

The Cely Letters 1472–1488, ed. Hanham, A.(Early English Text Society 273, 1975)

Chronicle of Adam of Usk, 1377–1421, ed. Given-Wilson, C. (Oxford, 1997)

Chronicles of London, ed. Kingsford, C.L. (1905)

Chronicles of the Revolution 1397–1400, ed. Given-Wilson, C. (Manchester, 1993)

The Crowland Chronicle Continuations 1459–1486, ed. Pronay, N. and Cox, J.C. (Gloucester, 1986)

Death and Dissent: The Dethe of the Kynge of Scotis and Warkworth's Chronicle, ed. Matheson, L. (Woodbridge, 1999)

'A Defence of the Proscription of the Yorkists in 1459', ed. Gilson, J.P., *English Historical Review* 26 (1911): 512–25

An English Chronicle of the Reigns of Richard II, Henry IV, Henry V, and Henry VI, ed. Davies, J.S. (Camden Society, 64, 1856)

English Historical Documents, vol. 4, *1327–1485*, ed. Myers, A.R. (1969)

The Fane Fragment of the 1461 Lords' Journal, ed. Dunham, W.H. (New Haven, 1935)

'Financial Memoranda of the Reign of Edward V. Longleat Miscellaneous Manuscript Book II', ed. Horrox, R., *Camden Miscellany* 29 (1987)

Fortescue, J., *On the Laws and Governance of England*, ed. Greenwood, S. (Cambridge, 1997)

Four English Political Tracts of the Later Middle Ages, ed. Genet, J.-P. (Camden 4th series 18, 1977)

Gesta Henrici Quinti: The Deeds of Henry the Fifth, ed. Taylor, F. and Roskell, J.S. (Oxford, 1975)

The Great Chronicle of London, ed. Thomas, A.H. and Thornley, I.D. (1938)

Historical Collections of a Citizen of London in the Fifteenth Century, ed. Gairdner, J. (Camden Society, new series 17, 1876)

Household Accounts from Medieval England, ed. Woolgar, C.M. (British Academy Records of Economic and Social History 17, 18, 1993)

The Household of Edward IV: The Black Book and the Ordnance of 1478, ed. Myers, A.R. (Manchester, 1959)

The Howard Household Books, ed. Crawford, A. (Richard III and Yorkist History Trust, Stroud, 1992)

Ingulph's Chronicle of the Abbey of Croyland, ed. Riley, H.T. (1859)

'John Benet's Chronicle for the years 1400 to 1462', ed. Harriss, G.L. and Harriss, M.A., *Camden Miscellany* 24 (1972)

Kingsford's Stonor Letters and Papers 1290–1483, ed. Carpenter, C. (Cambridge, 1996)

Letters and Papers illustrative of the Wars of the English in France, ed. Stevenson, J. (2 vols in 3, rolls series, London, 1861–4)

Letters of Margaret of Anjou, ed. Monro, C. (Camden Society, 86, 1863)

Marcher Lordships of South Wales 1415–1536: Select Documents, ed. Pugh, T.B. (Board of Celtic Studies History and Law Series 20, Cardiff, 1963)

Materials for a History of the Reign of Henry VII, ed. Campbell, W. (2 vols, rolls series, London, 1873–7)

More, T., *History of King Richard III* (Yale Edition of the Complete Works, New Haven, 1963)

Original Letters illustrative of English History, ed. Ellis, H. (11 vols in 3 series, 1824–46)

Parliamentary Texts of the Later Middle Ages, ed. Pronay, N. and Taylor, J. (Oxford, 1980)

The Paston Letters 1422–1509, ed. Gairdner, J.G. (6 vols, London, 1904)

Paston Letters and Papers of the Fifteenth Century, ed. Davis, N. (2 vols, Oxford, 1971–6)

'The Petition of Edmund Dudley', ed. Harrison, C.J., *English Historical Review* 87 (1972): 87–90

The Plumpton Correspondence, ed. Stapleton, T. (Camden Society, 4, 1839)

Plumpton Letters and Papers, ed. Kirby, J.L. (Camden 5th series 8, 1996)

The Politics of Fifteenth Century England: John Vale's Book, ed. Kekewich, M.L., Richmond, C.F., Sutton, A.F., Visser-Fuchs, L. and Watts, J.L. (Richard III and Yorkist History Trust, Stroud, 1995)

'Private Indentures for Life Service in Peace and War 1278–1476', ed. Jones, M. and Walker, S., *Camden Miscellany* 32 (1994)

Proceedings and Ordinances of the Privy Council of England, ed. Nicholas, N.H. (7 vols, London, 1834–7)

The Reign of Henry VII from Contemporary Sources, ed. Pollard, A.F. (3 vols, London, 1913–14)

Richard III: The Road to Bosworth Field, ed. Hammond, P.W. and Sutton, A.F. (1985)

Rolls of Parliament (6 vols, Record Commission, London, 1767–77)

Select Documents of English Constitutional History 1307–1485, ed. Chrimes, S.B. and Brown, A.L. (1961)

Smith, T., *De Republica Anglorum*, ed. Dewar, M. (Cambridge, 1982)

Stonor Letters and Papers 1290–1483, ed. Kingsford, C.L. (Camden 3rd series 29, 30, 1919); *Camden Miscellany* 13 (1924)
Testamenta Vetusta, ed. Nicolas, N.H. (2 vols, London, 1826)
Three Chronicles of the Reign of Edward IV, ed. Dockray, K. (Gloucester, 1988)
The Usurpation of Richard III, ed. Armstrong, C.A.J. (2nd edn, Oxford, 1969)
Women of the English Nobility and Gentry 1066–1500, ed. Ward, J. (Manchester, 1995)

Secondary sources

Much of the most important work of the past twenty years has been first or subsequently published in collections of essays. In general, collections have been listed below, rather than specific essays. The place of publishing is not specified if the item was published in London.

Acheson, E., *Leicestershire in the Fifteenth Century, c.1422–c.1485* (Cambridge, 1992)
Allmand, C.T., *Henry V* (1988)
Allmond, R.A. and Pollard, A.J., 'The Yeomanry of Robin Hood and Social Terminology in Fifteenth-century England', *Past and Present* 170 (2001): 52–77.
Archer, R.E. (ed.), *Crown, Government, and People in the Fifteenth Century* (Stroud, 1995)
Archer, R.E. and Walker, S.K. (eds), *Rulers and Ruled in Late Medieval England* (1995)
Armstrong, C.A.J., *England, France and Burgundy in the Fifteenth Century* (1983)
Arthurson, I., *The Perkin Warbeck Conspiracy 1491–99* (Stroud, 1994)
Baldwin, J.F., *The King's Council in England during the Middle Ages* (Oxford, 1913)
Bean, J.M.W., *The Estates of the Percy Family 1416–1537* (1958)
—— *From Lord to Patron: Lordship in Late Medieval England* (Manchester, 1989)
Bellamy, J.G., *Bastard Feudalism and the Law* (1989)
—— *Crime and Public Order in the Late Middle Ages* (Toronto, 1973)
—— *Criminal Law and Society in Late Medieval and Tudor England* (Gloucester, 1984)
—— *The Law of Treason in England in the Later Middle Ages* (Cambridge, 1970)
Bennett, M., *Community, Class and Careerism: Cheshire and Lancashire Society in the Age of Sir Gawain and the Green Knight* (Cambridge, 1983)
—— 'Edward III's Entail and the Succession to the Crown, 1376–1471', *English Historical Review* 113 (1998).
Britnell, R.H., *The Closing of the Middle Ages? England, 1471–1529* (Oxford, 1997)
Britnell, R.H. and Hatcher, J. (eds), *Progress and Problems in Medieval England* (Cambridge, 1996)
Britnell, R.H. and Pollard, A.J. (eds), *The McFarlane Legacy: Studies in Late Medieval Politics and Society* (Stroud, 1995)
Brown, A.L., 'The Commons and Council in the Reign of Henry IV', *English Historical Review* 79 (1964): 1–30

—— *The Early History of the Clerkship of the Council* (Glasgow, 1969)

—— *The Governance of Late Medieval England 1272–1461* (1989)

Bush, M.L., *The English Aristocracy: A Comparative Synthesis* (Manchester, 1984)

—— 'Tax Reform and Rebellion in Early Tudor England', *History* 76 (1991): 379–400

Carpenter, C., *Locality and Polity: A Study of Warwickshire Landed Society 1401–1499* (Cambridge, 1992)

—— *The Wars of the Roses: Politics and the Constitution in England, c.1437–1509* (Cambridge, 1997)

Castor, H., *The King, the Crown and the Duchy of Lancaster: Public Authority and Private Power 1399–1461* (Oxford, 2000)

Chrimes, S.B., *English Constitutional Ideas in the Fifteenth Century* (Cambridge, 1934)

Clayton, D.J., Davies, R.G. and McNiven, P. (eds), *Trade, Devotion and Governance: Papers in Later Medieval History* (Stroud, 1994)

Clough, C.H. (ed.), *Profession, Vocation and Culture in Later Medieval England* (Liverpool, 1982)

Collins, H.L., *The Order of the Garter 1348–1461: Chivalry and Politics in Late Medieval England* (Oxford, 2000)

Curry, A.E. and Matthew, E. (eds), *Concepts and Patterns of Service in the Later Middle Ages* (Woodbridge, 2000)

Davies, R.G. and Denton, J.H., *The English Parliament in the Middle Ages* (Manchester, 1981)

Davies, R.R., *The Revolt of Owain Glyndŵr* (Oxford, 1995)

Dobson, R.B. (ed.), *Church, Politics and Patronage in the Fifteenth Century* (Gloucester, 1984)

—— *Church and Society in the Medieval North of England* (1996)

Dunham, W.H., ' "The Books of Parliament" and "The Old Record", 1396–1504', *Speculum* 51 (1976): 694–712

—— *Lord Hastings' Indentured Retainers 1461–83* (New Haven, 1956)

Dunn, D.E.S. (ed.), *Courts, Counties and the Capital in the Later Middle Ages* (Stroud, 1996)

Eccleshall, R., *Order and Reason in Politics: Theories of Absolute and Limited Monarchy in Early Modern England* (Oxford, 1979)

Edwards, J.G., *Historians and the Medieval English Parliament* (Glasgow, 1970)

—— *The Second Century of the English Parliament* (Oxford, 1979)

Elton, G.R., 'Tudor Government: Points of Contact: I– III', *Transactions of the Royal Historical Society*, 5th series 24–26 (1974–6)

Field, P.J.C., *The Life and Times of Sir Thomas Malory* (Cambridge, 1993)

Given-Wilson, C. *The English Nobility in the Later Middle Ages* (2nd edn, London, 1996)

Goheen, R.B., 'Peasant Politics? Village Community and the Crown in Fifteenth-Century England', *American Historical Review* 96 (1991)

Green, R.F., *The Crisis of Truth: Literature and Law in Ricardian England* (Philadelphia, 1999)

Griffiths, R.A., *King and Country: England and Wales in the Fifteenth Century* (1991)

—— (ed.), *Patronage, The Crown, and the Provinces in Later Medieval England* (Gloucester, 1981)

—— *The Reign of King Henry VI 1422–61* (2nd edn, Stroud, 1998)

Griffiths, R.A. and Sherborne, J.W. (ed.), *Kings and Nobles in the Later Middle Ages* (Gloucester, 1986)

Griffiths, R.A. and Thomas, R.S., *The Making of the Tudor Dynasty* (Gloucester, 1985)

Gross, A.J., *The Dissolution of the Lancastrian Kingship. Sir John Fortescue and the Crisis of Monarchy in Fifteenth-Century England* (Stamford, 1996)

Grummitt, D., 'Henry VII, Chamber Finance and the New Monarchy', *Historical Research* 72 (1999): 229–43.

Gunn, S.J., 'The Courtiers of Henry VII', *English Historical Review* 108 (1993): 23–49

—— *Early Tudor Government 1485–1558* (Basingstoke, 1995)

—— 'The Structures of Politics in Early Tudor England', *Transactions of the Royal Historical Society*, 6th series 5 (1995): 59–90.

Harriss, G.L., *Cardinal Beaufort: A Study of Lancastrian Ascendancy and Decline* (Oxford, 1988)

—— (ed.), *Henry V: The Practice of Kingship* (Oxford, 1985)

—— 'Political Society and the Growth of Government in Late Medieval England', *Past and Present* 138 (1993): 28–57.

—— 'Preference at the Medieval Exchequer', *Bulletin of the Institute of Historical Research* 30 (1957): 17–40.

Harvey, I.M.W., *Jack Cade's Rebellion of 1450* (Oxford, 1991)

Heal, F. and Holmes, C., *The Gentry in England and Wales 1500–1700* (Basingstoke, 1994)

Hearder, H. and Loyn, H.R. (eds), *British Government and Administration* (Cardiff, 1974)

Hicks, M.A., *Bastard Feudalism* (Harlow, 1995)

—— 'Bastard Feudalism, Overmighty Subjects, and Idols of the Multitude during the Wars of the Roses', *History* 85 (2001): 386–403.

—— *False, Fleeting, Perjur'd Clarence: George Duke of Clarence 1449–78* (1st edn, Gloucester, 1980; rev. edn, Bangor, 1992)

—— (ed.), *Profit, Piety and Professions in Later Medieval England* (Gloucester, 1990)

—— (ed.), *Revolution and Consumption in Late Medieval England* (Woodbridge, 2001)

—— *Richard III* (2nd edn, Stroud, 2000)

—— *Richard III and his Rivals: Magnates and their Motives during the Wars of the Roses* (1991)

—— 'The 1468 Statute of Livery', *Historical Research* 64 (1991)

—— *Warwick the Kingmaker* (Oxford, 1998)

Hilton, R.H., and Aston, T.H. (eds), *The English Rising of 1381* (Cambridge, 1984)

Holt, R. and Rosser, G. (eds), *The Medieval Town: A Reader in English Urban History 1200–1500* (Harlow, 1990)

Horrox, R.E. (ed.), *Fifteenth-century Attitudes: Perceptions of Society in Late Medieval England* (Cambridge, 1994)

Hurstfield, J., *Freedom, Corruption and Government in Elizabethan England* (1973)

Jewell, H.M., *English Local Administration in the Middle Ages* (Newton Abbott, 1972)

Johnson, P.A., *Duke Richard of York 1411–60* (Oxford, 1988)

Jones, M. (ed.), *The Gentry and Lesser Nobility in Late Medieval Europe* (Gloucester, 1986)

Jones, M.K. and Underwood, M.G., *The King's Mother: Lady Margaret Beaufort, Countess of Richmond and Derby* (Cambridge, 1992)

Jurkowski, M., Smith, C.L. and Crook, D., *Lay Taxes in England and Wales 1188–1688* (PRO Handbook 31, Kew, 1998)

Keen, M.H., *Chivalry* (New Haven, 1984)

—— *Nobles, Knights and Men-at-Arms in the Middle Ages* (1996)

Kermode, J.I. (ed.), *Enterprise and Individuals in Fifteenth-Century England* (Stroud, 1991)

Kirby, J.L., 'Councils and Councillors of Henry IV, 1399–1413', *Transactions of the Royal Historical Society*, 5th series 14 (1964): 35–65

—— *Henry IV of England* (1970)

Lander, J.R., *Crown and Nobility 1461–1509* (1976)

—— *English Justices of the Peace 1461–1509* (Stroud, 1989)

—— *The Limitations of English Monarchy in the Later Middle Ages* (Toronto, 1989)

McFarlane, K.B., *England in the Fifteenth Century* (1981)

—— *Lancastrian Kings and Lollard Knights* (Oxford, 1972)

—— *The Nobility of Later Medieval England* (Oxford, 1973)

McIntosh, M.K., *Controlling Misbehavior in England, 1370–1600* (Cambridge, 1998)

Maddern, P.C., 'Honour among the Pastons: Gender and Integrity in English Provincial Society', *Journal of Medieval History* 14 (1988): 357–71

—— *Violence and the Social Order: East Anglia 1422–42* (Oxford, 1992)

Mertes, K., *The English Noble Household 1250–1600: Good Governance and Politic Rule* (Oxford, 1988)

Moreton, C., *The Townshends and their World: Gentry, Law and Land in Norfolk c.1450–1551* (Oxford, 1992)

Morgan, D.A.L., 'The King's Affinity in the Polity of Yorkist England', *Transactions of the Royal Historical Society*, 5th series 23 (1973): 1–22

Musson, A., *Medieval Law in Context: The Growth of Legal Consciousness from Magna Carta to the Peasants Revolt* (Manchester, 2001)

Myers, A.R., *Crown, Household and Parliament in Fifteenth Century England* (1985)

Orme, N., 'The Culture of Children in Medieval England', *Past and Present* 148 (1995)

—— *Medieval Children* (2001)

Ormrod, W.M., *Political Life in Medieval England, 1300–1450* (Basingstoke, 1995)

Payling, S.J., 'The Ampthill Dispute: A Study in Aristocratic Lawlessness and the Breakdown of Lancastrian Government', *English Historical Review* 104 (1989): 881–907

—— 'County Parliamentary Elections in Fifteenth-Century England', *Parliamentary History* 18 (1999): 237–57

—— 'Murder, Motive and Punishment in Fifteenth-Century England: Two Gentry Case-Studies', *English Historical Review* 113 (1998): 1–17

—— *Political Society in Lancastrian England: The Greater Gentry of Nottinghamshire* (Oxford, 1991)

Pollard, A.J., *John Talbot and the War in France 1427–1483* (1983)

—— *Late Medieval England 1399–1509* (Harlow, 2000)

—— *North-Eastern England during the Wars of the Roses: Lay Society, War and Politics 1450–1500* (Oxford, 1990)

—— 'The Northern Retainers of Richard Nevill, Earl of Salisbury', *Northern History* 11 (1976): 52–70

—— (ed.), *Property and Politics: Essays in Later Medieval English History* (Gloucester, 1984)

—— *Richard III and the Princes in the Tower* (Gloucester, 1991)

—— (ed.), *The Wars of the Roses* (Basingstoke, 1995)

—— *The Wars of the Roses* (Basingstoke, 1988; 2nd edn, 2001)

Powell, E., 'After "After McFarlane": The Poverty of Patronage and the Case for Constitutional History', *Trade, Devotion and Governance*, ed. Clayton, D.J., Davies, R.G. and McNiven, P. (Stroud, 1994)

—— 'Arbitration and the Law in England in the Later Middle Ages', *Transactions of the Royal Historical Society*, 5th series 33 (1983): 49–67

—— *Kingship, Law and Society: Criminal Justice in the Reign of Henry V* (Oxford, 1989)

Pugh, T.B., *Henry V and the Southampton Plot of 1415* (Gloucester, 1988)

Rawcliffe, C., 'The Great Lord as Peacekeeper: Arbitration by English Nobles and their Councils in the Later Middle Ages', *Law and Social Change in British History*, ed. Guy, J.A. and Beale, H.G. (1984)

—— 'Parliament and the Settlement of Disputes by Arbitration in the Later Middle Ages', *Parliamentary History* 9 (1990)

Richardson, H.G. and Sayles, G.O., *The English Parliament in the Middle Ages* (1981)

Richardson, M., *The Medieval Chancery under Henry V* (List and Index Society, special series 30, 1999)

Richmond, C.F., *John Hopton: A Fifteenth-century Suffolk Gentleman* (Cambridge, 1981)

—— *The Paston Family in the Fifteenth Century* (3 vols, Cambridge 1990–6; Manchester, 2000)

—— 'When did John Hopton become blind?', *Historical Research* 60 (1987): 102–6

Rosenthal, J.T., *Nobles and the Noble Life, 1295–1500* (1976)

Rosenthal, J.T. and Richmond, C.F. (eds), *People, Politics and the Community in the Later Middle Ages* (Gloucester, 1987)

Roskell, J.S., *The Commons in the Parliament of 1422* (Manchester, 1954)

—— *The House of Commons 1386–1421*, vol. I (Stroud, 1992)

—— *Parliament and Politics in Late Medieval England* (3 vols, London, 1981–3)

Saul, N., *Richard II* (1997)

—— 'Richard II and the Vocabulary of Kingship', *English Historical Review* 110 (1995): 854–77

Rowney, A. 'Arbitration in Gentry Disputes of the Later Middle Ages', *History* 67 (1982): 367–76.

Sayles, G.O., *The King's Parliament of England* (1975)

Sherborne, J.W., *War, Politics and Culture in Fourteenth-Century England*, ed. Tuck, A. (1994)

Slack, P. (ed.), *Rebellion, Popular Protest, and the Social Order in Early Modern England* (Cambridge, 1984)

Stone, L., *The Crisis of the Aristocracy 1558–1641* (Oxford, 1965)
—— *The Family, Sex and Marriage in England 1500–1800* (1977)
Storey, R.L., *The End of the House of Lancaster* (1966)
Strohm, P., *England's Empty Throne: Usurpation and the Language of Legitimation 1399–1422* (New Haven, 1998)
Taylor, J. and Childs, W. (eds), *Politics and Crisis in Fourteenth Century England* (Gloucester, 1990)
Thomson, J.A.F. (ed.), *Towns and Townspeople in the Fifteenth Century* (Gloucester, 1988)
Virgoe, R., *East Anglian Society and the Political Community of Late Medieval England*, ed. Barron, C., Rawcliffe, C. and Rosenthal, J.T. (Norwich, 1997)
Walker, S.K., 'Rumour, Sedition and Popular Protest in the Reign of Henry IV', *Past and Present* 166 (2000): 31–65
Warner, M.W. and Lacey, K., 'Neville vs. Percy: A Precedence Dispute *circa* 1442', *Historical Research* 59 (1996): 207–17
Watts, J.L., 'The Counsels of King Henry VI c.1435–41', *English Historical Review* 16 (1991): 279–83
—— (ed.), *The End of the Middle Ages?* (Stroud, 1998)
—— *Henry VI and the Politics of Kingship* (Cambridge, 1996)
Wilkinson, B., *Constitutional History of England in the Fifteenth Century (1399–1485)* (1964)
Wolffe, B.P., 'Acts of Resumption in Lancastrian Parliaments, 1399–1456', *English Historical Review* 73 (1958): 583–616
—— *The Crown Lands 1471–1536* (1970)
—— *Henry VI* (1981)
—— *The Royal Demesne in English History* (1971)
Woolgar, C.M., *The Great Household in Late Medieval England* (1999)
Wright, S.M., *The Derbyshire Gentry in the Fifteenth Century* (Derbyshire Record Society viii, 1983)

INDEX

Howard, John Lord (d. 1485) 106,
  121, 142, 151, 163
Thomas, earl of Surrey (d. 1524)
  163
Hugford, John 160
Humphrey, duke of Gloucester
  (d. 1447) 34, 41, 42, 49, 56 59,
  128, 135, 136, 186, 191
Hungerford family 16, 65–7, 71–3,
  147
  Eleanor, Lady Moleyns (d. *c.* 1476)
    72
  Frideswide 16, 68, 72
  Joan 144
  Leonard 67
  Margaret, Lady Hungerford and
    Botreaux (d. 1478) 63, 65, 71–2
  Mary, Lady Hastings 66, 72
  Robert Lord Hungerford
    (d. 1459) 71
  Robert Lord Moleyns (d. 1464)
    31, 72–3, 177
  Sir Thomas (d. 1398) 79
  Sir Thomas (d. 1469) 65, 72
  Sir Walter (d. 1516) 72
Hurstfield, Prof. Joel 131, 137
Husy, William, chief justice 123, 139
Hyde, James 144

Idle (Yorks.) 155
Idley, Peter 54
Ilderton, Isabel 158
indentures of retainer *see* bastard
  feudalism
inheritance 15, 40–4, 62–70, 150, 188,
  194 *see also* lineage, primogeniture
Ireland, Irish 48, 120–1, 135, 197,
  209, 212–13

James, Mr M.E. 12, 176
Jersey, isle of 204
Jewell, Dr Helen 79
Joan of Arc 14, 186
John, of Gaunt, duke of Lancaster
  (d. 1399) 41–2, 46, 147, 153
John, duke of Bedford (d. 1435)
  41–2, 49, 151, 185–6, 207
judicial system 2, 24 *see also* justice, law
just cause 150
just war 119

justice 24, 31, 38, 89, 94, 122, 139,
  175–6, 181–3, 199–201 *see also*
  arbitration, law
justices of the peace 111–12, 142,
  155, 160, 166–7, 170, 182–3

Kebell, Thomas 147
Kemp, John, archbishop of York 23
Kent, kentishmen 86–9, 116–18,
  136, 194, 199–200
  earldom of 16
Kidwelly (Wales) 114
King, Oliver, bishop of Bath and
  Wells 78
king, kingship: *de facto* & *de iure* 45–6,
  135, 203, 210, 214–15
  see also affinity, allegiance,
  coronations, crown, dynasticism,
  Edward III, IV, V, Henry IV, V,
  VI, VII, VIII, household,
  legitimacy, monarchy, Richard II,
  III, succession
kingmaker *see* Neville families
king's evil 29
king's peace 24
King's two bodies 28, 45–6
Kinsman, Simon 156
Kleineke, Dr Hannes 126
Knaresburgh (Yorks.) 146, 154, 160
Knowle (Warw.) 171

Lancaster, duchy 48, 148, 209
  dukes 52 *see also* Henry IV, V, VI,
    John
  palatinate 114
  retainers 128
Lancastrian 16, 40–4, 73, 131, 144,
  162, 187–8, 191, 193, 202, 212,
  215–16, 208 *see also* Henry VI
Lander, Prof. Jack R. 32, 105, 126
Langland, William 11, 76, 121
largesse 57, 60–2
Laslett, Prof. Peter 2, 56
law 8, 15, 24–7, 31, 38, 40, 94, 109,
  121–6, 168, 175, 199 *see also*
  justice
legal consciousness 8, 124
legisperit 143, 147 *see also* law
legitimacy 28, 40–4, 56, 202 *see also*
  succession

BIBL
LONDON
UNIV
SHL
WITHDRAWN